Steering the Stone Ships

The ship is built. The voyage has hardly begun.
Through history the stone prow will break
Or lie becalmed
Or skirt uncharted reefs and quicksands
Or be shaken by tempests and maelstrom.

George Mackay Brown, *Celebration of Magnus* (1987)

An understanding of the lives of bygone men is not to be had
without a knowledge of how they earned their daily bread and
found their pleasures, how they believed and thought of God, or
did not.

Andrew Drummond and James Bulloch,
The Church in Late Victorian Scotland 1874–1900 (1978)

Steering the Stone Ships

The Story of Orkney Kirks and People

Jocelyn Rendall

Drawings by Crispin Worthington

SAINT ANDREW PRESS
Edinburgh

First published in 2009 by
SAINT ANDREW PRESS
121 George Street
Edinburgh EH2 4YN

ISBN 978 0 7152 0908 0

British Library Cataloguing in Publication Data
A catalogue record for this book is available from the British Library.

It is the publisher's policy to only use papers that are natural and recyclable and that have been manufactured from timber grown in renewable, properly managed forests. All of the manufacturing processes of the papers are expected to conform to the environmental regulations of the country of origin.

Typeset in Palatino by Waverley Typesetters, Fakenham
Manufactured in the United Kingdom by Bell & Bain Ltd, Glasgow

Contents

Foreword

Orkney is marked not just by rich ochre fields but also by stones and ships. Some of the stones are ancient, such as the village of Skara Brae, which predates the Pyramids. Ships brought Vikings to Orkney; and, when Magnus, who would become Orkney's saint, saw six more than the agreed two ships come sailing towards Egilsay for a so-called peace conference, he recognised the arithmetic of death and prepared himself for martyrdom. Ships carried many Orcadians to Canada to work for the Hudson's Bay Company; wrecks of ships, overwhelmed by storms or blown up by submarines, lie in lonely Scapa Flow.

It is no surprise, then, that Orkney's George Mackay Brown turned to images of stones and ships so often in his poetry and prose, or that his dying vision was of ships coming into the harbour of his beloved Hamnavoe (Stromness).

Here's part of his exquisite poem about St Magnus Cathedral, titled 'The Kirk and the Ship':

> *Masons from Durham, strange speakers,*
> *Squared the blocks rough-hewn.*
> *They chiselled their marks, setting stone on stone.*
> *And the Kirkwall villagers*
> *Paused, and shook wondering heads, and went on.*
>
> *And the kirk grew, like a lovely ship*
> *Freighted with psalm and ceremony, blissward blown …*
> *Pillars soared up, red as fire or blood.*
>
> *And in one they laid*
> *Their martyr, Magnus: his breached bellchambered bone.*

There were many stone ships in Orkney over the centuries; and Jocelyn Rendall tells of their voyages through time, often in troubled waters. There are some wonderful tales about the crews – the faithful, adventurous, eccentric, imaginative, half-mad, devoted, sometimes confused disciples of Jesus Christ in this northern archipelago. Among the cast of characters in this superb book, you will meet two rival preachers in Birsay who raced each other on horseback to claim a church for their followers, the feisty and fearsome women of Stromness who heckled an unpopular clergyman foisted upon them, the minister in Sanday who was sent to prison for his robust advocacy of land reform, the laird whose sins of the flesh helped pay for his church balcony, the charismatic preacher who impregnated the daughter of his session clerk and ended up in prison in Turkey; and the saints, heroes and unsung team players who served and sang on board their chosen denominational vessel, praying that it was indeed blissward blown.

Jocelyn Rendall is a fine researcher and an elegant and amusing writer. Her book not only fills a gap in Orkney's many-layered history; it will be appreciated and admired by many readers who have never set foot on these far-flung isles.

RON FERGUSON

Acknowledgements

So many people have had a share in making this book. A very big Thank You to Crispin for the wonderful illustrations; to Ron Ferguson for writing the Foreword; and to Anna Ritchie, Graeme Brown, Elizabeth Beaton and William Thomson for reading drafts and generously giving their time to steering my course through historical straits and narrows.

My debt to George Mackay Brown is obvious, and I am very grateful to Archie Bevan and the Estate of George Mackay Brown for their kind permission to quote frequently from his works. I am also grateful to Alison Fraser for permitting me to reproduce photographs and drawings from the collection of the Orkney Library and Archives, to David Mackie for copying them, and to all the staff in the Archives for providing such a helpful haven in which to research this book.

I would also like to thank all the people in Orkney who kindly allowed me to visit the private chapels in their homes and gardens; the Trustees of the Strathmartine Trust who assisted me with a grant; and all the team at Saint Andrew Press, especially Anne Muir for enjoying this story in the first place and for her patient and perceptive editing.

The stone ships would never have been launched without my friends, who made invaluable contributions of enthusiasm. For Neil, who had to live with the ships' stormy journeys for so long, and for Charlotte, Janis and Robert who kept me going with encouragement and hospitality, my special thanks and love.

Finally, I would like to thank my mother, who first took me time-travelling, and led the way with such indefatigable enthusiasm and curiosity.

Text Acknowledgements

The author gratefully acknowledges the following for their permission to quote their material in this book.

The extracts from the works of George Mackay Brown are reproduced by kind permission of the Estate of George Mackay Brown.

The extracts from *Scotland and the Abolition of Black Slavery* by Iain Whyte and from *Scotland's Best Churches* by John Hume are reproduced by kind permission of Edinburgh University Press.

The extracts from *A Flame in the Shadows* and *Low's History of Orkney* by Olaf Cuthbert are reproduced by kind permission of Olaf Cuthbert.

The extracts from *The Orcadian* and *The Orkney Herald* are reproduced by kind permission of the editor, *The Orcadian*, Kirkwall.

The extracts from *Orkneyinga Saga* are from the edition translated by H. Pálsson and P. Edwards, first published by the Hogarth Press and reproduced by permission of The Random House Group Ltd.

The extracts from *The Church in Late Victorian Scotland 1874–1900* by Andrew Drummond and James Bulloch are reproduced by permission of Saint Andrew Press.

The extracts from *Circle of Light* by Alison Gray and from *The Little General and the Rousay Crofters* by William P. L. Thomson are reproduced by permission of John Donald, an imprint of Birlinn Ltd. The quotations from *History of Orkney* and *The New History of Orkney* by William P. L. Thomson are reproduced by permission of Birlinn Ltd (www.birlinn.co.uk)

The extracts from *Njal's Saga,* translated by Magnus Magnusson and Hermann Pálsson (© Magnus Magnusson and Herman Pálsson, 1960), and from *Eyrbyggja Saga,* translated and introduced by Hermann Pálsson and Paul Edwards (© Herman Pálsson and Paul Edwards, 1972, 1989), are reproduced by permission of Penguin Books Ltd.

The extracts from *The Architecture of Scottish Post-Reformation Churches* by George Hay, from *Four Centuries of Scottish Psalmody* by Millar Patrick and from *A History of the Vikings* by Gwyn Jones are reproduced by permission of Oxford University Press.

The extract from *A Golden Treasury of Irish Poetry AD 600–1200* (© David Green and Frank O'Connor 1967) is reproduced by permission of PFD (www.pfd.co.uk) on behalf of the Estate of Frank O'Connor.

The extract from *A Church History of Scotland* by J. H. S. Burleigh is reproduced by kind permission of John K. Burleigh.

List of Illustrations and Credits

Unless otherwise stated, photographs used in this book are by the author, Jocelyn Rendall and sketches and watercolours are by Crispin Worthington. Both Jocelyn Rendall and Crispin Worthington retain the copyright on these images.

The following shorthand for credits is used:

OLA   reproduced courtesy of Orkney Library and Archive.

NMS   reproduced courtesy of the Trustees of the National Museums of Scotland.

RCAHMS   reproduced courtesy of the Royal Commission on the Ancient and Historical Monuments of Scotland.

PSAS   reproduced courtesy of the editor of the Proceedings of the Society of Antiquarians of Scotland.

Colour plates

1. St Mary's, Burwick, (i.e the bay of the burgh or fort), South Ronaldsay

2. St Michael's Kirk, Harray
   Many early churches were built on or near the remains of brochs, pragmatically making use of their building stone, their strategic location and their traditional role as the 'power-centres' of the surrounding area. The graves at St Michael's crown the mound of a prominent broch that once dominated the fertile lands around the Harray Loch.

3. St Boniface Kirk and the site of 'Munkerhoose', Papay

4. The Castle of Burrian, Westray
   Life in the Papay monastery, surrounded by fertile farmland, must have been relatively comfortable, but monks also spent periods of time in retreat, or as a penance, on stack-sites like the Castle of Burrian.

5. Silver crucifix from Birka *(Birka Museum)*
   This silver crucifix made around AD 900 was found in the important Viking trading port, Birka, in Sweden. The stylized figure is the earliest image of Christ found in Scandinavia.

6. Window in St Magnus Kirk, Birsay, detail
   St Magnus reading his psalter in a longship during the Battle of the Menai Straits. Stained glass window designed by Loveday MacPherson, made by Alexander Strachan and given by members of the congregation in 1904.

7. The Brough of Birsay from Birsay
   After his murder, St Magnus was carried to Birsay to be buried in Thorfinn's Christskirk, but it is uncertain whether the 'fine minster' was built on the Brough or on the Birsay mainland.

8. The Round Church, Orphir
   St Nicholas' kirk at the Bu', Orphir, built by Earl Hakon around 1123.

9. Corn Holm from Copinsay
   In 1774, George Low found a ruined chapel still standing here and 'the obscure foundations of small buildings, possibly the cells of ecclesiasticks'.

10. Crosskirk, Westray
    Crosskirk, or the Westside kirk, at Tuquoy. The east end, with its arched doorways and window, is part of the twelfth-century kirk built by the wealthy Norse farmer whose hall has been excavated on the shore below. The low walls are all that survive of the eighteenth-century extension.

11. Carved panel in Old Hoy kirk
    The carved panels in the pulpit were originally in the (now ruined) parish kirk near the Bu'. The monogram commemorates Mastery Henry Smythe, minister of Hoy and Graemsay 1621–32.

12. The Covenanters' Memorial, Deerness
    The Memorial was built by public subscription in 1888 to commemorate the tragedy of 1697, when over 200 Covenanter prisoners-of-war were shipwrecked and drowned in Deer Sound.

13. St Mary's, Swandro, Rousay
    The present thirteenth-century kirk, near the old farm of Skaill, replaced a much earlier one, built close to a Norse leader's 'skali' or hall.

24. The chapel at Westness, Rousay
   The chapel in the grounds of Westness House was converted from an engine shed in the early twentieth century, and furnished by the Grant family.

25. The kirkyard at Warbeth, Stromness
   The well-to-do of nineteenth-century Stromness lie as tightly packed in the graveyard as their houses are in the town, and as close to the sea which brought them their wealth.

26. The Old Hackland Kirk, Rendall
   The extensive parish of Rendall was without a kirk after St Laurence fell into ruin in the 1790s. The Hackland kirk was built in 1845 in a desperate attempt to stop the haemorrhage of people to the Free Kirk by providing more churches, but too late to serve this purpose.

27. The Parish kirk and the ruined Secession kirk in Eday
   The Free kirk (now the parish kirk) and the Secession kirk, built in 1831 for 300 people, perched on a heather-covered hill above it. This was probably the only site that the congregation could obtain from the heritors, but it certainly would have dominated the surrounding landscape!

28. The Free kirk, Sourin, Rousay
   The abandoned hulk of the Free kirk was the scene of the Rev. Archibald MacCallum's impassioned speeches on land reform and the centre of resistance to General Burroughs.

29. Detail of stained glass window in the Episcopal Chapel in Graemeshall, Holm
   A splendidly indignant dragon is trodden underfoot by St Margaret of Antioch. Another window shows a pearl necklace, a Graeme family heirloom which was sold in order to build the chapel.

30. St Peter's, Skaill, Sandwick
   The parish kirk at Skaill where James Tyrie began his ministry amidst violent demonstrations by the women of Sandwick and Stromness. The coastal location of many kirks made them useful for other purposes: in 1771 Tyrie found room in St Peter's to store a shipwrecked cargo of linseed and gin. (Tyrie's kirk was rebuilt in 1836 and restored by the Scottish Redundant Churches Trust in 2003).

31. The Italian Chapel, Lamb Holm
   The chapel was created out of two Nissen huts by Italian prisoners-of-war, 1943-45. Early photographs show it surrounded by immaculately neat gravel paths and formal parterres of grass and flowerbeds.

32. Memorial to the Longhope lifeboat disaster, Osmundwall, Walls
Above the war-graves in Osmundwall kirkyard, the bronze figure of a lifeboatman gazing out to Scapa Flow commemorates the tragedy of the Longhope lifeboat disaster in 1969. The monument is surrounded by the graves of the eight men who died when the boat overturned in 60-foot waves.

33. Celebrations at Golgotha Monastery, Papa Stronsay
The members of Golgotha Monastery come from all over the world. In 2003, they hospitably invited the people of Stronsay to join them in their celebrations of the 25th anniversary of Father Michael Mary's ordination, and some of the monks performed a haka, a traditional Maori dance of welcome.

34. The Moncur Memorial Church, Stronsay
Few ministers can have had such an extravagant memorial as this church. Alexander Moncur built it in 1955, in memory of his mother, Eliza Moncur, and his grandfather, the Rev. James Mudie, who was minister of the UP kirk in Stronsay 1825–60.

35. St John's, North Walls
The attractive St John's mission kirk was built in 1883 by public subscription as a counter-attraction to the nearby Free kirk. It retains all its original oil lamps and furnishings.

36. The old parish church at the Bu', North Hoy
St Nicholas beneath the Hoy hills has one of the loveliest situations in Orkney. It 'fell down of itself' in 1786 and was only partially restored.

Illustrations within text

Invitation to Time-Travellers

I desire an Ark to carry this people
To Golden Jerusalem
George Mackay Brown (2001)

A great stone ship that will carry the people of Orkney through the turbulent tides of history: this is the vision of St Magnus Cathedral that Earl Rognvald outlines *to an Itinerant Builder of Churches*, in a poem by George Mackay Brown.[1] He commissions an Ark to be built in Kirkwall, but an Ark is not only a ship. It is built to protect the people within it from the chaos and catastrophe outside. It carries them forward to new beginnings. It houses a community. The members of that community may often seem thoroughly ill-assorted (like the diverse animals – from aardvarks to armadillos – that entered Noah's Ark) and sometimes have difficulty getting on together for the length of the voyage, but they are all travelling to the same final destination. Since Christianity first came to Orkney, around fourteen centuries ago, many smaller arks have been launched on every island in the archipelago and have had an enormous influence in shaping their history. I was curious to know more about the voyage – and the passengers.

From hermitages on wind-blasted holms to dour nineteenth-century preaching barns; from a splendid cathedral founded by a Norse earl to a Nissen hut painted by Italian prisoners during the Second World War; from city kirks, built for huge and earnest Presbyterian congregations, to a diminutive Roman Catholic chapel converted from a byre: the Orkney 'arks' come in all shapes and sizes. Some survive only as a ridge in a green field or as a half-forgotten name, or as a gaunt shell with boarded windows, but others are newly built or being renovated for the future. Many are very lovely in their island landscapes. The Norse church on the Brough of Birsay, with its magnificent views of the dramatic coast from

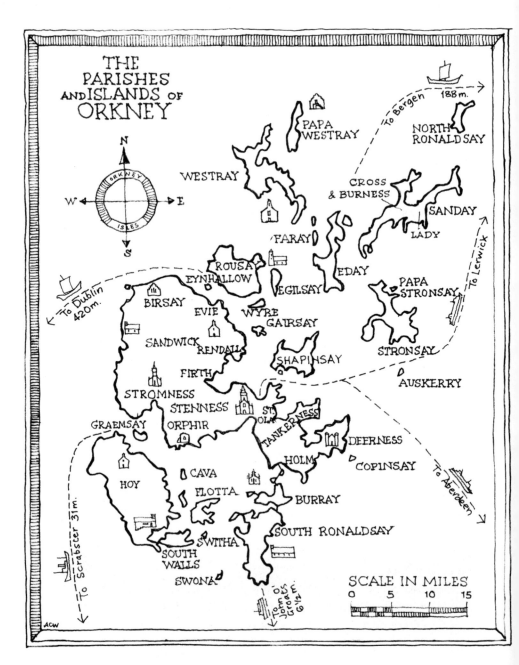

FIGURE I.1

Map of the parishes and islands of Orkney

Costa to Marwick Head; the lichen-encrusted walls of St Mary's, growing out of the rocky shore on Rousay; and – seen from far off – the slim finger of the round tower of St Magnus on Egilsay: they link hill and shore, island to island like a chain of beacons.

If one traced the network of churches right around Orkney, one would be walking in a far more ancient sacred landscape, because Christianity never broke the invisible thread that ties a people to a special, potent place. Almost invariably, the first churches were built on sites that had been spiritual and secular 'power-centres' long before the arrival of the first missionaries, and generation after generation rebuilt them with the same stones.

St Mary's in Burwick, on the southmost tip of South Ronaldsay, stands near the place where Pictish kings held their coronation ceremonies, and guards the footprint stone in which they stood to take their kingship oath. Some thousand years after the Picts, the people of the parish utterly

FIGURE I.2

The 'footprint stone' in St Mary's Church in Burwick is evidence that this was an ancient and important ceremonial site. Stones like these were used in coronation rites, the new king symbolically stepping into the footprints of his ancestors.

refused to leave their kirk, even though it was a roofless ruin, or allow their minister to lead Sunday worship anywhere else more waterproof or convenient. It was not merely a building to shelter them from the elements, it was the sacred centre around which their community had revolved for centuries. It anchored them in the landscape which had belonged to their ancestors: to abandon it was to be cast adrift.

Orkney's prehistoric monuments are so impressive and well-documented that our Neolithic ancestors often feel quite familiar, but ironically, those who lived much closer to us in time and culture yet left a less dramatic impact on the landscape, remain frustratingly elusive. The crosses carved in stone by Christian Picts trace the spreading of the faith across the islands, but the people themselves – the passengers in the first arks – remain shadowy and anonymous. Archaeology offers tantalising clues, but few certainties, and it is only in the late Norse period that *Orkneyinga Saga* fills the stage with a full cast of heroes and villains, saints, assassins and church-builders.

The saga was written in Iceland long after the events it describes, but it brings the Norse earls loud and large into the places we know today: Earl Sigurd accepting baptism at the point of the sword at Osmundwall, St Magnus butchered on Egilsay, Earl Hakon's drunken Christmas at Orphir, Earl Rognvald drawing up plans for his new cathedral in Kirkwall.

After all the blood and bluster of *Orkneyinga Saga*, late medieval Orkney falls very silent again, and even the sixteenth and seventeenth centuries, which were times of great political and social upheaval, have left little to tell us about the lives of ordinary people in Orkney let alone their thoughts and opinions. We do not even have their churches: there is a large gap between the fine Romanesque buildings of the twelfth century and the plain Presbyterian ones of the nineteenth. After the Reformation, the Kirk was so impoverished that, when new churches were built, they were constructed on such a shoestring budget that they were soon in ruins. In compensation, the Presbyterian bureaucracy generated paperwork on a generous scale. In the meticulously kept records of Kirk Session and Presbytery meetings, the people of Orkney speak out: arguing with one another, discussing local events and those in the much wider world; and at last emerge into history as real individuals, warts and all.

It was in the pages of the North Isles Presbytery records that I first came upon that insufferable character, Thomas Traill of Holland in Papa Westray, and his almost equally quarrelsome and unprincipled offspring, and realised that these sources had far more to offer than merely Church history. In fact, the minutes of Kirk meetings, far from being as dull as they sound, are wonderful social documents of the Upstairs-Downstairs world of Orkney society. Upstairs, the lairds and gentry are involved in, and arguing about, the politics and issues of the day, against a background of a long-running soap opera of parish life downstairs. Who was quarrelling with, or sleeping with, whom? Who stole peats, or let their cow into their neighbour's corn, or was seen kissing behind the fish-barrels? It is a veritable Orkney *Eastenders*. In *Orkneyinga Saga*, it is the rich and famous who have most of the speaking parts, but in the Kirk records we hear the voices of farm-servant and fisherman, housewife and apprentice and maid, as well as those of laird and merchant and minister.

In all these sources, it is obvious that the Kirk played a huge role in shaping our mental, as well as our physical, landscape. For centuries it was not merely the place of Sunday worship, but the centre of the parish's social, as well as its religious, life. Before there were newspapers (*The Orcadian* was first issued in 1854), it was at the kirk that one learned the national and international news. It was from bulletins issued by the General Assembly and read out in pulpits that Orcadians learned of the progress of the Jacobite Rebellion, or of the terrifying events of the French Revolution; of famine in Ireland, or of the appalling condition of slaves on the American plantations. It was, also, through the Kirks that people involved themselves with these issues: with prayer, with collections for the victims of disaster and with petitions to Parliament. Until the Education Act in 1872, it was not the State but the Churches that provided the only schools, and often the minister provided the only available medical knowledge as well.

The Kirk Sessions operated as a local police force, punishing petty crime and antisocial behaviour as well as moral lapses that we would regard today as entirely private issues. Until the Welfare State came into being, they also provided the only assistance that the very poor, the sick, the unemployed, or the physically or mentally disabled could hope for. Before community centres were built in the late twentieth century, the kirk buildings were usually the only place large enough to hold community meetings or social functions: the concerts and 'soirées' that were such an important part of parish life. Up to the present day, those holding every shade of belief or unbelief end up side by side, gathered companionably together into the continuum of history in the parish kirkyard.

In the eighteenth century, it was the ministers who brought the enquiring spirit of the Scottish Enlightenment to Orkney. Men like

George Low, William Clouston and George Barry – well-educated, curious, articulate – studied, and wrote brilliantly, on the history and natural history, geology, antiquities, agriculture and economy of their parishes. How little we would know about their times without them, and how much more slowly Orkney would have been modernised in the nineteenth century without the progressive and politically radical ministers of the Dissenting churches, who championed improved education, the extension of the franchise and the cause of land reform. Buildings and beliefs can be abandoned, but the role of the Kirk in the islands' history cannot be airbrushed away; one might as well try to describe Orkney without mentioning the sea.

Of course, the Kirk's influence was not all beneficial, and the stern censoriousness of the Kirk Sessions and the sectarian intolerance in the past seem particularly unattractive to us today. However, if many episodes of Kirk history are far from edifying, some are certainly entertaining. Who would not have enjoyed the scene in St Magnus on the Sunday in 1702 when the Rev. Thomas Baikie – still with his nightcap on, for he had just been roused from his sickbed – and Mrs Baikie attacked the rival minister who had started to take the service, and dragged him bodily from the cathedral pulpit?[2] Another drama to relish is the momentous Sunday in 1843, when the Church of Scotland minister and his rival, the young Free Kirk minister, preached simultaneously inside and outside the Harray kirk, and then leapt on their horses and raced each other at a gallop to get to the Birsay kirk first, pursued by a cheering crowd laying bets on who would win.[3] Anyone who expects a book about churches to feature people being well-behaved will be very disappointed.

Ruins and empty buildings need not be dead; they can be a bridge to connect us with other lives, other times. A silent tumble of stones or a medieval church, bright with colourful hangings, warm with candlelight, brimming with the sounds of harp music and psalm-singing? It depends on one's point of view. It is for us to make the leaps of imagination and listen to the voices of the past – but, even in churches, the voices are those of any ordinary human community, and one must not expect to encounter people more than occasionally at prayer. One will also hear plenty of gossip, scandal, argument, violence and moments of pure comedy.

For every Orkney schoolchild, the voices at St Magnus Kirk on Egilsay must be those of armed men, raised in fear or anger, followed by the crack of an axe on a man's skull. At the Brough of Deerness, a faltering line of pilgrims shuffle up the rock steps to the chapel on bleeding knees.

In Westray's Crosskirk, loud-mouthed seafarers brag of their adventures on the way to Jerusalem, or self-important lairds argue over who has the right to the best seat. At St Peter's in Skaill, there's a screech of Sandwick women, threatening to tear their unpopular minister in pieces. The hulk of the old Free kirk in Rousay, wrecked in a sea of meadowsweet at Sourin, was once the flagship of those who fought for land reform, and against the tyranny of a laird: one can hear mutterings of defiance among the wreckage. They are scenes in the continuing drama of Orkney life, in which those of us who live here all have small parts to play and, though most of the other characters happen to be dead, they do not have to be silent.

I undertook to research the stories of the Orkney kirks, and the part they played in the islands' history, as a voyage of discovery, without any particular destination in mind or preconceived idea of what I would find on the way. Inevitably, I found that there are many times when archaeology and historical record fall far short of offering certain answers to the questions with which one tries to prise open the past, and the only tools one is left with are best-guessing and imagination. These, I am aware, are dangerous. 'If a man once embarks upon the ocean of speculation, there is no saying to what shores of error he may drift in the uncharted currents of conjecture.'[4]

With this fearful warning in mind, I apologise in advance for the errors into which I will inevitably drift. This is not a voyage with a fixed schedule, but a suggested itinerary for time-travellers, whether exploring Orkney by foot, bicycle, car, or from an armchair. It is best to leave behind heavy baggage, and as many prejudices as possible, before embarking.

CHAPTER 1

Heroes, Hermits and Obstinate Pagans

Legends of the saints endure because we all need holy people. The saints are heroes, symbols of what could be possible; a reminder that everything cannot be reduced to manageable, cerebral categories, and that there is a dimension beyond what our logical minds dictate.

Esther de Waal (1991)

*I*n 1923, some men digging a new grave in the kirkyard in Papay, one of the smallest and most northerly islands of the Orkney archipelago, struck a large stone with their spades. They brought to the surface a thin slab, almost two feet long, with a cross incised on it in fine, precise lines, as if drawn with a compass. It is the earliest piece of hard evidence that, at least 1,300 years ago, Christianity had spread to the Northern Isles.

To travel to the time when the first 'arks' were built in Orkney is to explore a region where saints and heroes abound, and the borders between history and legend shift elusively in the North Atlantic mist. In the background are the figures of giants – St Ninian, St Patrick, St Columba. The life of Patrick, a fifth-century Briton captured as a boy by Irish pirates, who escaped from slavery to convert the people of Ireland single-handedly, reads like an adventure story, but the facts are as astonishing as his miracles. Within a hundred years of his death, there were churches and monastic communities in every part of Ireland. Irish missionaries were travelling to other parts of the British Isles and to far-flung corners of Europe, where Christianity had been driven out by 'barbarian hordes' after the collapse of the Roman Empire. At the same time as St Columba (c. AD 521–97) was preaching Christianity in western Scotland from his base on Iona, his contemporary St Columban was crossing Gaul and establishing monasteries as far afield as the Apennines in northern Italy. The Celtic heroes of ancient Ireland stride out of pagan legend and into the pages of history as larger-than-life Christian holy men who were also extraordinarily intrepid adventurers and explorers.

While missionaries like Columban were actively engaged in the world, there were also the 'peregrini' or wandering hermits who fled as far as possible from it. Seafarers such as St Brendan the Navigator sailed to inhospitable and uninhabited corners of the North Atlantic. Equipped with small boats and enormous faith, they pushed out the boundaries of the known world in their quest for 'a desert in the ocean', dealing briskly with tempests, monsters and pagans on the way. By AD 700, they had reached the Faeroes and, a little later, Iceland, and it would be very surprising if Irish curraghs did not also land on Orkney and Shetland islands on the way. We have 'embarked upon the ocean of speculation', and the only landmarks are traces of hermitages, perched precariously on cliff-tops and sea-stacks, and a scattering of crosses, carved in stone.

The names of the heroes who first preached Christianity in Orkney are unknown, but their mission must have been a dangerous one. Iceland and the Faeroes were empty islands when the itinerant monks first landed there, and they settled undisturbed until the Vikings made their abrupt entrance on the scene. Orkney, on the other hand, had long been inhabited by people with sophisticated religious beliefs of their own. There is no reason to imagine that the local pagan priests would have given a warm welcome to visiting Christian missionaries. When St Columba made a diplomatic visit to King Bridei of the Picts in Inverness, he was challenged by extremely resentful druids. Columba impressed Bridei by upstaging the druids' miracles, and putting the Loch Ness Monster to flight with a wave of his cross, but his actions would have hardly endeared him to his hosts. The point of the story is that he was undertaking a hazardous journey in enemy territory.[1]

Columba was at Bridei's court at the same time as the ruler of Orkney, which seems to have been a province of Pictland at the time. Clearly, Columba realised that Christian monks risked being put to death by hostile Picts, for he asked Bridei to command this man to ensure the safety of his friend Cormac and his companions if they landed in Orkney on their travels.[2]

St Columba was an aristocrat and clearly a political figure as well as a religious leader – generations of clergy would adopt this role model – but he was not typical of his time. Most of his followers removed themselves from the secular world to live in poverty and seclusion. It is entirely due to the monks that so much of pagan Irish legend and poetry has survived, because they wrote down the oral traditions. Fortunately, much of their own poetry has survived too, and it is full of delight in the created world and contentment with a life of tilling the soil, netting fish, gathering berries and enjoying birdsong and the change of the seasons.

> A full household could not be more lovely than my little oratory in
> Tuaim Inbir with its stars in their order, with its sun and its moon ...
> A house where rain does not pour, a place where spear-points are not
> dreaded, as bright as in a garden with no fence about it.[3]

Characteristic of this poetry is its sheer cheerfulness. In the margin of the manuscript he was copying, one eighth-century monk wrote about his enjoyment of sitting in his scriptorium working at his books while his pet cat worked at keeping the mice down. It ends:

> So in peace our tasks we ply,
> Pangur Ban, my cat, and I;
> In our arts we have our bliss,
> I have mine and he has his.[4]

If the missionaries who came to Orkney were men like these, there is no doubt that they were carrying the *gospel*, literally, *good news* to the islands. At a time when 'conversion' all too often meant a military campaign of brutal subjugation, for political ends, the Irish monks seem to have genuinely embarked upon their amazing journeys for the love of God. Somehow, their spiritual descendants in every generation hung on to their message, even though, over the following centuries, the good news often seems to have been hijacked by politicians for secular ambitions, forgotten in the Church's own political entanglements, or distorted into news that was not good at all.

King Bridei was not sufficiently impressed by Columba's miracles to be converted, but his successors saw that Pictland's political credibility lay in its becoming part of the rapidly expanding militant empire of 'Christendom'. In the machinations of early medieval power-politics,

FIGURE 1.1
This unusually large iron handbell (9 inches/22.5 cm high) was deliberately buried in a stone cist in a Christian cemetery at the Knowe of Saevar Howe, Birsay. Bells like this were used by Celtic clergy and were greatly venerated for their association with the holy man to whom they had belonged. Was it buried to protect it from damage or theft by raiders? (After Anderson)

secular rulers and the Church found a mutual advantage in supporting one another. The Church gained land and protection, so that it could support itself and expand its influence, in return for gilding the role of the ruler with Divine Authority, and providing a literate civil service for his administration.

The Picts, at this stage, were a powerful and artistically accomplished people. Their ruling class had sophisticated tastes and cultural links beyond Scotland, especially with Northumbria which was a flourishing Christian kingdom and a remarkable centre of culture. When the Pictish kings became Christian, it is likely that the people in the territories under their control would soon have been persuaded, or compelled, to follow suit. It is a less romantic picture of 'conversion' but, while salt-soaked monks like Columba's friend, Cormac, may have been the first to preach the gospel in the Northern Isles, it was probably only when political pragmatism persuaded the rulers to adopt the new beliefs that missionaries had any real chance of survival and success.

Carved crosses trace their journeys across Orkney, from South Ronaldsay to the Brough of Birsay in the west, and North Ronaldsay and

Papay on the northern edges of the archipelago. They are clear statements that 'Christians Were Here', but 'conversion' is unlikely to have been as straightforward an affair as history often presents it: accomplished on a precise date, rather like Britain going over to decimal currency. One tries to imagine the scene: strangers land on the beach, expound complex metaphysics in a foreign language and, against all the odds, the locals are so impressed that they abandon their old gods and sign up for baptism. If this is what happened, it was an astonishing event, but it is much more likely that conversion was a gradual and piecemeal process.[5]

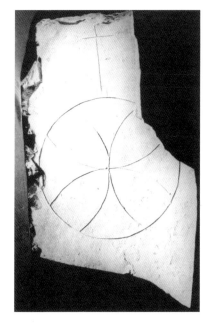

FIGURE 1.2
Probably the oldest cross-slab found in Orkney, from St Boniface kirkyard, Papay. In style it is very similar to crosses found at Whithorn and on the Isle of Bute. (NMS)

In the conflict between Christianity and paganism, however, Christianity had a significant advantage. It was not just a new set of religious ideas and practices, but a cultural package that had originated in the Mediterranean world and had brought from there two powerful tools for controlling the media: literacy, and a long tradition of representational art. The Romans had used portraiture and figural sculpture extensively for commemoration and propaganda, and Christian artists inherited their techniques and used them to convey their own message. Before the arrival of Christianity, the human figure was hardly ever portrayed in Scotland,[6] and the decorative, abstract art of the Celtic world, which was used with such superb skill to embellish weaponry and jewellery, was quite unsuited to narrative. In a nutshell, the core message of Christianity is that God lived on earth as a man, and the story of his life could be told in books and in pictures that a child, or an illiterate Pict, could understand. The Picts quickly adopted the idea of narrative art for their own secular propaganda, and there is every reason to imagine that they would have decorated the inside of their churches, even if only small and simple buildings, and painted the story of the gospels on the walls.

Although the Pictish churches have disappeared, the crosses indicate where some of them stood, and their names have sometimes lingered at the sites. These are clues that we can use in reconstructing the impact of Christianity on Orkney society. The church of St Boniface in Papay, for example, was built in the middle of an important settlement that surrounded a huge broch (presumably, once a chieftain's headquarters) and on some of the best land in this very fertile island. In a short time, those first pioneering missionaries had evidently become 'Establishment', and were held in such esteem by the chiefs and landowners that they were given some of the most valuable real estate available.

This theory is reinforced by the place name. *Papey*, island of the *papar*, Christian 'fathers' or priests, is the name the Norse gave to the isle. It is significant that all the places that they associated with *papar* are such good farmland that the Norse earls promptly appropriated them for their own estates. (The two *Papeys* were later named Papa Westray and Papa Stronsay to distinguish them, but Papa Westray is still invariably called Papay by its inhabitants.)[7]

The settlement surrounding St Boniface disappeared long ago, but the name 'Munkerhoose' survives,[8] suggesting that there was a monastery here as well as a church. It is unlikely that the monks who lived here, in such an accessible and upmarket location, led an entirely contemplative life. Perhaps, as in many later monasteries, they provided services to the local community in the way of education and medical care, and were repaid in manual labour in cornfield or fishing ground. In other parts of Europe the Church often founded monasteries as base-camps for missionary forays into heathen territory, and the choice of the dedication to St Boniface, coupled with St Tredwell for the chapel a mile away, suggests that this is what happened on Papay. According to medieval legend, a Pope Boniface travelled to Scotland from Rome, to lead a highly successful mission to Pictland. Among his entourage was a 'noble virgin abbess Triduana', the Latinised form of Tredwell.[9]

For seafaring clerics, Munkerhoose was strategically placed to be a springboard for missionary activity in the Northern Isles. In good summer weather, a day's sailing would take them to sheltered landings in places like St Ninian's Isle or Papil in Burra on the west coast of Shetland, which is exactly where we find evidence of Christian settlement in the eighth century. This scenario is guesswork, but plausible. What is puzzling is that the Shetland Christian sites are so much richer than those in Orkney. Papil and Bressay and St Ninian's Isle have produced splendid carved crosses and 'corner-post shrines' (stone caskets for preserving the bones of saints), but no shrines have been found in Orkney at all, and nothing remotely comparable to the magnificent collection of silver which someone buried under the floor of the chapel in St Ninian's Isle around AD 800.

In comparison to the crosses commissioned by wealthy Shetlanders, the simple incised crosses from Orkney are, frankly, bottom of the market. Only the altar-stone from Flotta, with its elaborate interlace, is characteristic of the high quality of Pictish sculpture. Even the Brough of Birsay, although it was clearly a high-status site, produced evidence of only modest wealth in comparison to the Pictish treasures found elsewhere. It seems that there was nothing showy or opulent about life in eighth-century Orkney.

If the wealthy had little disposable wealth, life for the poor must have been precarious. There is tree-ring evidence that Ireland suffered a period of exceptionally severe climate between AD 648 and 720; there were also outbreaks of plague in the 660s. Presumably, Scotland suffered similar conditions at the same time, and crop failure, famine and unrest would have followed. This could explain the Picts' savage military expeditions into Orkney.[10] There are terse statements in Irish Annals that Orkney was 'destroyed' by King Bridei II in 681, and that another war was 'fought in the Orkneys' in 709.[11] Is it possible that a defeated and demoralised people, disillusioned with their gods, were more receptive to a new message, offering them at the least the hope of a much better life after death? Wars could certainly have left the islands so impoverished that no local leaders had the resources to commission expensive sculpture, but monastic communities may have played a useful role in bringing lands

FIGURE 1.3

The superbly carved altar frontal found in Flotta. Jo Ben's sixteenth-century 'Description of the Isles of Orkney' refers to a large church in Flotta where three crosses 'were overturned for the wall-builder'. Were there originally other Pictish carved crosses of this quality that were destroyed at the Reformation? (Ian Scott/RCAHMS)

which had been ravaged by war back into agricultural production. It was normal for monasteries to support themselves by farming, and recent research has suggested that the *papar* may even have innovated improved agricultural techniques.[12]

At the Papay Munkerhoose, with their church in the protective shadow of a powerful chieftain, their granaries filled with corn from their fertile fields, we can picture the early missionaries leading relatively comfortable lives. Other places tell other tales. At the little chapel in St Tredwell's Loch, one can imagine something of the difficulties they faced in combating pagan beliefs and practices that were so old and so deep-rooted that the Church found them impossible to eradicate. Local chiefs could control their own subjects but not, perhaps, the hostilities of the ancient gods.

The chapel, perched on top of an Iron Age fortification on a small islet, was an important focus of pilgrimage right down to the eighteenth century and we know something of the customs that were observed here. The ritual sunwise circuits of the loch, the coins and pebbles left as offerings, are typical of many sacred wells and lochs in other parts of Scotland, but they all have a strong savour of something far, far older than Christianity. Throughout the Bronze Age and Iron Age, lakes, rivers and wells were frequently places of worship, and the practice of making votive offerings to the gods by depositing precious objects in these places seems to have been widespread and long-lasting. Innumerable hoards of stone axes, amber beads, weapons of iron and bronze, silver cauldrons and other valuable objects have been excavated from Europe's bogs and lakes. It has been said that the Romans were so well aware of this practice that, after conquering Gaul, they put up these sacred lakes to auction and 'many of the purchasers found quantities of solid silver in them'![13]

The astonishingly rapid spread of Christianity masks the fact that, in traditionally polytheistic societies, the acceptance of a new god is not necessarily the same as discarding all the old ones, and the obstinate survival of paganism is lamented by generations of churchmen. In the sixth century, the Christian historian, Gildas, complained that British pagans paid 'divine honour' to hills and wells and rivers, and that their idols 'almost surpassed in number those of Egypt'![14] A hundred years later, a Church Council in Rouen was denouncing all those who offered vows and gifts to trees or wells. Four hundred years on, King Cnut found it necessary to pass a statute forbidding the 'barbarous adoration' of the sun and moon, fire, mountains, stones and trees. Some thousand years after the arrival of Christianity in Scotland, the Presbytery of Dingwall

FIGURE 1.4
St Tredwell's Loch and Chapel, Papay, in winter.

was hearing that: in the parish of Gairloch, bulls were sacrificed, fertility offerings of milk were poured on the hills, sacred wells venerated and chapels 'circulated sunwise ...'.[15] While the Church denounced such customs, they always seemed to slip in again by the back door, and we will find Orkney ministers trying to put a stop to the rituals at St Tredwell's and other pilgrimage sites more than two centuries after the Reformation.

It is understandable that the arrival of Christianity did not put an instant end to pagan beliefs. There were, after all, very few missionaries engaged in the difficult and dangerous task of reaching communities spread over vast tracts of often hostile territory, and the early Church was forced to be somewhat pragmatic. Rather than antagonising potential proselytes by destroying a sacred shrine, its strategy was to build a church on or near it. Pope Gregory the Great (c. AD 540–604) sent instructions to St Augustine of Canterbury that he should not destroy heathen temples if they were well-built and could be usefully recycled into churches. The feast days of saints were to be held on the days of pagan sacrifice, so that the new converts did not feel deprived of festivals and holidays.[16]

St Tredwell's name in *Orkneyinga Saga*[17] is 'Trollhoena', the Norse 'troll' element suggesting wickedness rather than sanctity, so she may well have started life in a very different guise, as a being to be feared and placated by the lochside. If she did, the chapel was probably built in an attempt to 'christianise' a popular pagan site. In effect, deities too stubborn to be removed were often camouflaged and enlisted into the ranks of Christian saints. The gods and spirits of the pagan world, the dryads and naiads of ancient Greece and the trolls of Scandinavia, were not so much vanquished by the triumph of Christianity as driven underground, from where they sometimes quietly re-emerged, respectable, and garnished with Christian halos.[18]

For some monks, however, combat with pagan gods was not enough of a challenge. Signs of hermitages have been found in the Northern Isles, in places that are far more difficult to reach, both physically and with the imagination. On bleak holms, remote headlands and precipitous stacks, hardline ascetics built their huts. In places such as the Castle of Burwick in South Ronaldsay in Orkney and – far more desolate – the seaward-sloping rock of the Kame of Isbister or the 'truly dreadful' stack of Clett of Birrier in Shetland, they deliberately turned their faces to the sea and their backs to the world.[19] Because the stack-sites are so difficult to access, very few have been excavated and dated. One of the few is Brei Holm off Papa Stour, which could only be scaled by an experienced climber who fixed ropes for the rest of the team. Late Iron Age buildings were found there[20] and, presumably, some at least of the Orkney sites are of similar date.

One cannot imagine monks still occupying these places during the Viking raids in the early ninth century, when they were fleeing from their outposts on North Atlantic islands, but it is quite possible that the eremitic tradition revived in more settled times. There are buildings on sea-stacks off Stronsay, on the puffin-thronged Castle of Burrian off Westray, and a tradition of a nunnery on the Holm of Aikerness, a bare sliver of rock almost swamped by the sea at high tide, where John Brand saw the ruins of a chapel as late as 1700.[21] It is not possible to prove that any of these places were inhabited by hermits, but the 'negative evidence' is compelling. Who else would choose to live a life of such incredible privation?

FIGURE 1.5
The Holm of Aikerness between Westray and Papay is almost covered by the sea at high tide, but the ruins of a chapel could still be made out on the holm in 1700.

When one looks at the stacks, it is more than the physical gap between one's standpoint and the hermit's outpost that is hard to bridge. One is baffled both by the logistics of their survival and also by a metaphysical gap: the yawning chasm between the twenty-first-century culture of self-indulgence and these enigmatic, poignant monuments to an almost incomprehensible ideal of extreme self-denial. There is a sense of dislocation. Celtic anchorites were the cultural heirs of the monks who practised unspeakable austerities in the Egyptian desert, or lived for years on pillars in Syria in the third century AD. Here, these figures of far away and long-ago are translated to the cold, wet reality of the North Atlantic, to a tiny parapet of wall on a wave-battered rock.

It is no wonder that medieval artists depicted the Desert Fathers being fed by a tame lion or a faithful raven. It is hard to imagine that their survival was possible without miraculous intervention, and this is equally true of hermits on sea-stacks. It has been suggested that they lived off seabirds,[22] which could have provided an adequate food supply for two or three months of the summer, although the mental image of a hermit on the Castle of Burrian simultaneously contemplating Creation and whacking puffins on the head is somewhat unsatisfactory.

In these places, more than anywhere, one can see the legacy of the Irish monks who scattered across the North Atlantic in search of solitude, settling in isolated islands and cultivating tiny gardens even among the rock pinnacles of Skellig Michael, the famous rock monastery off the coast of Kerry in Eire. The literature of Celtic monasticism is full of their stories, but extremism was not the norm. The ideal was a life in which activity within the world and retirement from it were held in balance. It was common for monks to withdraw to solitary places for periods of contemplation (between missionary journeys, for example, or during the fasting season of Lent) but these were temporary retreats. Those like St Brendan, who spent years sailing the Atlantic in search of yet greater hardship and isolation, were famous because they were the exception, not the rule.

If we see the hermitage sites as outposts of the monasteries rather than alternatives to them, it is a little easier to understand how people could have survived in such hostile places. It would have been quite feasible for the Stronsay stack-sites to have been supplied by monks from Papa Stronsay, and the Westray site by monks from Papay. One imagines baskets of food being hauled up the cliffs from a small boat bobbing in the waves below. However, even if the hermits lived here only for periods of retreat, or penance, and in the summer months, it is still hard not to be moved by these places. They must have endured long days of driving rain, of total isolation in fogs, of gales when the turbulence of wind and water severed their small hut from everything but the elements. It was in such intense experience of the created world that they found themselves closest to God. From these lonely, salt-drenched rocks, the words of the psalm must often have ascended into the wind: 'If I take the wings of the morning, and dwell in the uttermost parts of the sea, even there shall thy hand lead me, and thy right hand shall hold me'.[23]

At all these places where we can find faint traces of the earliest churches or hermitages, we can come a little closer in the imagination to the people who built them, but we are still left with unanswered questions. Although the irrepressibility of the ancient gods may have caused it some problems, the Pictish Church in Orkney appears to have been well established – until it was engulfed in the early ninth century by the incoming tide of Vikings. Clearly, the invaders swept the islands

FIGURE 1.6
There is just room for a small hut on the top of this stack off the east coast of Stronsay, protected by a parapet of drystone walling.

back into paganism for a time, but how thoroughly did they obliterate the Christian culture that they found? Were the churches destroyed, the clergy slaughtered, and the memory of Christianity well and truly forgotten for two or three centuries, or was there a degree of toleration and coexistence? The huge preponderance of Norse place names certainly suggests that colonisation was swift and wholesale, but the Picts are notorious for inspiring controversy, and academic opinion is hotly divided as to whether they were annihilated by the Vikings or whether there was a degree of rapprochement between the two cultures.

Interpreting the past is a highly subjective business. Orkney historians such as Storer Clouston in the 1930s and Hugh Marwick in the 1950s saw the Norse period as a Golden Age, and were inclined to whitewash Viking belligerence. More recent historians have been less enthralled by the glamour of rape-and-pillage cultures. Marwick thought that the long tradition of veneration for sites such as the Brough of Birsay was proof that the Norse invasion caused no break in Christian tradition,[24] but it is hard to imagine that the same Vikings who looted churches and murdered clergy so enthusiastically up and down the seaboard of the British Isles would have resisted this temptation in Orkney. Churches and monasteries were obvious targets for pillage after all: they were often coastal, staffed by unarmed men, and housed precious objects like chalices and books. Vikings may not have had much use for manuscripts, but their jewelled and metal bindings were good hard currency.

However, it is unlikely that the invaders slaughtered the inhabitants of Orkney *en masse*. When they settled the islands, they would have needed women, servants, and farmers and artisans who would produce taxable wealth, and in all these respects the Picts were much more useful to them alive than dead. If this was the case, many a second-generation Viking settler would have been rocked in his cradle by a Christian Pict. Nor would the Norse have had any motivation for persecuting Christians to extinction just because of their beliefs. They were accustomed to a variety of gods in their pantheon, and one suspects them of being more interested in loot than in metaphysics. Christian crosses were evidently still being carved in Orkney in the pagan ninth and tenth centuries.

Recent excavations have suggested that there was little continuity of Pictish and Norse occupation at either domestic or ecclesiastical sites in Orkney, but rather that the Norse reoccupied sites that had long been abandoned.[25] This supports the record of Orkney being 'destroyed' by war, and suggests that, when the Norse arrived, the native population may have been so reduced that they were able to offer little resistance. If they were quickly assimilated by the invaders, their disappearance from history is easier to understand. However, despite all the blood and ink that has been spilled on the subject, the fate of the Picts and the *papar* has still not been entirely resolved. They had already faded into legend by the twelfth century, when the writer of the *Historia Norvegiae* could remember only that the Picts were little people who lived underground, and that the *papar* wore white robes, and from their dress and their books were clearly 'Africans adhering to Judaism'![26]

CHAPTER 2

A Saga of Saints and Retired Pirates

To stand by Thor and Odinn in these late days was to be a dog howling in the wilderness.

Gwyn Jones (1973)

In the year AD 995, Earl Sigurd of Orkney was at Osmundwall in the island of Walls, busy with preparations for his annual trip plundering along the coasts of Scotland and Ireland. Three ships lay at anchor in the bay, and the crescent of white sand was heaped with stores: casks of water, barrels of dried meat or fish, spare sails, shields, as his men made ready for a season of Viking activity.

Presumably, none of them had heard word of the approach of the Norwegian Viking, Olaf Tryggvason. After four years spent looting along the British seaboard, Olaf had been baptised a Christian, and he was heading homeward from Ireland with his ambition set on the crown of Norway and his soul freighted with a new faith. His encounter with the pagan Earl Sigurd is described in *Orkneyinga Saga*.

When Olaf's fleet of five ships suddenly appeared, rounding the sheltering arm of Cantick Head, Sigurd and his men found themselves trapped in the narrow bay. Olaf, wanting no trouble from Orkney while he was occupied with securing the Norwegian throne, took full advantage of his situation. He sent a messenger to Sigurd, asking him to come over to his ship:

'I want you and all your subjects to be baptised' he said when they met. 'If you refuse, I'll have you killed on the spot, and I swear that I'll ravage every island with fire and steel'. The Earl could see what kind of situation he was in and surrendered himself into Olaf's hands. He was baptised ... After that, all Orkney embraced the faith.[1]

FIGURE 2.1
'Olaf sailed east with five ships ... at Osmundwall he ran into Earl Sigurd, who had three ships and was setting out on a viking expedition ...'.

Olaf went on his way, and continued to bludgeon people up and down the Norwegian coast into his particularly militaristic version of Christianity. Obviously, his new beliefs did not cramp his lifestyle, so why did Olaf – and other Vikings – claim 'conversion'?

It may have been a shrewd political move to gain support from the Christian rulers of England and Ireland. It may have been his Irish wife who pushed Olaf towards baptism, and, like many other powerful and violent men, he gave into domestic pressure. Or had it, quite simply, become fashionable to be Christian?

> We need not assume that Olaf had much awareness of the doctrinal aspects of the Christian faith, and on the most favourable witness he appears little touched by its spiritual values. But ... like other travelled vikings he had observed at first hand the dignity, wealth and ceremonial of the Church in other countries. Here was a splendour, an enrichment and fellowship, from which the northern barbarian stood excluded.[2]

Did Earl Sigurd's unexpected christening really lead to the conversion of Orkney? It is hard to imagine the whole population suddenly queuing for mass baptism, and probably reality was a little less dramatic than the saga suggests. The earls may have remained heathen until the end of the first millennium, but many of their subjects had come into contact with

Christianity, perhaps on trading voyages to Ireland, much earlier than this. In the ninth century, Norse men and women had been buried at Westness in Rousay with their armour and jewellery, in traditional, pagan manner. By the mid-tenth century, however, grave goods were going out of fashion which suggests that Christian burial practices were being adopted long before the events in Osmundwall.[3] It is likely that new and old beliefs coexisted for some time. A complete break with the old gods must have seemed a high-risk strategy, and Helgi the Lean, the Icelander who 'believed in Christ but invoked Thor for sea-journeys and times of crisis',[4] was probably one of many who preferred to hedge their bets.

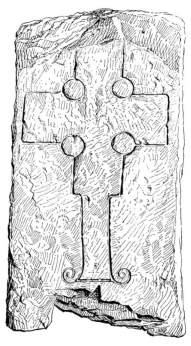

FIGURE 2.2

The ninth-century cross found at Osmundwall, on the shores of Kirk Hope, is evidence of a church here long before Sigurd's unexpected baptism. (PSAS)

When Orkney men and women did 'embrace the faith', what did that mean to them? The Christ who stares out at us from the pages of early Irish gospel books, or from Scandinavian metalwork, is disconcertingly unfamiliar. Centuries of Christian art have accustomed us to a repertoire of easily recognised images, but these figures are alien, created by minds inhabiting a totally different thought-world from our own, and wrought by hands that seem more used to beating intricate patterns out of metal than representing the human form. The Christ that the Norse encountered in the gospel stories had not yet been frozen into the rigidity of Byzantine icons, had never been cradled by serene Renaissance Madonnas in immaculately clean stables, nor sanitised by sentimental Victorian portrayals of Gentle Jesus Meek and Mild. They would have seen the coarse-handed carpenter, the miracle-worker and healer, only through the lens of their own fierce past. They probably understood the many agricultural parables much more vividly than we

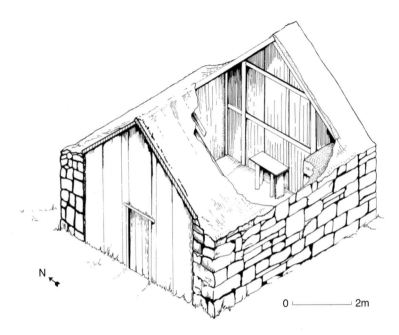

FIGURE 2.3
Reconstruction by Norman Emery of the timber chapel excavated on the Brough of Deerness. It was built in the later tenth century (more evidence that Christianity was being practised in Orkney before Sigurd's conversion in AD 995), of vertical planks, with the side walls clad in stone.
(C. D. Morris/PSAS)

do, and resonated to the disciples' fear as they lost control of their fishing boat in a sudden storm. They would have recognised the familiar figure of the man stripped and beaten by thieves, even if perplexed by the rescuing Good Samaritan. When we stand in the ruins of Norse churches, we have to make a leap of the imagination to connect with the people who built them and, first, we need to release our preconceptions of Christianity from its cultural packaging.

FIGURE 2.4
St Magnus Kirk, Egilsay, sketched by Hibbert in 1822, when the kirk was still in use.

There is nothing in the ensuing blood-soaked pages of *Orkneyinga Saga* to suggest that conversion in any way inhibited the earls and their followers from pursuing their customary activities with their customary relish, but the fatal meeting at Osmundwall does mark the beginning of a new era in Orkney's history. In 1014, Earl Sigurd terminated a classic Viking career under the raven banner of Odin in the battle of Clontarf in Ireland. It was the last great pagan mêlée to take place in the British Isles, recounted to an accompaniment of showers of boiling blood, weapons fighting in the air, a web of human entrails woven by the Valkyries and an orgy of pagan symbolism quite undiluted by the water of baptism.[5] A few decades later, Orkney gained a bishopric and its first cathedral. It owed these milestones to the surprising accident that Sigurd's son, Earl Thorfinn the Mighty – after a lifetime devoted to war, pillage and fratricide – somehow evaded a violent death and lived long enough to retire from his Viking career and devote his last years to legislation, ecclesiastical administration and architecture.

> By now [Thorfinn] was finished with piracy and devoted all his time to the government of his people and country and to the making of new laws. He had his permanent residence at Birsay, where he built and dedicated to Christ a fine minster, the seat of the first bishop of Orkney.[6]

Were Christkirk and the bishop's palace built on the green slopes of the tidal island that is the Brough of Birsay, with its defensible position and sweeping views? Or were they in the settlement of Birsay on the mainland shore, where St Magnus Kirk stands on older foundations remembered as Christkirk? Archaeology yields few certainties and a minefield of academic disagreement, but if we cannot be certain of the site, the saga's vivid descriptions make it easy for us to catch a glimpse of the ruthless, ugly earl, overseeing the building of his new minster from under his bushy eyebrows, or feasting with his companions in his hall.

'He was unusually tall and strong, an ugly-looking man with a black head of hair, sharp features and bushy eyebrows, a forceful man, greedy for fame and fortune.'[7] Reared in Scotland at the court of his grandfather, Malcolm, King of Scots, Thorfinn would have been familiar with Christian teaching from childhood, but he took readily to the family profession and was leading his own gang of Vikings as a precocious teenager. In a series of brutal campaigns in Scotland and the Hebrides, he enlarged the territory under Orkney control to the greatest extent it ever reached. His power-struggles against his relatives ended in 1046, when he became sole earl of Orkney by murdering his nephew, Rognvald Brusason.

After that, although he still kept his hand in by going on Viking expeditions from time to time, Earl Thorfinn found time to pay State visits abroad. According to *Orkneyinga Saga*, he was not only warmly welcomed by the kings of Norway and Denmark and by the Holy Roman Emperor in Germany, but was also received by the Pope in Rome 'and received absolution from him for all his sins'.[8] (It is an intriguing thought that Thorfinn may have knelt in St Peter's side by side with Macbeth. They were in Rome at the same time, and expiated their respective murders of Earl Rognvald and King Duncan at Easter 1050.)[9] Always astute, Thorfinn had secured not only his place among the crowned heads of Europe, but also his seat in the Christian Valhalla.

If Earl Thorfinn's support of Christianity appears pragmatic rather than spiritual in motivation, nonetheless it was significant in terms of bringing Orkney back into the mainstream of European culture. In the Modern Europe in which he was anxious to be included, paganism and piracy were outmoded. Modern rulers governed Christian countries with a clerical bureaucracy, rather than with fire and sword. A pilgrimage to Rome was as much *de rigueur* for young aristocrats in the eleventh century as the Grand Tour was in the eighteenth. More prosaically, Thorfinn's new laws were probably designed to bring Orkney into line with current Euro-legislation by banning pagan practices such as exposing unwanted infants to die, or eating horseflesh, which was traditionally consumed at ritual feasts after the animals had been sacrificed to the gods. Thorfinn also requested a bishop for Orkney, and the Pope appointed Thorolf as the first resident bishop. There had been some itinerant bishops before this, like 'Fat Henry' who was sent from Iceland, but he was a dissolute character. 'Delighting in the pestiferous habit of drunkenness and gluttony, he died at last through surfeit', and that is all we know about him.[10]

Earl Thorfinn made Birsay into a permanent base both for the earldom and for the bishopric, and Orkney was brought into the vast international organisation of the medieval Church, successively a part of the archdioceses of Hamburg-Bremen in Germany, York in England, Lund in Sweden, and Nidaros (Trondheim) in Norway in little more than a century! The splendid minster and Earl's and Bishop's Palaces, built side by side, were a symbol of the alliance of Church and State which was to be such an apparent strength and fatal weakness in the Church in the centuries to come. From this time on, the bishop had his own palace, his own cathedral and his own estates, and so he became an increasingly rich and powerful personality. A little later, we find Earl

Rognvald taking the bishop with him as an interpreter when he travelled abroad. A great advantage in employing clergy was that they spoke and wrote a common language, Latin, and could be dispatched anywhere to negotiate political or commercial deals. Without its own well-educated clergy, Orkney would have remained a backwater with no part to play in world affairs, not at all what Thorfinn's ambition demanded. By the time he died, he was an acknowledged head of a Christian state, ruling a relatively peaceful Orkney which he had transformed 'from a nest of pirates into a Christian earldom which aspired to be fully integrated into European Christendom'.[11]

Earl Thorfinn was buried in his own kirk in Birsay in 1065, and the peaceful earldom he had achieved disintegrated in the rivalry between his sons, and then his grandsons, which culminated in the murder of Earl Magnus on Egilsay, fifty years later. Paradoxically, it was this bloodshed which was to inspire some of Orkney's finest cultural achievements. In the twelfth century, the splendid round-towered St Magnus Kirk was built on Egilsay, and St Magnus Cathedral soared out of Kirkwall with all the vigour and splendour of fully-formed Romanesque architecture. At last,

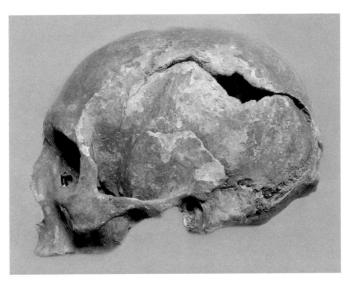

FIGURE 2.5
The axe-blow can be clearly seen on the skull of St Magnus. His bones were hidden for safety in a pillar of the cathedral choir, at the time of the Reformation, and only rediscovered in 1919. (Tom Kent/OLA)

instead of trying to mentally reassemble buildings out of fragmentary clues, we can stand in solid stone walls.

First, however, since everything revolves around him for a time, we need to focus on Orkney's patron saint.

> St Magnus, Earl of Orkney, was a man of extraordinary distinction, tall, with a fine, intelligent look about him. He was a man of strict virtue, successful in war, wise, eloquent, generous and magnanimous, open-handed with money, sound with advice, and altogether the most popular of men.[12]

The first 'Life' of St Magnus – upon which all the saga accounts were based – was written only about twenty years after his death, but by that time memory of the man Magnus Erlendsson was already confused in a tangle of legend and hagiography, piety and political propaganda. There is probably little we can know of him for certain other than that he was Earl of Orkney from about 1105, sharing the earldom with his cousin, Hakon, until an axe on Egilsay dispatched him into immortality in 1115 or 1116. Through *Magnus Saga* and *Orkneyinga Saga*, however, the saint comes down to us in a sequence of well-known images, clear and bright as stained glass windows.

First we see the young Magnus, launched unwillingly in the king of Norway's battle-fleet, standing in the king's longship reading a psalter, while all are hacking and hewing around him.[13] The following years that Magnus spent in Scotland or England are skipped over in the sagas, as are the disastrous years of the 'cloven earldom', when Orkney disintegrated into faction and ruin.

> The islands are in trouble.
> Fire in the thatch, blood on the shore,
> Their tables and cupboards empty,
> Weeping at every doorstep.[14]

The drama of the saga, however, is not in the earl's life but in his last moments before his death. A peace-parley between the rival earls had been proposed: both were to come with two ships to Egilsay, neutral territory, and thrash out their differences with words and pen, instead of the bow and the sword. The innocent Magnus came first, then treacherous Hakon arrived with eight fully-manned warships. Magnus was as defenceless as a sacrificial victim. He spent the night praying in the church and, skilfully, the saga-writer parallels his last hours with the betrayal and arrest of Christ. In the morning, Hakon's men surrounded him. They had determined to leave the isle with only one earl alive, but none of them was anxious to be remembered as the one who slaughtered an innocent man. Lifolf, the butcher, is compelled to wield his axe. 'Stand in front of me and strike me hard on the head', said Magnus, 'it's not fitting for a chieftain to be beheaded like a thief.'[15]

The axe-blow on Egilsay was only the beginning. Magnus was carried to Birsay and buried in the cathedral built by his grandfather, Thorfinn. That, Hakon must have fervently hoped, would be the end of his rival, but Magnus proved to be far more potent a figure dead than alive.

> Not long after the burial, a bright, heavenly light was often seen over Magnus' grave. Then people in peril started praying to him and no sooner did they pray than their troubles came to an end. People would sense a heavenly fragrance near his grave and the sick recovered their health.[16]

Secretly at first, the lame, the lepers, the blind began to make their way to Birsay.

A cult of St Magnus the Martyr must have been a serious political embarrassment to Earl Hakon and his party, and Bishop William did his best to suppress it – until he was struck blind in his own cathedral, and recovered his sight only when he had groped his way to Magnus' grave and vowed to translate the relics to a shrine. The news that Earl Rognvald, Magnus' nephew, was on his way back to Orkney to claim his share of the earldom may not have been unconnected to the bishop's change of mind. William was anxious to be found backing the right horse and, some twenty years after the murder, the bones of Magnus were ceremoniously placed in a shrine above the altar.

The pilgrims flocking to Magnus' shrine brought money to the church and a busy prosperity to Birsay, but it was short-lived. With the decline of the Viking trade routes round the western coasts of Scotland, Birsay had become isolated, and a small but strategically located market town called *Kirkjuvagr* (Kirk Bay) was growing. St Magnus himself evidently shared the view that Birsay was no longer important enough to house his shrine. He appeared in a dream to a Westray farmer called Gunni, and demanded to be removed to the new town. '(Gunni) set out right away for Birsay, where he told his dream at Mass to the whole congregation, in front of Earl Paul ...' When Earl Paul (Thorfinn's great-grandson) was defeated by Earl Rognvald in 1136 and 'disappeared', Birsay ceased to be a residence of the earls. It became an estate of the bishopric, but it was no longer the power-centre of Orkney.[17]

Our next image of the journeys of Magnus is of a splendid procession winding the twenty miles from Birsay to Kirkwall: Bishop William on horseback at the head, gorgeously clad in episcopal robes, the reliquary containing the saint's remains carried, shoulder-high, to the church of St Olaf, where it was placed above the high altar.[18] There it remained, until the first stage of the cathedral that Earl Rognvald founded was completed, and the relics could be enshrined in the choir. For over 400 years, the bones of Magnus remained at peace in the cathedral, but at the Reformation they were removed from their shrine and hidden, to save them from being thrown out in the zeal of the reformers. Their hiding place was unknown until, in 1919, a cavity was discovered in one of the piers of the choir, and inside it a wooden box containing the bones of a male skeleton. The skull had been smashed with a great blow to the head.

The story of Magnus can easily be read in terms of political history. The Norse had nothing to learn in the way of media-spin, and a miracle-working saint in the family was obviously a convenient asset to Rognvald when he was staking his claim to the earldom. Yet, in practice, it makes

FIGURE 2.6
St Magnus Kirk, Egilsay. By the time Capt. W. G. Burke made this sketch in 1875, the roof and the top of the tower had fallen in. (RCAHMS/Society of Antiquaries)

little difference whether Magnus was really a saintly individual or just another leader assassinated in a coup. What mattered to the ordinary people who made their hopeful pilgrimage to his shrine was that he was remembered as caring for them, and for giving his life for the healing of Orkney. The Orcadian poet, George Mackay Brown, rediscovered Magnus as inspiration and paradigm: the innocent man whose self-sacrifice paves the way to peace and renewal. In a profound insight, Brown ends his book *Magnus* with a story of a miracle, but not one that happens to anyone important, devout, or even remotely deserving. The tinker, Jock, lights his stump of tallow candle on Magnus' tomb with a half-believing prayer, and the bitter-tongued, cynical, thieving 'bag of sins', Blind Mary, recovers her sight on the Birsay shore.[19]

As well as being Orkney's patron saint, Magnus was popular in Norway and in all its colonies. Five churches were dedicated to him in Shetland, two in Caithness, seven in Iceland and a cathedral in the Faeroes, which was given a finger-bone of the saint. (When the bones of Magnus were rediscovered in Kirkwall, the appropriate phalange was missing from the skeleton.)[20] In Orkney, he is remembered at the places connected with him: in Egilsay, Birsay, Kirkwall and also in Stronsay. St Magnus Day commemorates the day of his death, 16 April, appropriately the Easter season of both sacrifice and renewal.

Orkneyinga Saga depicts the twelfth century in Orkney as a more or less continuous rampage of blood-feud and violence. Apart from Earl Rognvald's taste for poetry, it gives little indication of a society with an interest in cultural attainments, so it is fortunate that we have the evidence of the very real architectural achievements of the time. With the exception of the cathedral, the Romanesque churches built by the Norse survive only in ruins, but they are beautiful and evocative buildings, their sturdy walls and round-arched doorways echoing the solidity and gentle curves of their island landscapes. It is appropriate that one of the finest, and certainly the most distinctive with its tall round tower, should be the church built on Egilsay to commemorate St Magnus.

Bishop William seems to have had a residence on Egilsay – this would explain the choice of the island for the earls' peace-parley – and it is likely that he had a major hand in the planning of the new church around 1136, when he was promoting the cult of Magnus. Even today in its abandoned, roofless state, Magnuskirk makes a powerful statement about the Church as a strong fortress against the anarchic world around it. It is built to impress: the design sophisticated, the masonry of high quality. If William

FIGURE 2.7

The medieval kirk at Stenness with its semicircular tower, drawn by George Law in 1774. Stenness Loch is in the background and the plum pudding marked B is Maeshowe! At D a couple are plighting their troth through the hole in the Stone of Odin. (OLA)

built it as part of an episcopal palace, the walls that are so silent now must have rung with the hubbub of a busy household, with the sounds of men shouting, horses clattering over cobbles, servants singing or cursing over work, as well as the serene chant of psalms from the choir. It is a large building, 19 metres long from east to west, and survives intact apart from the flagstone roof and the top of the elegant tower, a slightly tapered cylinder that originally rose to a neat cone 19 metres above ground.

The lost storey may well have held bells, perhaps as much to sound alarm if an enemy was sighted, as to call to Mass. The church was a sanctuary: its doorway has a bar-hole so that the door could be locked from the inside with a heavy beam of wood.[21] In the unsettled times which *Orkneyinga Saga* describes, it is not surprising to find some of the churches stoutly built, as if to provide a defensible refuge as well as a place of worship. The semicircular tower of the old Stenness church was built with walls as much as five feet thick, like a castle keep,[22] and Tammaskirk in Rendall also had a tower. It may have been built as a mainland stronghold by the notorious pirate, Svein Asleifson, whose hall on the island of Gairsay lay opposite the Rendall shore.[23]

From the gallery in St Magnus Kirk one could reach a chamber above the chancel. This room may have served as a dwelling for a priest: clergy, then as now, had to travel between islands and stay overnight. Alternatively, it may have been a treasury for the church valuables, and medieval charters give an idea of what one might have seen in an important church like St Magnus. The contemporary church of Eyre in Iceland, for example, owned 'hangings all round the church, two bells, a silver chalice, four altar-cloths, four candlesticks, three hand-basins, three incense vessels and one fire-bearer, three rood crosses and one picture'.[24] In twelfth-century Orkney, one might well have felt the need to lock away a silver chalice and temptingly portable candlesticks.

The closest parallels to the Egilsay round tower are found in churches around the North Sea coasts, which would have been known to Orkney architects through trading links. In East Anglia, there are over a hundred churches with round towers attached, and the same design is found in northern Germany and southern Scandinavia.[25] A splendid Romanesque church with two round towers at the west end, capped with little cupolas just like the tower of St Magnus when it was complete, was still

FIGURE 2.8
St Mary's Kirk, built at the important Norse farm of Skaill in Deerness in the twelfth or thirteenth century. George Low thought it 'the most remarkable country Kirk in these isles' when he drew it in 1774, but it was described as 'ruinous' shortly afterwards and demolished. (OLA)

standing in Deerness when George Low, the Birsay minister, drew it in 1774. In Shetland, St Magnus in Tingwall and St Laurence in Papil were also fine 'steeple-kirks'.[26] All of these were demolished in the 1780s or 1790s, a period that perhaps only the 1960s equalled for its architectural vandalism.

CHAPTER 3

Jerusalem-faring and Church-building

I went the blue road to Jerusalem
With fifteen ships in a brawling company
Of poets, warriors, and holy men.

George Mackay Brown (1971)

*A*fter murdering his cousin, Magnus, on Egilsay, Earl Hakon Paulsson decided that discretion dictated an extended trip away from Orkney. 'Hakon set out on a long journey overseas and travelled south to Rome. His pilgrimage took him beyond to Jerusalem, where he visited the holy places and bathed in the River Jordan as is the custom of palmers.'[1] So Hakon knew, at first hand, the round Church of the Holy Sepulchre in Jerusalem, the most sacred site in Christendom and the ultimate goal of the medieval pilgrim. He returned from his journey around AD 1120 and consolidated his respectability by building a copy beside his own house in Orphir.

In the twelfth century, when enthusiasm for the Crusades was at its height, round churches were quite fashionable in Western Europe, but Hakon's St Nicholas is the only, fragmentary, survival in Scotland. The circular nave was six metres in diameter and roofed with a dome. Plastering survives on the internal walls of the semicircular apse, and undoubtedly the whole church was originally plastered and painted in bright colours. This spectacular building stood complete until 1757, when the nave was demolished and the stone used to build a new parish church. The apse was spared only because the workmen found the thick walls so strongly cemented together with lime mortar that they were extremely hard to knock down.

FIGURE 3.1
St Nicholas Church at the Bu', Orphir, built by Earl Hakon.

In *Orkneyinga Saga*, the 'great drinking hall' at the earl's residence is the scene of several unpleasant episodes that occurred during Christmas Feasts.[2] After Earl Hakon's death, the earldom was divided between his sons Harald and Paul, and quarrelling and bloodshed immediately broke

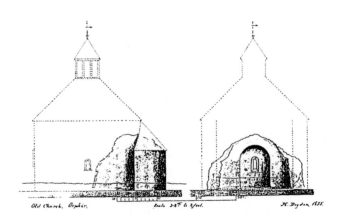

FIGURE 3.2
Reconstruction of Orphir Round Church by Sir Henry Dryden. (OLA)

out between their factions. The earls' mother and aunt, Helga and Frakkok, decided to put an end to the fighting in characteristically ruthless fashion, but their plan went hideously wrong. The following Christmas, Earl Harald was busy preparing for the feast at his hall in Orphir while Helga and Frakkok were occupied sewing an embroidered shirt as a present for his brother, Earl Paul. Harald came into the room and insisted on trying on the shirt despite their frantic protestations, and immediately suffered an agonising death. A few years later, Earl Paul was hosting the Christmas feast at Orphir and, as the story progresses, one can see that the proximity of hall and church was essential to the lifestyle. In the morning, the guests attended Matins, 'and then, after High Mass, they settled down to a meal. After they had carried on drinking for some time they went out for Nones, then came back and drank toasts from horns ... they kept drinking till Vespers ...' In-between stumbling in and out of divine service, Svein Breast-Rope and Svein Asleifarson broke into a drunken quarrel which ended with an axe in Breast-Rope's head on the way to Vespers.[3]

FIGURE 3.3

Several churches were built in Britain on a circular plan, imitating the Holy Sepulchre Church in Jerusalem. One of the few surviving is the Church of the Holy Sepulchre in Cambridge, consecrated in 1101.

Circular churches built in the first half of the twelfth century survive in Denmark, and these are the closest parallels to St Nicholas in Orphir. One is the chapel of St Michael in Halsingborg Castle, and all are small buildings, intended for the private use of royal or aristocratic circles rather than for public worship.[4] This is probably how St Nicholas functioned as well – the fuddled congregation present at Christmas Mass would have been Earl Paul's well-lubricated entourage.

Not only the earls but also their leading men and, sometimes, groups of the wealthier farmers, built their own chapels for their families and dependants – and funded a priest to say Mass in them. More than 200 chapel sites have been identified, most of them close to large farms or settlements, and anyone who visited Orkney around 900 years ago would have found a chapel in virtually every well-populated area. There were good pragmatic reasons for being a benefactor to the Church. According to *Eyrbyggja Saga*: 'The priests promised each farmer as many places in Heaven as there was standing room in any church he might build, and this proved a great inducement to them to put up churches.'[5] The Norse – who were hard-headed traders, after all, as well as farmers and pirates – cast the Almighty as a decent sort of chap who would overlook a spot of pillage and rapine if he was bought off with a nice church. Not only was it a good insurance policy for the next world, but also an opportunity to enhance their own prestige in this one by showing themselves off as men of sophistication who knew about the architectural styles that were fashionable abroad.

FIGURE 3.4
Twelfth-century window in Crosskirk, Westray.

Saints were also subject to fashion. The cult of St Nicholas was in vogue throughout Europe from the eleventh century onwards, and many of the Orkney churches with his name are associated with the earldom.

Saint Nicholas keepes the Mariner from danger and diseas
That beaten are with boystrous waves, and tost in dredfull seas.[6]

As the patron saint of seamen, it is not surprising to find that St Nicholas became a favourite in Orkney, but as a historical figure one can say almost nothing about him except that he was Bishop of Myra in Lycia (southern Turkey) in the fourth century AD. The main thread of the traditional story of his life is that he was persecuted as a Christian under the emperor Diocletian, but survived, and at an early age was made bishop of Myra, where he was buried. He was revered even in his own lifetime because of his generosity to the poor and his compassion for anyone in need. By the sixth century, there was a church in his honour in Constantinople.

By the tenth century, the Greek wife of the Holy Roman Emperor had brought the cult of St Nicholas to Germany. The relics of a popular saint were of huge value in attracting the tourist trade, and so the cities of Bari and Venice vied with each other to obtain his body. In 1087, merchants of Bari succeeded, by a combination of deception and force, in spiriting away the saintly corpse – which made Bari one of most important pilgrimage centres of medieval Europe, and enormously rich.

Few saints have so often been depicted in art, or been adopted as patron saint by so many places or groups of people. The most frequently depicted scene from his life shows Nicholas looking through a window into a room where three young women lie in bed. A bag of gold is in the bishop's hand. He had heard their sad story: their father was so poor that he could afford no dowry to enable them to marry, and so they were doomed to be sold into slavery. Nicholas tossed a bag of gold through the window for the oldest daughter's dowry, and repeated the kind action for the others. He is the patron saint of marriageable women, mariners, prisoners, children, bakers, merchants, pawnbrokers ...

There were 400 churches dedicated to St Nicholas in England alone. He was the patron saint of Greece, Naples, Sicily, Lorraine and countless cities in the west, including Aberdeen. Nowhere, however, was he as popular as in Russia. Before the Revolution of 1917, so many pilgrims flocked to Bari that a Russian church, hospital and hospice were built there!

As well as four parish kirks on Orkney dedicated to St Nicholas, there were several chapels, including one on the small island of Papa Stronsay. Here was discovered tangible evidence of those medieval journeys to the Mediterranean. When the site was excavated (1998–2000), a fragment of green porphyry was found beneath the twelfth-century church – one of those tiny objects that opens a magic window on the past. *Porfido verde antico* was quarried in Greece until the late fifth century and exported to Rome to decorate important buildings such as temples and, later, polychrome shrines and altars in churches. Pieces of this porphyry were valuable souvenirs to medieval pilgrims, proof of having visited the Holy City. Through how many hands might this small scrap of stone have passed on its journey from the Laconian hills to Papa Stronsay?[7]

A number of Orkney men must have accompanied Earl Hakon and Earl Rognvald on their voyages to the Holy Land (in about 1120 and 1152) and one imagines that tales of their sightseeing tours of Jerusalem circulated freely around the Orkney hearths when they came home

FIGURE 3.5

A twelfth-century Norse leader of considerable importance ended his days under this hog-backed tombstone in St Boniface kirkyard, Papay. The design imitates a Norse longhouse, roofed with overlapping wooden shingles. The red sandstone is not local but has been imported from another island (possibly Eday).

again, and lost nothing in the telling. Even for such hardened sailors and fighters, this must have been an immensely long and dangerous journey, sailing out of the northern fogs and gales to the heat and dust of the coast of Palestine. Ever since 1095 when the first Crusade was launched, thousands of people had set out from every corner of Europe for the Holy Land, far more of them dying on the way of hunger or disease than in battle. Some genuinely believed that they were going to rescue the holy places from the clutch of the infidel. For many more, it was an excuse for adventure, or a chance to advance themselves. Others were simply so destitute that they had nothing to lose. When there was no Crusade to join – as in Earl Hakon and Earl Rognvald's time – the arduous pilgrimage to Jerusalem earned a major reward. For those who actually made it to the city, the Pope had promised a 'plenary indulgence' – a fast-track ticket to heaven when they died, with no tedious kicking of the heels in purgatory. For most of the earls' followers, the possibility of evading the eternal consequences of their many violent sins, while enjoying a major piratical binge, must have seemed extremely attractive.

One result of pilgrims travelling to the places associated with Christ's life and death is that the dedication of churches to the Holy Cross became popular in the Northern Isles at this time. Westray's fine Crosskirk was built

1. Many early churches were built on or near the sites of brochs, as St Mary's Burwick, South Ronaldsay

2. The kirkyard at St Michael's, Harray

3. St Boniface Kirk and the site of the 'Munkerhoose' (monastery), Papay

4. The 'Castle of Burrian' heritage site, Westray

5. Silver crucifix from Birka, Sweden, c. AD 900

6. Window in St Magnus Kirk, Birsay (detail)

7. The Brough of Birsay from Birsay

8. The Round Church, Orphir

9. Corn Holm from Copinsay

10. Crosskirk, Westray

11. Carved panel in Old Hoy kirk pulpit

12. The Covenanters' Memorial, Deerness

13. St Mary's, Swandro, Rousay

14. St Mary's, Pierowall, Westray

15. The chapel on the Brough of Deerness

16. Crannog in Wasbuster Loch, Rousay

17. The Moodie Mausoleum, Osmundwall

18. St Peter's, Eastside, South Ronaldsay

FIGURE 3.6

St Peter's Church on the Brough of Birsay commands a wonderful panorama of Orkney coast from Costa to Marwick Head and stands in the middle of an extensive Pictish and Norse settlement. It must have been an imposing building, with its semicircular apse, and a tower, or even two towers, at the west end.

beside a splendid hall at Tuquoy, discovered when massive lime-plastered masonry was seen eroding out of the cliff-face.[8] The high-quality artefacts which were excavated there may have been the property of Thorkel Flayer, whom *Orkneyinga Saga* describes as a Westray farmer and 'a very able man, but overbearing'.[9] (He came to a nasty end, despite the church.)

Crosskirk has long been abandoned to wind and sea-spray, and to the sound of arctic terns screaming above their nests on the shoreline in early summer; but its rubble walls were stoutly built and much of the twelfth-century work survives, while the walls of the eighteenth-century extension stand only a foot or two high. The round arches of the door and the narrow window in the south wall are built not of dressed stone, but simply of thin flagstones set on edge and wedged into place. The view is wonderful. Through the window, the lord of Tuquoy would have looked straight across the Westray Firth to the tower of St Magnus on Egilsay, or watched the dark sails of longships rounding Rousay's Faraclett Head.

With its little square-ended, barrel-vaulted chancel and flagstone windows, and with its lovely seaward view, Crosskirk is typical of the medieval churches that survive. It is also one of a number of churches that started life as private chapels, built by wealthy men, and were later designated as parish churches. This explains why so many of these old kirks are situated beside the sea, and right on the periphery of their large parishes. St Mary's at Skaill in Deerness,[10] St Mary's at Skaill in Eday, St Mary's at Skaill in Rousay and St Peter's at Skaill in Sandwick were all built beside a Norse leader's *skali* or hall. Later generations were reluctant to move a church from its ancient site, however inconvenient it was for most of the population, and so they were always rebuilt in exactly the same place.

These kirks that we can see today represent only a fraction of those that existed in medieval times. Most are now invisible under present-day fields and farms, but their names have often survived, and so we know who were the most favoured saints. St Peter was a common dedication. It was to his apostle, Peter, that Christ said: 'On this Rock I will build my Church', and on many an Orkney rock small Peterkirks were raised. However, by the time of the twelfth-century building boom, by far the most popular dedication was to the Virgin Mary. There are thirty-three parish kirks and chapels dedicated in her name in Orkney.[11] Interestingly, but inexplicably, she is not nearly so popular in Shetland!

> All things rising, all things sizing
> Mary sees, sympathising
> With that world of good,
> Nature's motherhood.[12]

It is particularly appropriate that so many 'Ladykirks' are beside the sea, for the 'Star of the Sea' was one of Mary's titles. In the New Testament, she is glimpsed only briefly after the well-known stories of Christ's nativity, but tradition snowballed. Soon, she had a detailed biography, and pilgrims to the Holy Land could expect to have the places associated with Mary's life and death pointed out to them by the tour guides. From the sixth century onwards, it was accepted doctrine that she did not die but was taken up bodily into heaven, and the 'Assumption' of Mary was, and still is in Roman Catholic countries, a major feast day of the Church. It is rare to find early churches dedicated in her name, but from the eleventh century onwards she became increasingly prominent in Christian art, literature and liturgy, and thousands of churches were built in her honour all over Europe.

In popular belief, Mary was the all-loving and all-merciful mother who would intercede with her Son on behalf of her petitioners. She had suffered the pain of human grief herself and sympathised with human suffering. Despite her virginity, Mother Mary inevitably took over some of the roles of the irrepressible pre-Christian fertility goddesses and, as the Church had totally failed to banish them altogether, it tried to sanitise their festivals by making them into celebrations of Mary. It was to Mary that women would bring their prayers for children, or for safe childbirth, and Orkney women were taking their petitions to St Mary's chapel in the small island of Damsay well into the eighteenth century.

While Mary, Peter and Nicholas were imported from Palestine and Turkey via continental Europe, there were other popular saints, such as Columba and Bride, who had travelled only from the west coast of Scotland and their native Ireland.

> Sanct Brigid, weill carvit, with ane kow
> With coistlie colouris, fyne and fair.[13]

Although Bride (or Brigid) was widely venerated, almost nothing is known about her, except the traditions that she founded a famous nunnery in Kildare, performed many miracles, and died c. AD 525. She is often depicted as a milkmaid, with a cow, and is addressed in many Gaelic incantations to protect the cows, or make them prolific, or let down their milk. It is understandable that she was so well-loved in Ireland and in the Highlands of Scotland, where wealth was reckoned in cattle, and cattle were as vital to both survival and status as they are among the African Masai today. Her cult must once have been important in Orkney, too, for the name Bride survives at chapel-sites on six islands.[14]

However, Bride is a more complex figure than the innocent cowherd. Her identity was sometimes blurred with that of a Celtic goddess, reviving a very ancient fire-cult. She is also closely associated with the Virgin Mary, and often addressed as the foster-mother of Christ. As pagan goddess and mother of God were almost equally disparaged by later generations of Presbyterian ministers, it is not surprising that they took a dim view of Bride, and that all her chapels have long since vanished.

After the Reformation, all ecclesiastical buildings other than the parish kirks were designated 'popish chapels', and abandoned, usually ending up as useful stone quarries. (St Nicholas on Papa Stronsay, for example, stood almost complete until the late eighteenth century, when the tenant demolished it to build a new barn.)[15] Yet we know enough about them to mentally recreate a medieval landscape dotted with Romanesque churches, some of them splendid with towers and steeples which must have been distinctive landmarks and seamarks. In the mind's eye, we can reclothe the bare grey stones with paintings and hangings, and fill the quiet walls with people, with psalm-singing and candlelight.

It is far harder to identify medieval monasteries in Orkney. They have left few traces other than a scattering of 'Monks'Houses'or'Munkerhooses' mapped on small islands and in the middle of empty fields.[16] Tumbled walls that can still be made out on islets, or on little promontories jutting into lochs, suggest places of retreat, perhaps hermitage,[17] but the far north of Scotland and the Northern Isles never had the agricultural wealth that underpinned the huge abbeys and monasteries that are still so spectacular, even in ruin, further south. The earls evidently directed their resources into the building of their cathedrals in Birsay and Kirkwall, rather than into great monastic houses. The chronicles of the Cistercian

FIGURE 3.7

Reconstruction drawing by Norman Emery of the Brough of Deerness, based upon survey. It shows the Brough before the land bridge at the neck of the promontory collapsed. The chapel is enclosed by a wall. (C. D. Morris/PSAS)

FIGURE 3.8
Eynhallow Church. (Wilfred Marr/OLA)

abbey of Melrose record the election of Laurence, 'abbot in the Orkneys', in 1175.[18] If there was a community in Orkney sufficiently prestigious for its leader to be headhunted by one of the great houses of the Scottish Borders, it is unfortunate that we have no evidence of where it was.

Although no distinctive monastic architecture survives in the Northern Isles, monasteries were such a major feature of life everywhere else in Christian Europe before the Reformation that it is inconceivable that they did not exist in some form. Most medieval orders did not live in total seclusion. They combined the unchanging routine of the 'offices' of prayers and psalms seven times a day with a working life – gardening, farming, teaching, medicine, book-copying, according to each monk's interest and ability – and used these skills to benefit the wider community.

> The monks in a green holm sing every day the sevenfold
> office. They wear the long bright coats of chastity,
> poverty, obedience.[19]

Men of all ranks were drawn to the cloister, some by a genuine vocation, some by the need to expiate past sins. For the poor, it provided at least relative security, and austerities no worse than those in the world outside.

For the secular rich, supporting the holiness of others was the next best thing to leading a holy life themselves, and much less uncomfortable. Even more than the average Christian, a Norse leader must have found Christ's commandments to love one's enemies and turn the other cheek when injured seriously incompatible with his followers' expectations of his role, and it is understandable that he would think that it was easier to fund professionals to do the prayer and poverty and peacemaking requirements on his behalf.

FIGURE 3.9
Eynhallow church, looking east through the nave. The fireplaces which were inserted when the church was a row of cottages can be seen through the chancel arch.

If the earls endowed a monastery, the most likely site is the Brough of Birsay where one of Earl Thorfinn's sons or grandsons built St Peter's church in the early twelfth century.[20] It was an impressive building, with a semicircular apse at the east end and perhaps a tower or towers at the west, and a connecting range of buildings surrounding a courtyard, just as in a monastic cloister. When Birsay was abandoned as a capital, and earl and bishop moved to Kirkwall with all their retinues and staff, the once-busy town must have been left quiet and empty, and the Brough a peaceful retreat, each high tide securing it from the clamour of the world.

FIGURE 3.10
The west door into the porch, Eynhallow church.

For those seeking a life of austerity, the shelterless plateau of the Brough of Deerness would have offered a greater challenge. All that is still clearly visible are the ruined walls of the little stone chapel, but aerial photographs show almost the entire plateau filled with rectangular buildings, laid out either side of a roadway in a regular pattern. The walls of the chapel still stood four or five feet high when Dryden surveyed it in 1866,[21] but after the Royal Navy had shelled it from the sea for target practice in the First World War, and the Army from the land in the Second, considerably less survived. (The theory that the 'circular depressions' near the chapel were traces of the beehive cells of a Celtic monastery[22] also took a battering, when it was concluded that most of them were shell-holes!)[23]

If the settlement was indeed a Norse monastery, it would be tempting to connect it with the wealthy Christian Norse family whose hall and farm have been excavated at Skaill, only one and a half miles away. It has been suggested that it belonged to Thorkel, the foster-father of Earl Thorfinn. Thorkel might well have felt that his prestige in this life would be enhanced, and his stake in the next made more secure, by founding a monastery on his own lands and providing for its community. However, it remains only a possibility. Even after the meticulous excavation of the chapel and enclosure by Dr Christopher Morris in 1975–6, the buildings on the Brough remain an enigma. 'Iron Age promontory fort, early Christian monastic site, Viking/Norse secular site with associated chapel, and Norse monastic settlement all remain possibilities and indeed are not mutually exclusive.'[24] What was needed to support the case for a monastery was a graveyard, preferably full of middle-aged and elderly male skeletons, but this crucial evidence was sadly lacking. Morris found very few graves in the enclosure, and some of these were of children.

Another possible site for a monastery is the small island of Corn Holm, linked by a causeway to Copinsay at low tide. It is hard to make out the traces of any buildings now, but the ruins of a chapel were still standing when George Low visited in 1774. He also saw traces of 'cells of ecclesiasticks',[25] and the Royal Commission on Ancient and Historical Monuments of Scotland's survey identified at least fourteen round or rectangular buildings similar to those on the Broughs of Birsay and Deerness.[26] The holm is fertile ground that has clearly been cultivated in the past and would have been well able to support a small community, possibly an outlier of a monastery on the Brough of Deerness.

Eyin Helga, the Holy Isle, is encircled by turbulent tides in the dangerous sound between Rousay and the Evie shore. 'Everyone who had been in the Orcades talked about Enhallow [sic], but no-one seemed able any more than ourselves to tell for what it was good'[27] wrote T. S. Muir after his visit in the 1880s, and he was not the only one to leave these ruins with a sense of bafflement and frustration. To wander through the labyrinth of rooms – so often altered – and the curiously primitive little doorways, is to find more questions than answers. Did the Norse call it Holy Isle because they found a monastery here? Was it, as Mooney passionately believed, an important monastery in the twelfth and thirteenth centuries?[28] Or did the monastery exist only in tradition and imagination, and the buildings just belong to a 'grange' or church farm on the bishopric estate?[29]

By the mid-nineteenth century, Eynhallow was a poor tenant farm, worked by four families who lived in a row of cottages on the south side of the isle. In 1851, tragedy struck when several of the inhabitants died in a fever epidemic. The survivors placed the bodies in empty boats that were towed back to the Rousay kirkyard, and the landlord, David Balfour of Trenaby, insisted that they abandon the infected houses. To prevent their reoccupation, he took off the roofs: half-hidden by partition walls and fireplaces and household furniture, were seen the arched doorways of a twelfth-century church.[30]

In 1894, Thomas Middlemore, a wealthy English industrialist then living at Westness in Rousay, purchased the island from David Balfour. Three years later, the Arts and Crafts architect, William Lethaby, was designing him a new home at Melsetter in Hoy, and Middlemore invited him to survey the Eynhallow ruins and 'tidy' the site. Lethaby attempted to disentangle medieval church and (presumed) monastic buildings from the sixteenth-century houses that were built in and around them, and shored up the south and east walls with the huge buttresses that are a Lethaby trademark. (He did the same at St Mary's at Skaill in Rousay, to prevent the west wall from sliding into the sea, and liked the shape so much that he used it on the brand-new chapel that he designed for Melsetter.)

The Eynhallow church is quite large, but there is no sophistication about its masonry, and the few pieces of red freestone used in its construction look like 'leftovers' from another building (perhaps St Magnus Cathedral) which have been reused wherever they would fit. The round archway into the nave is crudely built of thin flags set on edge, but when the church was altered, an attempt was made to follow changes of architectural fashion in more cosmopolitan centres by creating a pointed version for the chancel. The hobbit-like west door of the porch is arched by the even more primitive expedient of leaning two slabs against each other. (The Royal Commission found the doorways narrower than in any building they had recorded!)[31] There is something deeply appealing about Eynhallow. One squeezes through the archaic little doors into 800 years

of human history compressed into its stout, weathered walls. Both monks, and the families who replaced them here, struggled with cold and hunger and the unrelenting effort to wrest survival from the gale-torn, salt-strewn acres. These stones do not tell of a monastery that was ever a wealthy foundation, but rather of a place of refuge from the tumult of elements and politics that raged outside.

CHAPTER 4

Launching the Ark

Rejoice. Saint Magnus kirk
Is launched on the ocean of time.
The dove sits furled in the stone rigging.

George Mackay Brown (1987)

*I*t is impossible to separate the story of the kirks built by the Norse leaders from the issues that dominated their lives: plots, treachery, assassination, the endless bloodshed as rival earls and their factions fought over the earldom of Orkney. When one stands in the serene space of St Magnus Cathedral, it is hard to believe that anything so lovely could have been conceived in such a welter of intrigue and violence. The building is magnificent, yet surprisingly intimate. There is no vastness of scale to overwhelm, no dizzying Gothic heights or unsettling virtuosity of tracery, but the reassuring solidity of sturdy, round columns and arches, and the warmth of soft red and ochre sandstone. Somehow, it is both thoroughly European and securely, and undefinably, as Orcadian as its own stones.

The story of the founding of the cathedral is told in *Orkneyinga Saga*. Twenty years after the death of Magnus on Egilsay, his nephew Rognvald Kolsson made a bid to claim Magnus' share of the earldom. Rognvald's claim was not particularly strong, and Earl Paul Hakonsson was already securely in control. Rognvald's first attack on Orkney ended in ignominious defeat. Clearly, he needed much stronger allies, and his father, Kol, urged him to seek a more persuasive backing than mere military force:

> Look for support where men will say the true owner of the realm granted it to you, and that's the holy Earl Magnus, your uncle. I want you to make

a vow to him that ... should you come to power, then you'll build a stone minster at Kirkwall more magnificent than any in Orkney, that you'll have it dedicated to ... Magnus and provide it with the all the funds it will need to flourish.[1]

To appreciate the subtlety of Kol's manipulation of the media, one has to go back to the scenes in Birsay before the translation of Magnus' relics to Kirkwall. The idea of presenting Rognvald as the legitimate heir of his saintly, martyred uncle was masterly, but, at the time the attempted coup was being planned, Magnus was not yet officially a saint, and Bishop William was a staunch supporter of Earl Paul ... until he visited Norway, shortly before Rognvald's invasion. As we have already seen, William returned to Birsay, and the miracle of his sudden blinding in his own cathedral and cure at Magnus' tomb brought about an abrupt volte-face.[2] Magnus was pronounced a saint, and the Church threw its considerable weight behind Rognvald. Clearly, the bishop was bought. Rognvald's vow to St Magnus just may have been literary shorthand for a promise to move the bishopric from rural Birsay to the town that was fast growing into the political and economic centre of the earldom, and to build a splendid new cathedral there.

FIGURE 4.1
A window in the north arcade of the cathedral choir.

With the help of Bishop William, the holy Magnus, and some very unholy alliances, Earl Paul was dispatched and, in 1136, Rognvald became sole earl. 'Not long after that, the ground plan of St Magnus' church was drawn up and builders hired for the work.'[3] In 1137, Rognvald laid the foundation stone – and, over the next years, work on the east end progressed so rapidly that it was ready for consecration, and for the translation of St Magnus' relics from St Olaf's kirk, in 1146. Five years later, the earl set out on his pilgrimage to the Holy Land, and Bishop William 'the Old' accompanied him as interpreter and right-hand man.[4]

(He had already been bishop for almost fifty years and had another seventeen to run!)

To make sure that his church would be as up-to-date as anything in Europe, Earl Rognvald looked south for inspiration and an experienced workforce. In Durham, a great cathedral had recently been built over the body of St Cuthbert, and stonemasons had brought Romanesque architecture to a breathtaking perfection, lightening the massive Norman pillars with an elegant new experiment in ribbed vaulting. A few decades later, they had moved tools and skills to Dunfermline Abbey, and by the time that Rognvald, Kol and Bishop William had drawn up their plans, they were ready to move north again.

There is no doubt that St Magnus Cathedral was intended to be a powerful status symbol. Rognvald's earldom was no backwater on the periphery of Europe. He would have been baffled by the modern perception that his territories were 'on the edge'. He ruled over a prosperous society. Kirkwall was a busy port and an international trading centre, and its leaders had travelled extensively and been received by Pope and Emperor. Rognvald himself had already explored the North Sea on trading trips and would soon be sightseeing in the Mediterranean on

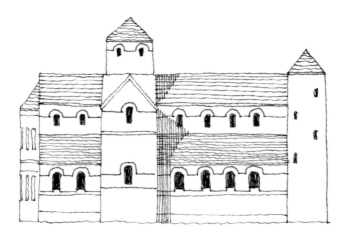

Figure 4.2

The cathedral as it was planned by Kol, Rognvald and Bishop William. In the next century, under Bishop Bjarni, the plan became grander, and the original, semicircular, apse was rebuilt as a much longer, square-ended choir.

his own journey to Constantinople and Jerusalem. He would have been aware that his contemporary, King David I of Scots, was creating a powerful kingdom in which the interests of Church and State were interlocked, and that he was winning support and prestige by his generous endowment of cathedrals and abbeys. The earl did not intend to be outshone.

The original choir was much shorter than in the present building, and it ended in a semicircular apse at the east end, where pilgrims could file thankfully past their goal – the shrine of Magnus, set in a magnificent jewelled and gilded reliquary above the high altar. The large roofed space of the nave proved useful for more secular purposes, such as storing the great sails of longships when they were in Kirkwall harbour.[5]

To imagine the cathedral that Earl Rognvald planned, it is necessary to strip away the clutter of later memorials and twentieth-century woodwork; to plaster the stone columns, and decorate them with striking red and black designs; and to visualise a space, not for sitting in rows and listening (an unlikely activity for Rognvald's followers), but for people on their feet and moving, in procession, pageant and pilgrimage. As in all medieval cathedrals, the original design was somewhat altered in the centuries that it took to complete the work, building being delayed by a faltering supply of money or motivation, by accidental destruction (the crossing collapsed in the 1170s and had to be extensively rebuilt), or deliberate demolition, as architectural fashions changed.

Work slowed down for a time after Rognvald's death, but surged ahead again under the talented and cultured Bishop Bjarni Kolbeinsson (1188–1223). He demolished the original apse and extended the choir, completed the transepts (his slightly pointed arches indicate the transition from Romanesque to Gothic), continued building the nave, and raised the elaborately carved west doorways, with arches picked out with alternate red and yellow sandstone. Bjarni also ensured that Rognvald (who had been assassinated in a scrap with an outlaw in Caithness in 1158) was duly appreciated by having him canonised too and his bones laid to rest in his cathedral.[6]

Rognvald would have been horrified if he had known that it would take 400 years for the nave to be finally completed, and that the steeple would be burnt down in 1671, and at what later generations did to the interior of his cathedral, but he would surely have been pleased by the idea that it would still be dominating Kirkwall 800 years after his death, and that St Magnus, even without his shrine, would be so well remembered.

FIGURE 4.3
The interior of St Magnus: the crossing. (OLA)

With their cathedral in use, if still far from complete, the earl and bishop must have faced the task of keeping it in funds, and it is likely that Orkney was first divided into parishes around this time – divisions that still prove administratively, and socially, useful 800 years on. (How would Orkney's social life function without all the inter-parish competitions between football teams, WRIs, Young Farmers' or Drama Clubs?) There were models to copy in other parts of Europe that had already developed a parish system, administered jointly by both civil and ecclesiastical authorities. The parishes were convenient units for the purpose of taking censuses, raising taxes, levying conscripts and so on, as well as for organising Church affairs. Churches would no longer be randomly built and funded by private individuals. They would be systematised, centralised and, most importantly, financed by general taxation.

The more important churches, like Crosskirk in Westray and the Round Kirk in Orphir, which became parish kirks, exacted from all their parishioners an annual payment of *teinds* (or tithes) – a tenth part of the hard-won produce of grain, or lambs, or wool, or fish, or eggs, or butter, or peat, or any other commodity that the community produced. Originally, the teinds were intended to be divided between the bishop, the parish priest and the poor, though it seems unlikely that this relatively sensible arrangement ever actually worked in practice. All over medieval Europe, a large proportion of these teinds were creamed off to support the large, prestigious abbeys and cathedrals, and little was left for the parish kirks, let alone the poor. This 'appropriation' of parish revenues happened all over Scotland, but to its greatest extreme in Orkney,[7] where an extraordinarily complicated two-tier system of 'parsonage teinds' and 'vicarage teinds' evolved, which makes the agricultural policies of twenty-first-century Brussels look straightforward in comparison.

Bishop William and his successors lived in considerable style, enjoying the revenues of the huge bishopric estate. As well as collecting teinds, the bishop had the income from lands given by the earls. This was increased, as time went on, by donations given to the Church by pious folk, in the hope of earning an easier passage in the next world for themselves, or for a deceased relative, or paid as a penalty for some sin. (The lands of the bishopric, Bishop Graham later remarked somewhat drily, 'grew daylie as adulteries and incests increased in the countrey'.)[8] By the time of the Reformation, the bishopric estate had engulfed much of St Ola and of the West Mainland (Birsay, Marwick, Costa and Evie) as well as lands in Westray, Rousay and Egilsay and across the Firth in Caithness.

Much of this money was channelled into St Magnus Cathedral, which must have grown steadily more magnificent over the centuries, as the building was completed and its ritual elaborated. When Mass was celebrated, in the flickering light of hundreds of candles:

the embroidered vestments of the clergy, copes, chasubles and dalmatics, would glow with colour as the procession proceeded up the nave to the sanctuary, led by the cross bearer, flanked by candlebearing acolytes and followed by the choir intoning the psalms or filling the ancient building with the harmonies of a sacred anthem.[9]

All this splendour had its running costs. A considerable staff of clergy was needed to look after the building, to teach the choristers to sing the anthems and the acolytes to say the correct Latin responses, to attend to the expensive beeswax candles and to wash the embroidered dalmatics ... not to mention saying Mass regularly at the innumerable altars. Today, one wonders where there would have been room for them all. Besides the High Altar and the great shrine to St Magnus, there were side altars to Our Lady, the Holy Trinity, St Andrew, St Nicholas, St Columba, St Olaf and at least a dozen other saints,[10] each demanding regular candle-lighting, prayers and dusting.

FIGURE 4.4
All the doors into the cathedral are embellished with superb decorative iron hinges, the designs varying on each door.

When Bishop Reid reorganised the cathedral chapter in 1544, his regulations provided for a staff of no less than twenty-seven clergy of different ranks and six boys! At the top of the hierarchy were the wealthy, well-connected and well-educated higher clergy who were often influential politicians. Robert Reid spent most of his time as Bishop of Orkney engaged in diplomatic missions in London and France. His successor, Adam Bothwell, had an impressive command of ancient and modern languages, and a Renaissance breadth of interests – his scientific curiosity earning him a reputation as 'a sorcerer and execrable magician'![11] Below the bishop were officials such as the Provost and the Archdeacon, who were both obliged to preach at least four times a year; the Precentor, who was responsible for the music and training the choirboys; and the Sub-Chantor, who played the organ. On the bottom rung of the clerical ladder, and social hierarchy,

FIGURE 4.5
The north door of St Magnus.

were the chaplains, thirled to the inexpressibly tedious-sounding job of saying Masses for the dead at a particular altar.

When not processing through the candlelit dimness of St Magnus, the clergy had humbler maintenance tasks to perform, and all were paid for by teinds from one of the parishes, or 'prebends' – revenues derived from parcels of Church lands, scattered through the islands, which had been 'appropriated' by the cathedral. There was the Treasurer, for example, drawing income from Stronsay, who looked after the bread and wine for the Mass, the wax and oil for the lights, and kept the large wardrobe of vestments in repair. He had an assistant, paid for by teinds from Sanday, who was responsible for the clock, and ringing the bells, and keeping the floor clean. Another 'prebendary' was the Master of Works who looked after the roof and windows.[12] All this drained income out of the parishes: money that might have been used to maintain their own kirk roofs and windows, or support a reasonably educated parish priest. Bishop Reid's foundation ensured that the cathedral would be magnificently staffed – and the country parishes totally impoverished. The clergy who were paid, out of the residue of the teinds, to serve in the parish kirks were often absentees, who preferred the relative luxury of

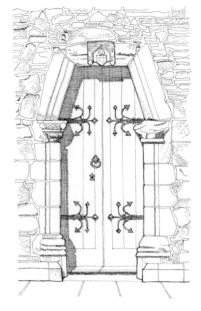

FIGURE 4.6
The south door of St Magnus.

Kirkwall to the hardships of the isles, and paid a very small sum to a curate to take their place.

Most of the inefficiencies and corruptions of the medieval Church that the reformers wanted to stamp out stemmed from this hopeless top-heaviness: a few extremely wealthy, top-brass clergy, living in luxury and processing in glorious vestments through the splendour of cathedrals and abbeys, while the majority of miserably paid and miserably educated parish priests functioned inadequately in their thatched-roof kirks and hovels of

FIGURE 4.7
St Magnus in the seventeenth century, drawn by the Rev. James Wallace,
the cathedral minister 1672–88. (OLA)

manses. At both ends of the economic scale, the system invited corruption. The poor clergy collected church livings out of necessity; the rich, out of greed. Often, the most lucrative appointments were given to royal family and 'favourites' who were not even clergy. Three illegitimate baby sons of James IV, for example, were provided for by some of Scotland's wealthiest abbeys. Church law, of course, forbade such scandals, but the rich were able to buy 'dispensations' from the Pope, which allowed them to set the law aside.

There were as many as thirty-six parishes in Orkney, often – as successive generations of clergy plaintively pointed out – encompassing several islands, widely separated by dangerous tracts of water. Because so much of Church income was allocated to supporting the cathedral and its clergy, there were never enough priests to provide one to every church, and it was more common for one man to serve several, travelling between them as often as the appalling roads, the stormy seas, and their own dedication allowed.

When we stand in the ruins of medieval churches, we can refurnish them in the imagination as they might have been before the Reformation. The stone walls were plastered and, in churches with wealthy patrons, like St Peter's on the Brough of Birsay, one can imagine them painted with colourful geometric designs, or warmed with woven hangings. On festival days, there would have been bright cloths on the altars, and special vestments on the priest. The smaller churches were probably very plain inside. There were no pews. The stone benches still in place along the walls of St Peter's provided the only seating, reserved for the elderly or infirm who 'went to the wall'. Most of the people stood, or brought their own stools, but there was little emphasis on preaching in pre-Reformation services, and congregations did not have to survive the hours-long marathon sermons inflicted by later ministers.

Without sermons, there was no need for the enormous pulpits that came to dominate Presbyterian churches. The focus of attention was the high altar in the chancel, where the priest said Mass, and even relatively small buildings had side altars as well, where candles burned constantly before statues of the Virgin or the patron saint. These images were far more than mere decoration. In a world where war, hunger and disease were the ever-present realities for most people, and medicine and social security did not exist, the saints offered the only hope that a sick child might be cured, or that the meal in the girnel might last the winter. Everyone who could afford it gave donations or bequests to pay for lamps, or for re-gilding a statue, or maintaining a light before it, hoping that, in return, the saint would answer their prayers or intercede for them in heaven.

All these – altars and candles, processions and ceremony, the shrines and relics and images, the musical instruments and the choir-boys trained to sing elaborate anthems – disappeared during the Reformation and the stormy decades that followed it. Stripped of much malpractice and corruption, but also of much sense of sanctity and beauty, Rognvald's Ark sailed out of the Middle Ages and into dark and turbulent waters.

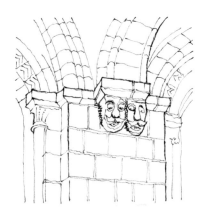

CHAPTER 5

A Wild Hogmanay?

Above the ebb, that gray uprooted wall
Was arch and chancel, choir and sanctuary,
A solid round of stone and ritual.
Knox brought all down in his wild hogmanay.

George Mackay Brown (1959)

*I*n the first half of the sixteenth century, pilgrims were still travelling to Kirkwall to visit the shrine of St Magnus, and the clear voices of the choristers from the 'Sang School' floated through the cathedral, over the murmuring of Masses for the souls of the dead. Outside on the streets, there were murmurings of a different kind. The trading vessels that docked at Kirkwall harbour were carrying a new cargo across the North Sea: *printed* religious books and pamphlets (the new technology had made them relatively cheap and readily available) and Bibles, translated from Latin into the English language. Travellers were stepping off the wharf below St Magnus laden with tales of extraordinary events abroad: of a wind of revolution blowing through the Church: of a German monk called Martin Luther who had dared to challenge its authority and criticise its corruption, and demand a return to the teaching of Scripture.

Long before Scotland became Protestant by Act of Parliament, Orkney folk must have listened in bewilderment as itinerant preachers at street corners dismantled the fabric of their world with a Bible. They taught that man was justified to God *by faith alone*, and neither the Pope's 'indulgences', nor pilgrimages to the tomb of St Magnus or even to Jerusalem, nor the relics of saints, nor the saying of Masses, were *of any use* in getting the faithless soul to heaven. Salvation could not be bought. It was a gift.

The Reformation brought profound social and cultural changes to Orkney, as well as religious ones, and it is tempting to see it as a decisive watershed, with history falling neatly, either side, into 'Catholic' and 'Protestant' compartments. In reality, history is much more untidy, and although the Reformation was a watershed, it was not a single event but a long and acrimonious process of transition. As in every other Christian country, genuine religious concerns were hijacked by political imperatives. In England, Henry VIII had led the country out of Catholicism, not from personal conviction, but because he could not deal with his marital problems without defying the Pope. Scotland, on the other hand, chose Protestantism in defiance of the monarch, and out of a sense of national identity. In the chaotic disintegration of Mary, Queen of Scots' reign, it was antagonism to the Catholic French, more than theology, that gave victory to the Protestant party. In 1560, the Scots Parliament adopted a Protestant Confession of Faith, and rejected the authority of the Pope, and forbade the saying of Mass – but Scotland certainly did not become Protestant overnight.

It is frustratingly difficult to find out what ordinary people in Orkney *thought* about the changes that were thrust upon them. Plenty has been written about what *happened* in terms of new laws in Parliament, or decrees hammered out in the General Assembly of the Church, but what was the gossip on the street in sixteenth-century Kirkwall? England, Denmark, Norway and much of northern Germany had been 'reformed' for a generation before 1560, so Protestant opinions had had plenty of time to circulate in Scotland, despite official attempts to stamp them out. In 1525, an Act of Parliament banned Lutheran books; in 1528, a young student who had aired the views of Luther in St Andrews was burnt at the stake. Did Orkney folk ask each other (as they certainly did elsewhere in Scotland): 'Why was Master Hamilton burned?' When the Scots Parliament made it legal for them to read the Bible in their own language in 1543, was the news welcomed, or was it totally irrelevant, as so few people could read anyway? 'James Skea, born in Orkney' had to flee to England in 1548 'for fear of burning for the Word of God',[1] so Protestant ideas must have been circulating in the islands, while they were still regarded as 'heretical', and long before they were imposed by law.

We can guess that there was fear, anger and confusion, but probably little realisation, at first, of just how profoundly the Reformation would disturb the social fabric. The Reformers did not see themselves as simply introducing new doctrines or new forms of worship, but as doing nothing less than designing a Christian society. In John Knox's blueprint for Scotland, the State would fund the Kirk adequately and support it in compelling people not just to be law-abiding, but to be *good*. With the wealth of the Kirk redistributed among the parishes, there would be a well-educated clergy and a programme of social welfare that would care for the poor and disadvantaged. There would be a school in every parish so that the laity could be educated. They would be able to read their own Bibles and service books and participate in the running of their parish kirks in a democratic fashion, choosing their own ministers and electing their elders every year.

Knox's vision, however, foundered on two familiar rocks: power-politics and funding shortfalls. His power-to-the-people ideas were quickly overturned by clergy who did not want to relinquish power,[2] and the idealistic programmes for education and social welfare were, to a large extent, derailed by the vested interests of the king, the landowners and even Protestant ministers, eager only to get their hands on Church property. The abbeys and monasteries were not demolished, but there was no attempt to recover all the wealth that they had 'appropriated'; it was simply whisked into private hands. Church revenues were either used to pension off those Catholic clergy who would not 'conform' to Protestantism, or pounced on by the king. Little was left to finance the running of the parishes. There was not even a budget for paying ministers' salaries or maintaining kirks and manses. It became the legal responsibility of the landowners, or 'heritors', to shoulder these costs, something the Orkney gentry were generally most reluctant to do. Not many heritors took such an extreme position as Lady Melsetter in Walls, who threatened to shoot the minister if he dared to ask for his stipend, but many were extremely grudging. By the eighteenth century, every church in Orkney was in a dangerously 'ruinous' condition, or totally derelict, because the heritors refused to pay their share of the repair bill.

Knox himself was bitterly disillusioned by what he saw as the incompleteness of the Reformation. For centuries after him, Scottish ministers, elders and congregations would struggle to provide kirk buildings, schoolmasters' salaries, charity for the needy and education for the poor out of their meagre resources. It is surprising that they achieved as much as they did.

The task of reforming Orkney fell, not to a firebrand like John Knox, but to its frail, cultured, intellectual bishop, Adam Bothwell. Bishop Bothwell had been appointed in 1559, at the height of the conflict between the

FIGURE 5.1

The great bell (1574 lbs) brought down from the cathedral tower in the course of restoration work in the early twentieth century. This was the bell that cracked when the steeple was struck by lightning in 1671, and was recast in Amsterdam. The inscription records that it was made by Robert Borthwick in Edinburgh Castle for 'Master Robert Maxwell Bishop of Orkney the year of God 1528' with a figure of St Magnus and the bishop's arms beneath. (Tom Kent/OLA)

Scots Protestant lords and the Queen Regent's Catholic faction and their French allies.[3] He had an adventurous journey to Orkney, being unlucky enough to be captured by the English fleet that had sailed into the Firth of Forth to support the Protestant party. His weeks as a guest of the English were a turning point. Bothwell left Edinburgh a Roman Catholic bishop and arrived in Orkney a 'reformed' one. Early in 1561, he announced his plans for the 'mutation of religion'.

The introduction of strange forms of worship is guaranteed to arouse resentment in any age, and the response to Bothwell was an angry demonstration by 'ane gret multitude of the commonis'. The bishop locked the door of the cathedral, and refused to allow Mass to be said. The people responded by crowding into a little chapel next to the bedchamber where the bishop was lying sick, forcing him to listen to a priest saying Mass and celebrating marriages according to the old rites he had forbidden![4]

Resistance did not last, however. The 'commonis' do not seem to have given trouble for long, and although there is no evidence that there was any great fervour in Orkney for 'reforming' religion, the landowners enthusiastically welcomed the opportunity to enrich themselves and their families with property confiscated from the Church. Gilbert Balfour, for example, grabbed a huge estate of former bishopric land in Westray and Papay. There is no point in dwelling unduly on the theological issues involved because, apparently, almost no-one did so at the time. Most of the Orkney clergy 'showed themselves to be more concerned with the pressing business of turning their livings into hereditary estates than with the niceties of theology'.[5]

The large-scale transfer of landownership probably did not affect the ordinary people very much: rents and taxes still had to be paid and, at first, they would not have noticed drastic changes in their kirks. There was far less destruction in Orkney than in many other parts of the country.

FIGURE 5.2

Detail of the tombstone of George Liddell of Hammer in St Magnus Cathedral, 1648. Characteristic of the times is the superb carving and the lugubrious inscription – it ends: 'none can make good the loss of time. Remember death' – and the 'reminders': the skull, spade, coffin, candlestick, funeral bell and hour-glass.

Because the Reformation was carried out by the bishop, the cathedral was not harmed. The magnificent shrines of St Magnus and St Rognvald were broken up, but the bones of the two saints were reinterred within columns of the choir. Altars and images were removed, but as there was no money to build new kirks, the old ones remained in use and were only gradually altered for Presbyterian worship.

In fact, there was a surprising degree of continuity, because most of the Orkney clergy 'conformed' to Protestantism and remained in their parishes. The huge upheavals that the Reformation caused elsewhere must have been relatively minor ripples in Stronsay and Eday, for example, where James Maxwell gave twenty years of service as a Catholic priest and a further thirty as a Protestant minister! On the surface, Orcadians were turned into Protestants with remarkably little resistance, but old beliefs endured, underground, and survived generations of ministers' attempts to extirpate the 'dregs of Popery' from the isles.

The Reformation made one significant difference to the personal lives of the clergy: they were now allowed to marry, and instead of remaining celibate or having 'housekeepers', could found respectable clerical dynasties. These were to play a major role in Orkney's subsequent history. The most important change for the people was that they were expected to participate much more in services, which were now read 'in the vernacular'. Formerly, the priest celebrated Mass at the altar, in Latin, but now Communion was to be *shared* by the people, seated round a table with the minister. For the first time, they heard the Bible read in an English translation, but Biblical English read by a Scots minister was hardly the vernacular of sixteenth-century Orcadians, who were still speaking a dialect strongly influenced by Norse, and one wonders if it was much more accessible to them than Latin!

Although St Magnus Cathedral was spared destruction at the Reformation, it had a narrow escape in 1614, during the battle between the supporters of Robert Stewart, the son of Earl Patrick Stewart, and the forces of the Earl of Caithness, who had been sent north to suppress Stewart's rebellion. Initially, the rebels held the excellent vantage point of the steeple, from which to snipe at the enemy. When the steeple was surrendered, the earl 'went about to demolesh and throw down the church, bot he wes with great difficultie hindered and stayed by the bishop of Orkney who wold not suffer him to throw it doun'.[6]

Even when there was no deliberate demolition, maintaining a large building such as the cathedral became virtually impossible when all the income that had previously supported it was diverted into private pockets. In a Session minute of 1658, we read that: 'the fabric had been partly maintained out of the Bishops revenues and partly by the fines of al adultries throughout the whole countrie. Both Mainland and Yles'.[7] The system of making sinners pay fines for their sins was a prudent way of keeping the cathedral coffers in funds for running repairs, but all the adulterers in Orkney could not possibly have paid for the rebuilding caused by major disasters, such as the fire in 1671.

> Quhilkday ther happened ane fearful and sad accident to this place to the great astonishment and terrification of all the beholders by thunder and lightning which fell upon the steeple heid of the Cathedral of Orkney.[8]

The wooden spire was destroyed and the three bells crashed to the ground, but the citizens of Kirkwall had had time to barrow in enough earth to break their fall, and only the largest was cracked. It was recast in Amsterdam, and the three bells were rehung in the new tower, a dumpy, slate-hung, wooden pyramid that was much shorter than the original spire.

FIGURE 5.3
The doorway of the mausoleum built by the Moodies of Melsetter at Osmundwall, carved with the inscription: 'Sole Deo Laus Honor et Gloria' (To God alone be Praise, Honour and Glory).

Most of the country churches built in the sixteenth and seventeenth centuries were small, straw-thatched and earth-floored, and long ago disappeared without trace. A few, like Ladykirk in Pierowall, Westray, which was rebuilt in 1674, were on a grander scale. Post-Reformation churches had no altar, and no need of a chancel at the east end for the Mass and, often, this area was converted into a laird's 'aisle' or wing – where the heritor's family could sit and hear the sermon, while maintaining a degree of social segregation from everyone else. At the end of their days, they would be buried in the aisle too, and Ladykirk has two superbly carved tombstones commemorating the Balfour and Sinclair families.

Whatever their immortal state, lairds were anxious to make their mark on this world even after their death. The largest landowners in the district of Walls, the Moodies,[9] built a family mausoleum that survives in the Osmundwall kirkyard: an attractive small building with crow-stepped gables and stone-flagged roof. 'Sole Deo Laus Honor et Gloria' (To God alone be Praise, Honour and Glory) is carved around the lovely round-arched doorway, but one cannot help wondering if seventeenth-century lairds like the Moodies were not more interested in opportunities to give praise and honour to themselves rather than to God. They were certainly reluctant to spend money on building parish churches of such a high standard of workmanship.

Defunct Moodies were not actually buried in the mausoleum but laid on stone slabs, to be mummified by the sea breezes. Evidently, they were not the only family to follow this custom. In 1774, George Low visited a tomb in Stroma, while he was researching his *Tour through the Islands of Orkney and Schetland*. He was told it had contained 'natural mummies' that had been a considerable tourist attraction, but he was disappointed to find the door broken and only bones left by the time of his visit.[10]

The words 'Memento Mori' (Remember Death), and the visual reminders – the skull and crossed bones, spade, coffin, candlestick, funeral bell and hour-glass – that occur on so many seventeenth-century tombstones are grimly appropriate, though death was so commonplace that one would have thought they were hardly necessary. The splendid seventeenth-century tombstones in St Magnus Cathedral are those of the bailies, and notaries public, and magistrates, and their wives – the rich and important of Kirkwall – but, even for them, life was often short and tragic. Many died in their thirties, having already buried most of their children. The stone of 'ane verteous and pious woman', Elizabeth Elphinstone, is typical. She died in 1680, aged 36. Of her nine children 'only 2 ar alyv and 7 lyes heir interd with her'. It seems significant that so few of these stones refer to a consoling belief in a happy afterlife. More often the inscriptions are a comment on the brevity of life and the tragedy of death and bereavement. 'O death how harsh how grievous are thy laws.' Always they end with the grim injunction: 'Memento Mori.'

It was a bleak time in Orkney history, beginning with the rapacious regime of the Stewart earls, Robert and his son 'Black Pate', whose oppressive taxation caused destitution. The country was also in the grip of the Little Ice Age: a period of exceptionally harsh winters and cold, wet summers, when crops never ripened and famine was a constant threat. In the 1630s and, again, in the 1690s, the Orkney harvest failed totally for several years in succession, and many of the poor died of starvation.[11]

With hunger and cold on the doorstep, there was no longer any consolation to be found in the kirks. In 1641, with the Puritan party in the ascendancy, Parliament passed the Act for Abolishing Monuments of Idolatry, and unleashed the smashing of images that reduced almost all medieval works of art to rubble and splinters. The Kirkwall Presbytery ordered the statue of St Peter in St Peter's kirk in South Ronaldsay to be burnt.[12] All over the islands, people watched in dismay and disbelief as the much-loved figures, that generations of their families had prayed before and cherished, were carried to the bonfire. The familiar paintings that had once added warmth and colour to their little kirks were whitewashed or mutilated, leaving scarred walls and ravished interiors. There was no longer the compassionate figure of the Virgin to light a candle to, and pray that the boat would come home safely, full of fish, or that the harvest would be gathered in before the storm. Statues, vestments, music, festivals … all the familiar traditions became 'popish superstitions', and were banished. People's lives must have been much bleaker too, with dancing and music expunged from their brief moments of leisure by stern Calvinistic ministers,[13] who harangued them at length about Sin, and the Discipline of the Kirk.

George Mackay Brown imagines the iconoclasts coming to the remote settlement of Rackwick in the island of Hoy:

> About that time a terrible thing happened. A dozen horsemen rode through the hills from Hoy. They dismounted at the chapel of Our Lady. The valley people heard the sounds of blows and smashing and dilapidation inside – it went on all morning. Presently some of the horsemen came out with bulging sacks and staggered with their loads to the edge of the crag and emptied them out into the sea below. A young man with a pale face stood at the end of the chapel and told the people that now they could worship God in a pure form; the Pope and his bishops had been cast down from their high Babylonish places; the idolatry of the Mass was abolished, abomination of desolation that it was; instead the unadulterated word would be preached to them, Sabbath after Sabbath, by him their new minister, in the kirk of Hoy five miles away …
>
> When the strangers had ridden off the Rackwick folk peered through the door of their chapel. The strangers had made it starker than any

stable. The sanctuary light was out. Altar, tabernacle, crucifix, the statue of Saint Magnus, the Stations of the Cross, were torn down. Their treasures were taken from them.[14]

In the bitterness of the seventeenth century, the original, liberating message of the Reformers soured into a dour and punitive religion. It was this cheerless institution, so strangely at odds with the New Testament, that added to the unhappiness of the time. The Kirk Sessions functioned like secret police in every parish, ferreting out Sin, and 'disciplining' culprits. All the activities in which people had found some comfort and distraction from the poverty and hardship of their lives became offences for which they were punished: the celebration of saints' days and holy days, or going on pilgrimage to a favourite chapel.

Misery and insecurity found an outlet, as they so often do, in the vicious hounding of scapegoats to blame for people's woes. It was the century of the witchcraft trials, when a number of women were tortured, 'wirreit at a staik, and brunt in ashes'. One of the most disturbing cases was the politically motivated trial of Alison Balfour, accused of plotting to murder Earl Patrick Stewart with witchcraft in 1594. Under the supervision of the minister of Orphir, the Rev. John Colville, Alison was hideously tortured and, when she refused to confess, her 81-year-old husband and her children were tortured as well. Finally, she 'confessed' and was strangled, and burnt at the stake.[15]

In other cases, the accusation seems to have been founded only on the dislike or spite of neighbours, perhaps because the women were bad-tempered, or antisocial, or begged for alms too importunately. The 'witches' were blamed for all the commonplace disasters of life in a rural community: a horse falling sick, a cow failing to give milk, a corn-kiln catching fire. David and Margaret Mowat in Birsay had three cows, of which one died in calving, another calved but never gave milk and the third 'four years past never tuik bull'. Not an unusual run of bad luck for a farmer, but a tragedy for a poor family and one that, in the seventeenth century, could only have been caused by witchcraft. For this, and similar 'crimes', Marable Couper and Anie Tailzeour were sent to the stake in 1624. The traditional story of Janet Forsyth, the 'Westray storm-wife', has an unusually happy ending. She was accused of causing deaths at sea by raising storms, and sentenced to death in 1629, but was rescued from her dungeon in Kirkwall by her long-lost lover, in the nick of time.

Others were not so fortunate, though the records of their trials reveal that their 'witchcraft' amounted to little more than folk remedies and harmless charms, and they were more often trying to help than hurt. Fisherman James Davidson, in Sanday, was complaining that he could not catch any fish. Marion Richart washed the feet of his cat in the water in which he kept his bait, and cast it after him when he went to sea, in order to change his luck. The records do not relate if James brought home a record catch, but Marion's life ended on Gallows' Hill in 1633.[16]

There was even more to worry people than the lack of milk or fish when the islands became fatally involved in the Civil War. In 1650, the Earl of Montrose landed in Orkney. He had raised a mercenary army in Sweden, in support of Charles II's attempt to regain his throne, but most of his ships were lost in the North Sea, and he arrived with only a remnant of his troops. The Royalist gentry of Orkney hastily mustered a force from their tenants, who marched with Montrose to meet Oliver Cromwell's army at Carbisdale in Sutherland. It was a crushing defeat for the Orkney troop of farmers and fishermen: 400 men died and as many were taken prisoner.[17] There was distress for the Orkney clergy as well. Almost all of them had signed a 'loyal address' to Montrose, expressing their horror at the execution of King Charles I the previous year and their loyalty to Charles II. For this, they were expelled from their kirks by the General Assembly.

Following Cromwell's successes, Kirkwall became a town under occupation, and suffered from the disruption to trade and the unpleasantness of a foreign army. The troops were garrisoned in St Magnus Cathedral, where they smashed the magnificent tomb of Bishop Thomas Tulloch, 'one of the most splendid canopied tombs in Scotland'.[18] The troops, on their part, were probably as disgruntled with their posting as troops on foreign service usually are. One Cromwellian officer vented his spleen at his 'banishment from Christendome' in a lengthy diatribe in verse, along the lines of the Second World War doggerel, 'Bloody Orkney', but much more scurrilous.[19]

The association with England during the Commonwealth period, and the occupation by Cromwell's forces, imported ideas which were thoroughly unwelcome to most Scots, especially those in the conservative North. They were horrified by the republicanism of the English Puritans, and by the anarchy of their churches which subdivided into Separatists, and Independents, and Anabaptists and so on, at every disagreement. The Cromwellian administration fostered schism by supporting extremist minorities, and while the Scots are often blamed for turning Protestantism into something stern and oppressive, it was the hated Cromwellians who introduced a grim interpretation of the 'Sabbath', based on rigorous observance. (The concept of the joyless Sunday was unknown to John Knox, who found a game of golf on a Sunday afternoon the ideal way to focus his mind on his evening sermon.)

Although Orkney was a long way from south-west Scotland, where the most savage episodes of the war between King and Covenanters were played out, Orcadians were made well aware of the brutality of that conflict. The National Covenant had been signed in 1638, to protect the 'true religion' of Scotland from King Charles I's attempts to bring it into line with English practices, but the Covenanters saw nothing inconsistent in entering the Civil War in order to force a Scots Presbyterian theocracy on England.[20] Long after the Civil War had ended in England, the Covenanters were fighting a bloody war in Scotland against Royalist forces. In 1679, an army of Covenanters was routed at the battle of Bothwell Bridge, and their leaders hanged. Some of the prisoners were condemned to be transported to 'some one or other of our plantations in America', but while rounding Orkney in a December storm, their overcrowded ship foundered off Deerness. Most of the crew escaped to safety, but over 200 prisoners, chained in the hold, drowned in Deer Sound.

Puritanical and ruthless, the Covenanters war-cry was 'Jesus, and No Quarter'; and they were totally without compunction in slaughtering anyone who opposed them, including women and children. It is certain that they would have been equally merciless to their prisoners, but it is still a chilling thought that William Paterson, who had the government contract to 'dispose' of the cargo in *The Crown*, expected to make a good profit by selling his captives as slaves and returning with his hold full of sugar and tobacco. From a proclamation issued by the magistrates of Kirkwall a week later, it seems that a few 'passengers' were suspected of surviving the wreck, and it is possible that some escaped – there were families in Deerness who claimed to be descended from Covenanters.[21]

Although it seems that Orkney people did not object much to being made into Protestants, they were not in the least unanimous about what kind of Protestants they should be. Throughout the seventeenth century, Scotland was torn by the conflict between the Episcopalians and the Presbyterians. This had nothing to do with different religious beliefs or forms of worship: kirk services in Presbyterian and Episcopal kirks were virtually identical. The issue was the timeless question of power, and who should wield it. The Episcopalians wanted the king to remain in ultimate charge of the Kirk, governing through the hierarchy of bishops and clergy who were his appointees. The Presbyterians wanted to shift power into the hands of *presbyteries* of ministers and elected elders, who were answerable, ultimately, to a General Assembly. In a politically unstable time, this was an extremely sensitive issue. Was the king's position divinely appointed, or a tyrannical autocracy? Were presbyteries accountable democracies, or hotbeds of anarchy?

King James VI regarded Presbyterians as little better than terrorists. He thought their ideas were totally subversive of royal authority and peaceful government: 'presbytery as well agree with monarchy as God with the Devil'. Subsequent history proved that he did have a point. His English subjects briskly followed the removal of bishops with the removal of the head of his son, Charles I, and the throne of his grandson, James II. From Church Records, we know that most Orkney lairds shared the king's prejudices, and we will see that they were often both vocal and violent in their expression.

The Reformation itself did not bring immediate, dramatic change to life in Orkney, but its long-term cultural impact was enormous: for better or worse, according to one's point of view. In the eyes of George Mackay Brown, a convert to Roman Catholicism, Scotland became a 'Knox-ruined nation',[22] shorn of poetry and mystery. For many Presbyterians, on the other hand, Christianity arrived for the first time in the sixteenth century, the previous thousand years or so being relegated to the realm of dark superstition. What is certain is that Luther's challenge to the Church created an intellectual climate in which no authority could hold a lid on enquiry, and criticism and debate. Without the unassailable Authority of

the One True Church, it was inevitable that Protestantism would splinter into its endless subdivisions, but also that the way would be open for the empirical curiosity, the insatiable appetite for gathering and testing knowledge that later characterised the Enlightenment. Without Luther and his followers, the eighteenth-century Orkney intellectuals who garnered information about the islands' history and economy, and the nineteenth-century radicals who transformed them politically and socially, could not have existed.

CHAPTER 6

Resorting in Pilgrimage

Then longe folk to goon on pilgrimages.

Geoffrey Chaucer (c. 1387)

Many of the customs of the medieval Church were banned by Act of Parliament after the Reformation, especially pilgrimages to shrines of the saints, and praying at chapels and holy wells – all religious observance, in fact, other than attending the parish kirk on the Sabbath or when commanded by the minister. The local bailie, or magistrate, and his officers were ordered to assist the Kirk Sessions in 'suppressing all idolatry, especially of walks and pilgrimages',[1] but evidently both the Act and the bailies were ineffective, because an edict of the Privy Council in 1629 threatened severe punishments for anyone caught 'resorting in pilgrimage to chappellis and wellis, *which is so frequent and common in this kingdome*, to the great offence of God, scandall of the kirk and disgrace of his Majesteis government'.[2]

The pilgrimage to St Magnus' shrine in the cathedral must have come to an end when the shrine was destroyed at the Reformation, but other parts of Orkney were less easy to police. To places like the ruined chapels on the Broughs of Birsay and Deerness, the island of Damsay, and St Tredwell's Loch in Papay, people continued to bring their prayers and petitions, despite all the threats from the Privy Council, local bailies and parish pulpits. With the 'official' church divided among itself and offering a sternly authoritarian, judgemental face, it is not surprising that popular religion went underground, and people looked to their banished saints and to their forbidden 'popish' chapels for comfort and consolation.

For the poor, who could not afford doctors, visiting and making vows at chapels thought to be particularly holy, or drinking or washing in the water from wells or springs associated with popular saints was often their only medicine. There were a number of healing wells scattered throughout the islands, one of the most frequented being St Magnus' Well in Birsay, a spring of clear water which gushed from the spot where the saint's coffin rested on its way from Egilsay to Christchurch.

Doing anything furtively in Orkney is virtually impossible even today, and anyone seen visiting these places risked punishment. In 1660, John Budge was in trouble with the Burwick Kirk Session for going to St Colm's chapel in Grimness when he was ill, and was made to walk from the south of South Ronaldsay to the north kirk (about 10 kilometres) to do penance

FIGURE 6.1

The water of St Magnus' Well in Birsay (where the saint's body was washed on its way to Birsay after his murder) was thought to have healing powers. The spring was also known to be an excellent source of pure water for making ale, or adding to whisky. The pump, added in 1906, does not function but people are still collecting water from the spring and some claim that it is medicinal, giving relief to sufferers from cancer and multiple sclerosis.

on his knees the following Sabbath.[3] One hopes that his visit to St Colm's had cured his sickness by then. The chapel dedicated to the Virgin Mary on the island of Damsay was especially popular with women and, as late as 1741, Elspit Bews and five companions from Firth parish were disciplined by the Kirk Session for travelling to it on the Sabbath. Elspit claimed that 'a Vision came to her in the night to go to the Chapel of Damsay and get her health' but visions did not get her out of trouble.[4]

People made their way from far afield to the healing waters of St Tredwell's Loch in Papay. St Tredwell, if hardly the best known of Scottish saints, is reasonably well documented, and we know that the sites associated with her were widely believed to offer miraculous cures, especially for diseases of the eyes. The little chapel dedicated to her on Papay was a popular pilgrimage site for many centuries. Both the eye-witness accounts and the coins found on the chapel floor testify that she was venerated there until at least the late eighteenth century. By 1841, however, the parish minister could write in his entry for the *Statistical Account of the Orkney Islands* that 'her fame is now passed away, and name almost forgotten'.[5]

> Saint Tredwell, als, there may be sene
> Quhilk on ane prick he baith her ene.

The name Tredwell seems to be the Scotticised form of Triduana ('three-day fast') and her story appears, with variants, in several late medieval sources.[6] In one version, she is described as a companion of St Regulus, who bore the relics of St Andrew from Greece to Scotland, and in another, as one of the followers of St Boniface, who led a mission from Rome to Pictland. All the sources agree, however, on the main feature of her story. She caught the attention of the Pictish king, Nechtan, who praised the beauty of her eyes. Triduana responded to his advances in summary fashion: she plucked out her eyes and dispatched them to the infatuated king skewered upon a twig.

Spared Nechtan's unwelcome attentions, Triduana settled down to a holy life in Rescobie in Angus, and died at Restalrig near Edinburgh where she was buried. A well sprang up near her tomb, and its waters became renowned for healing those who suffered from afflictions of the eyes. The cult of St Tredwell was flourishing by the beginning of the thirteenth century, and several chapels were dedicated to her up the east coast of Scotland, as well as the one in Papay. According to *Orkneyinga Saga*,

Bishop Jon of Caithness was healed at her shrine after being mutilated by Earl Harald Madadarson in 1201:

> Earl Harald took the bishop captive and had his tongue cut out and a knife driven into his eyes, blinding him. While he was being tortured, Bishop Jon kept praying to the holy virgin St Tredwell, and when they set him free he went over to a hillside where he asked a woman to help him ... The bishop was taken to where St Tredwell rests, and there he was restored to health both in speech and sight.[7]

It is curious, in the light of this gruesome story, that Tredwell was so highly venerated in Orkney, the home of the earl responsible for the bishop's brutal treatment.

Bishop Jon may have been taken to the saint's shrine in Restalrig, where James III later built a magnificent and highly innovative hexagonal, two-storeyed royal chapel over the relics of 'this most holy virgin (who) was in great honour among the Scots for the sanctity of her life and the glory of her miracles'.[8] Until the Reformation, people flocked there 'to Sanct Tredwell, to mend thair ene', as Sir David Lindsay wrote in 1554,[9] but only six years later the first General Assembly ordered that the kirk 'as monument of Idolatrie, be razed and utterly casten downe and destroyed'.[10] The well, however, survived, and the edict of the General Assembly evidently had no effect on its healing powers. As late as 1840, its waters were being collected and sold in Leith 'to clarify the vision of the dwellers of that enlightened burgh'.[11]

As a saint credited with healing eye-diseases, therefore, Tredwell had a long history in Scotland, but her origins remain a bit murky. It has already been suggested that her name in the original text of *Orkneyinga Saga*, 'Trollhoena', sounds distinctly pagan rather than saintly. The story of the holy virgin discouraging an unwanted suitor by plucking out her own eyes is a carbon copy of the legend of the much better-known St Lucy, a very popular saint in medieval Scandinavia. The pagan name and the recycled story and the association with a sacred lake all arouse suspicion that Trollhoena/Tredwell may originally have been a pre-Christian cult figure, disguised in the borrowed clothes of an early Christian martyr.

A conspicuous promontory juts into the water of St Tredwell's Loch from the east shore, a small mound that many centuries of occupation have littered with an untidy tumble of stones. Possibly it was originally a crannog, an artificial island-fort. Three hundred years ago, it was still an islet reached by stepping stones, but gradually fallen stones and invading segs (the yellow flag-iris), have anchored it to the shore, and now you may wade there in early summer through waves of marsh marigolds and meadowsweet. A stretch of battered walling indicates the Iron Age building at the core of the mound, crowned by the lichen-covered ruins of the little chapel on the summit.

Its massively thick walls still stand some five feet high in the north-west corner, and immediately outside this gapes the uninviting entrance to a long subterranean passage. William Traill, the teenage son of the laird, explored it in 1879,[12] and he also cleared the tumbled walls of the chapel and found the bones of a woman in a stone grave beneath the floor. A few feet west of the chapel, one can see the remains of a tiny cell, perhaps a shelter for a priest, or for pilgrims.

The chapel is medieval, but the earliest reference to it is in the sixteenth-century *Description of Orkney* by Jo Ben. For an account of the pilgrimage rituals we have to wait for the visit of the Rev. John Brand,

FIGURE 6.2
Aerial view of St Tredwell's Loch and Chapel, Papa Westray. The waters of the loch were renowned for their healing powers, especially for eye-diseases. The remains of the chapel are in the centre of the perimeter wall (the wall and circular sheep-fold are much later), on top of an Iron Age building.

published in 1701. Brand was touring the islands on official business: he was a member of the General Assembly of the Church of Scotland Commission investigating 'the state of religion and morals in these parts'. At St Tredwell's, Brand found exactly the sort of thing he had come to put a stop to: 'Heathenish and Popish rites yet remaining in the Orkney Isles.'[13] However, he was sufficiently intrigued to write a detailed description of what he saw. The chapel was already a ruin at the time of his visit, but despite the threats of lairds and fulminations of Presbyterian ministers, the local people still regularly turned down the old road known as Messigate (the Mass Road) to worship in its roofless walls and, especially during Lent and on Easter Sunday, boats could be seen converging on Papay from other isles.

It was St Tredwell's reputation for healing disease that brought people in such numbers to her chapel and loch. 'The present Minister of Westra told me', wrote Brand:

> that such as are able to walk, use to go so many times about the Loch, as they think will perfect the Cure, before they make any use of the Water, and that without speaking to any, for they believe, that if they speak, this will marr [sic] the Cure.

After circling the loch in silence (this was no small matter, as one circuit is a walk of more than three miles over rough ground), the supplicants washed themselves in the water and left some possession at the loch ('as old Clouts and the like'). Despite Brand's scepticism, it is clear that he was impressed by the minister's testimony of recent cures: 'A Gentleman who was much distressed with sore eyes, went to the Loch and Washing there, became sound and whole ...'[14]

It was not only those hoping for a cure that came to St Tredwell's. Those who had been sick, or who had been in danger at sea, made vows to visit the chapel, if they were saved.

> And when they go to the Chappels to pay the Vows taken on, they use to lay several Stones, one above another, according to the number of Vows which they made; some of which heaps we saw in St Tredwells Chappel. And none must go empty handed, but leave behind them something, either a piece of Money, or of Bread, or a Stone.[15]

When the Rev. George Low toured the islands in 1774, he claimed that these rituals were practised 'only by a few of the oldest and most ignorant of the inhabitants', but probably the improvements in medicine, hygiene and nutrition which made eye-disease far less common had as much to do with St Tredwell's redundancy as the opposition of the Kirk. When William Traill cleared the floor of the chapel during his excavation in 1879, he found thirty copper pennies, halfpennies and farthings from the reigns of James VI, Charles I, George II and George III: proof that coins were left there until the late eighteenth or even the early nineteenth century.[16] It seems that 'the oldest and most ignorant' clung to their 'superstitious practices' for much longer than the ministers liked to admit.

The rituals practised at St Tredwell's have many parallels. The custom of circumambulating a sacred place, especially a holy well or loch, and of leaving small offerings, was widespread throughout Scotland and far beyond, and seems to have been hardly diminished by the zeal of the Reformers to exterminate 'popish superstitions'. At the beginning of the eighteenth century, contemporary with Brand's visit to Orkney, Martin Martin found people performing sun-wise circuits of sacred wells throughout the Western Isles. At Loch Siant in Skye, for example:

> they move thrice round the Well, proceeding Sunways from East to West …This is done after drinking of the Water; and when one goes away from the Well, it's a never-failing Custom, to leave some small Offering on the Stone which covers the Well. At St Katherine's Well in Eigg, all of them made the Dessil [Gaelic *deasail* or 'to the right hand'] of going round the well sunways, *the priest leading them.*[17]

At a healing well in Islay, he found pins and needles, the direct descendants of the offerings of pins found in Bronze Age wells. There is a tradition of pilgrims to St John's Chapel in Dunnet, Caithness walking around the loch,[18] and there are Orkney parallels too. The custom of leaving gifts of small coins or pebbles was also practised at the chapel on the Brough of Deerness and, in 1640, a Rousay woman, Katherine Craigie, was accused of trying to cure a sick neighbour by making her walk with her 'about the Cross Kirk of Wasbuster and the Loch of Wasbuster' in silence and before sunrise.[19] This was one of the crimes for which Katherine was tried for witchcraft and burnt at the stake, and yet, sixty years later, we have Brand's evidence that the custom was still frequently practised on Papay. He disapproves, but the fact that he describes the rituals as misguided, rather than criminal, suggests a considerable change in attitudes in the second half of the seventeenth century.

The Rev. James Wallace, the cathedral minister, also wrote about the pilgrimages that were popular in Orkney at this time:

Anciently, as they are yet in great measure, they were much given to Superstition ... But the Chapels to which most frequently they made their Pilgrimage were to the Chapel of the Brough of Birsa and to the chapel of the brough at Mulehead in Deerness ...[20]

Just half a mile south of Mull Head, at the eastern extremity of the Deerness peninsula, rises the large rock-tower that is the Brough. As you approach it, the ruined chapel appears as a low mound on a grassy headland, and its dramatic location is only evident when you are a couple of stones'-throw away and see the land drop away abruptly in front of you. The Brough was once connected to the mainland by a narrow neck of land, but at some stage in the medieval period – certainly before the sixteenth century – this bridge subsided into the sea, so that the only

FIGURE 6.3
The steps to the Brough of Deerness, which pilgrims climbed on hands and knees.

access is by descending to the shingle beach of Large Burra Geo and climbing up again by a narrow path.

On a fine day, the Brough is easily reached, but when a blustery gale is besieging the stack and drenching the rock steps with spray, you appreciate the dramatic physical separation from the mainland that isolated the little chapel, perched on its wind-battered eyrie, from the secular world. The narrow path has been worn by the feet – and even the knees – of generations of pilgrims, who made this painful ascent up the sharp rocks to make their prayers more efficacious. Jo Ben described the scene in the sixteenth century:

> In the north part of the parish there is in the sea a natural rock where the people on hands and knees ascend to the top with great difficulty. On it is a chapel called the bairns of Brugh. Hither flock together from various islands men, youths, boys, old people and servants innumerable, in truth coming with naked feet ... they ascend praying.[21]

The name that Ben heard as 'bairns' was surely a derivative of the Old Norse *boen-hus*, a prayer-house or chapel.[22] Near it was a well of fresh water. Here, according to Ben, 'the people on bended knees with clasped hands, without confidence in the God that is, supplicate the bairns of Brugh with many incantations, throwing stones and water behind them and walking twice or thrice round the chapel'. These are very similar rituals to those that Brand witnessed at St Tredwell's Loch in Papay in 1700, and also at the old church in Weisdale in Shetland, which was 'much frequented by the Superstitious Country People who light candles therein, drop money in and about it, go on their bare knees round it, and to which in their straits and sickness they have Recourse ...'[23]

In the course of Dr Morris's excavation (1975–7), pebbles were found on a gravel path round the Deerness chapel, corroborating Ben's description and, as at St Tredwell's, many small copper coins of the seventeenth and eighteenth centuries. It is interesting that none of the coins is earlier than 1640: possibly this reflects simply a lack of coins at a time when a money economy was practically non-existent, but it may also represent a shift in the beliefs of the pilgrims. The custom of throwing stones or water behind them sounds like a magical rite, a method of getting rid of evil by transferring it to the stone, while the money may be offered to reinforce a prayer for some benefit, or as a thanksgiving for a blessing received. Usually seventeenth-century copper coins are badly worn, but those that Morris found at Deerness showed very little wear, suggesting to him that they were the best available and had been carefully selected.[24]

Jo Ben takes a dim Protestant view of pilgrimages, and is unimpressed by the rituals at the Brough. 'Here they do not worship god purely', he ends his description primly. Most of our information on the survival of medieval customs comes from the distinctly hostile pens of Presbyterian ministers, who are, at best, caustically dismissive of anything they can label as 'popish' or 'heathenish' superstition. They are also anxious to emphasise that, under their stern ministerial influence, such customs are dying out. 'For some time past they have begun to see the folly of a practice, so repugnant to the spirit of rational religion', sniffed the Rev. George Barry in 1805,[25] but the embarrassingly late coin of 1860 is evidence that traditions died hard. 'At the present day', wrote the historian John Tudor in 1883, 'no inhabitant of the parish ever visits the chapel without leaving some offering behind.'[26]

The Brough is one of the most evocative of Orkney's Christian sites, but also one of the most tantalising. Both literature and archaeology have trailed intriguing clues as to the people who lived here, and why, and when, but have left so many questions unanswered. It is a place to explore with the imagination, to watch through mist and salt-spray the slow file

of pilgrims – the old, the maimed, the sick – approach on bleeding knees. From the safe fold of the chapel, the vast view of sky and sea and island has changed little since their time, save that, to the north, wind turbines now break the horizon, and the sun glints on the white arms of giant steel idols, flailing in slow circles on Rothiesholm Head.

CHAPTER 7

Feuds and Formidable Women

The reformation in Scotland being made by a popular tumult and rebellion ... some of our fiery ministers ... began to fantasy to themselves a democratic form of government.

King James VI (1598)

*T*he pilgrimages give us an insight into the hold that the 'old religion' had on the hearts and minds of ordinary people long after the Reformation. The furtive visits to the island of Damsay or to the ruins of hillside chapels, the vows to the Virgin Mary and prayers to outlawed saints, the painful progress to the Brough of Deerness or the silent procession round St Tredwell's Loch were all performed in defiance of the authority of lairds and ministers, and risked punishment by the Kirk Session or even the civil courts. They all speak eloquently of how desperately people needed a source of spiritual comfort and consolation in their hard and hungry lives, and how dismally the 'official' Kirk was failing to provide it.

It is not difficult to understand why. The acrimony of the religious and political conflicts of the seventeenth century continued to poison the Kirk well into the eighteenth century, and many ministers seem to have been busy stirring the controversy. Not only was the Kirk serving up a religious diet that was decidedly thin on comfort and consolation, but society was divided into two hostile camps. To understand the ferocity with which the Episcopalians and Presbyterians attacked each other, we have to take a large leap of imagination backwards out of our multicultural, multifaith society into a time when there was really no concept that one nation *could* contain separate churches. No-one in Scotland in the seventeenth century could have imagined a situation in which belief was regarded as a personal and private affair. In fact, far from being thought politically correct, toleration of religious diversity was regarded as positively reprehensible.

When the Protestant monarchs, William and Mary, came to the thrones of England and Scotland in 1689, supplanting the deposed Roman Catholic James VII, they were persuaded that it was impossible for the two countries to peacefully accept the same kind of Church. In the 'Revolution Settlement' of 1690, Presbyterianism was finally recognised as 'the only government of Christ's Church' within Scotland, and Commissioners like John Brand, who described the rituals at St Tredwell's Chapel, were sent around the country to make sure that every pulpit was filled by an 'appropriate' minister. However, Orkney and much of northern Scotland were very conservative. Most of the gentry and many ministers were loyal supporters of the Stewart kings and staunchly Episcopalian. Fourteen of the eighteen Orkney ministers refused to accept the Settlement and resigned. The Commissioners replaced them with men of impeccably Presbyterian credentials, and the lairds, predictably, loathed them on principle.

If the party labels are unfamiliar to us, the conflict between national and religious loyalties is not. The Jacobite rebellions, and rumours of rebellions and French invasions, fuelled Presbyterian suspicion that all Roman Catholics and Episcopalians were potential traitors, who would put loyalty to their religion, and to foreign co-religionists, before their country's fragile peace. The situation was similar to the nervousness in England in the 1980s after the IRA bombings, when any stranger speaking with an Irish accent was liable to be suspected of being a terrorist.

Episcopalians, on the other hand, saw Presbyterians as plunging the established order into political and social anarchy. The 'episcopacy' of a laird like Thomas Traill was less a matter of religion – he was a most irreligious man – than an inherited accessory of the landed class. Bishops represented traditional values: they had always been drawn from the upper classes, and could be expected to uphold the landed interest in Parliament and in their sees. 'Presbytery', on the other hand, was not only politically dubious, but produced the appalling situation in which Kirk Sessions, consisting of ministers and of elders who might be elected from the 'trading and inferior sort',[1] could sit in moral judgement over their social superiors. Most of the Orkney lairds would have agreed wholeheartedly with Charles II's famous aphorism that 'presbytery was not a religion for gentlemen'. In their after-dinner conversations, one scents, through fumes of port and tobacco, a strong whiff of reds-under-the-beds.

As a result of this head-on collision of prejudices, the records of eighteenth-century Orkney Presbytery meetings often read like the script of a surprisingly violent soap opera, but with a much more imaginative use of invective. Some of the more colourful scenes arose out of the ministry of the Rev. William Blaw in Westray and Papay. He had the misfortune to be married to the sister of the choleric and vitriolic Thomas Traill, who was one of the principal heritors. The Kirk Session had bravely attempted to rebuke Traill for his flagrant and repeated sins, and 'ever since he hath carried on an implacable hatred to the Minister'. Their feud splatters many pages of densely written Presbytery minutes with distinctly unecclesiastical epithets. In 1719, Blaw reported that, among many other things, the laird never attended the kirk, refused to pay his tithes or the fine still owing for his father's sin of fornication, and forced his servants to work on Sundays.

> Thomas Traill of Holland, casting off all fear of God and regard to man, does not only remove seats in the Church, yea and the Pulpit at his own hand and Dispose of money collected for the poor as he thinks fit, but

FIGURE 7.1

St Boniface, Papa Westray, the scene of violent disputes between the minister and the laird's family in the eighteenth century. From the stair Thomas Traill's factor would give orders to the tenants for the following week's work in his fields.

also does most wickedly prophane the Sabbath by calling his Servants to the house upon the same and then and there contriving and commanding all the work that is to be done all the week after.[2]

Traill's response was to call his brother-in-law a 'Knave', a 'Witless Villain', a 'Coal-Stealer' and other uncomplimentary things in 'scurrilous and bantering language'.

It was Blaw's attempt to discipline Traill's son, Peter, for his sexual misdemeanours that provoked an extraordinary scene one Sunday in June 1718. Peter and his father and brother threatened the minister in the St Boniface kirkyard:

> using Dreadfull oaths and horrid Imprecations. The Minister begged for peace: Holland I pray you commit no more riot, for there is too much sin committed this day already, there hath been such swearing and cursing in the Kirkyard as might make the Kirk to sink with us all as the ground did to Sodom ... [Traill] swore with a dreadfull oath that he should close up the Kirk door, and break the bottom of the Boat that should bring the Minister to the Isle, and then like one mad he ran to the shoar, and took away the four oars of the Boat that had brought the Minister over, and beat some of the Boatsmen and swore if any man took the minister over and gave him lodgeing in the Isle he should presently be putt out of it.

Whenever Blaw came over from Westray to take a service at St Boniface, he had to moor his boat at 'the Minister's Flag' and walk two very rough miles along the shore to the kirk, because the laird would not allow him to set foot on his land.[3] The story is part of the folk-memory of Papay.

By law, the heritors were supposed to provide the stipends of the ministers and pay for the upkeep of the kirks and manses, in proportion to the value of their own property, but the Orkney gentlemen were adept at evading these responsibilities and some of them went out of their way to make life as difficult as possible for the unfortunate clergy. The Moodies of Melsetter in Walls, for example, were avowed Jacobites. In 1726, the Rev. John Keith complained to the Presbytery that 'My condition in the ministry in the island of Walls these eighteen years bygone has been a Labyrinth of oppressions, oppositions, Defamations, Pleas and Processes for a Stipend'.[4]

Cristiana Crawford, Lady Melsetter, 'whose blood-pressure was high, and whose life-style was intemperate',[5] was a redoubtable enemy. She carried on the feud to the extent of forbidding any of her tenants to work for Keith, so he was unable to get anyone to cut his peats, ferry him from the island or help his wife in the house. (She had her knife in Mr Pitcairn, the Hoy minister, too, and stole and destroyed his peats for good measure.) She locked up the parish school, fined the miller for grinding Keith's corn, intercepted the minister's post, and loudly defamed his character: 'when in Kirkwall he drinks whole nights in his Boots, as his landlady can witness'.[6] The climax to their war came on a Sunday in 1730. Lady Melsetter came to the kirk of Walls:

> in such a furious manner as is almost incredible ... she beat at the Church door with her whip ... then entered ... and broke forth into most base and upbraiding language to your Petitioner in the pulpit ... and passing up the Church to the minister's seat, abused his children, loudly saying, 'O ye sons and daughters of Belial!' And when without doors she was heard curse saying, 'the Devil break your Minister's neck, and the Devil break all your necks that comes to hear him ...' Some days afterward ... she sent George Jameson to tell me that she had four charged pistols prepared for me and any messenger that came firth to crave my stipend from her ...[7]

In 1730, a delegation from the Synod of Orkney succeeded in making a formal reconciliation between Keith and Cristiana, but she persisted in being reluctant to pay his stipend and relations between them remained strained. Astonishingly, he survived another sixteen years in his unenviable post!

The rivalries between Presbyterian and Episcopalian ministers led to many an episode of pure farce that it is impossible to believe were not relished for their entertainment value at the time. On a January Sunday in 1702, Thomas Baikie, Presbyterian minister of St Magnus Cathedral, was ill in bed in his house in Broad Street, with no-one to take his place in the pulpit. To the great consternation of himself and his wife, they heard the cathedral bell ringing and from their window saw the congregation streaming into service. Bundling her sick husband into his clothes with all possible speed, Mrs Baikie hurried him into St Magnus, still with his nightcap on, where they found his Episcopalian rival, John Wilson, officiating, 'and they two violently pull'd Mr Wilson out of the Pulpit'.[8]

Poor Baikie had other Episcopalian thorns in the flesh. Mr Fullerton, schoolmaster at Kirkwall Grammar School before he became minister of Westray in 1689, circulated scurrilous 'reproachful rhyms' about him, which were probably sung at inappropriate times and places by cheeky schoolboys.[9]

John Wilson and his successors, James Lyon and George Spence, held Episcopalian services in a meeting-house in Anchor Close, attended by a number of the most influential Orkney families: Feas of Clestrain, Baikies of Tankerness, Stewarts of Brough and 'unquestionably the most considerable part of Kirkwall'.[10] The local Presbytery would have liked to banish them, but the magistrates did not dare take on such a formidable coalition, and so ministers of both persuasions operated side by side, sniping at one another at every opportunity. In 1712, Parliament passed the Act of Toleration, allowing Scottish Episcopalians freedom of separate worship. It was the end of the tenaciously held belief that One Nation meant One Church, and extremely unpopular. Thomas Baikie reacted with a frenzy of intemperate language in the pulpit, denouncing Episcopalians as 'Baal-worshippers'! Even his congregation thought he had gone too far.

FIGURE 7.2

This 1733 tombstone is set in the north wall of the old kirk at the Bu', Hoy. The same delightfully naïve 'ionic columns' occur on a (much more damaged) stone in the Warbeth kirkyard, probably carved by the same sculptor.

For the next few years, the Episcopal Church enjoyed its only period of peace in the eighteenth century, and the Feas built a handsome Gothic-style chapel at Stove in Sanday. Then, in 1715, the Jacobites raised their standard of rebellion and the Orkney Episcopalians immediately broadcast their support. At the Market Cross in Kirkwall, 'Mr Drummond read a paper proclaiming the Pretender King', and Lyon and Spence, conspicuous in their preaching gowns, drank the health of James VIII.[11] The failure of the Rising put a swift end to toleration. Many Episcopalian clergy in Scotland were imprisoned or fled the country, and even in Orkney they were forced to keep a lower profile than previously.

It was after the suppression of the 1745 Jacobite Rebellion, however, that the laws against Episcopalians became really savage. Episcopalian meetings at which more than four persons were present became illegal. Any minister convicted of breaking this law was to be transported to the American plantations for life. Even the members of his congregation were liable to be arrested and sentenced to six months' imprisonment for a first offence, or two years for a second. Many meeting-houses were burnt, and the clergy forced 'to sculk where they best could, that they might not fall into the soldiers hands'. In Kirkwall, the meeting-house was divided into two flats with a hole cut in the floor, so that four persons could meet in the upper room and the rest of the congregation hear the service from below.[12]

While a number of the Orkney gentry had Jacobite sympathies – several North Isles lairds were convicted of corresponding with Prince Charles Edward during the '45, and suffered in consequence[13] – to most ordinary people the Risings meant only the awful spectre of civil war, and in the Kirk records of the time we can read their very real fear that 'popery' threatened peace and stability. The fear of 'Jacobites' was exploited by the media, to bolster support for the dynasty of rather unattractive kings from Hanover. In case popular suspicion of Roman Catholics should flag, the General Assembly sent out frequent bulletins to be read in all the churches, demanding the punishment not only of 'papists' themselves, but of any who 'supply, entertain, or furnish meat or drink to them or keep correspondence with any priests, Jesuits or trafficking papists'. Protestants would be prosecuted if they even employed a Catholic servant.[14]

In 1743, the Rev. James Tyrie stepped off the ferry from mainland Scotland into this well-stirred hysteria. He had been brought up a Roman Catholic, but 'had renounced the Errors of Popery' and been employed by the Church of Scotland at Fort William. Realising that his services were of little use there, because he had no Gaelic, he was sent to Orkney where he helped out as a missionary. In 1746, the parish of Cross and Burness in Sanday became vacant, and Tyrie was 'presented' to the living by the Earl of Morton.[15] The earl was the 'feudal superior' of Orkney, which entitled him both to feu duties, payable by all the landowners, and also to 'patronage' of all the kirks, or the legal right to nominate a minister when a parish became vacant.

The choice of Tyrie provoked uproar in Sanday. To just what extent he was unacceptable because of his former Catholicism, or simply because a local man, George Traill of Hobbister, was popularly expected to be the next minister, it is hard to say, but it brought into infuriated focus the people's resentment of a system which allowed a minister to be imposed upon a congregation against their wishes. The North Isles Presbytery complained to the General Assembly, but their letter did not reach Edinburgh because of the war: 'all the north of Scotland was overrun by the Rebels, whereby everything was in the utmost Disorder and Confusion; no correspondence was possible by Land and scarce any occasions offered by sea ...' Under pressure, the Presbytery backed down and appointed Tyrie, but when the time came for the heritors and elders to 'take him by the hand' in the customary gesture of acceptance, they all defiantly left the church, and only Morton's agent remained to shake poor Tyrie's hand.[16]

Even after his induction, the row continued unabated, and Tyrie must have been glad when he was transferred to the Mainland parishes of Stromness and Sandwick in 1747. Not a soul in Sanday objected to his going, but if his short stay there had been stormy, he had much more violent scenes to face in his new charge. In June, he went to the Stromness church to celebrate a marriage, but 'he was in a tumultuous manner opposed by a multitude of women' who barricaded the doors of the church against him, so that he was obliged to perform the wedding service in the churchyard. The sheriff had to be called to restore order, but the viragos of Stromness 'continued all the more outrageous and used several threats against the Presbytery if they should attempt to settle Mr Tyrie'.

Notwithstanding this inauspicious beginning, the Presbytery prepared to formally admit him at the Sandwick church, taking the precaution of ensuring that Ross, the sheriff, would be there as bodyguard. However, the Sandwick women were prepared, and had gathered to heckle. One of them struck Ross on the face when he remonstrated with them. 'A numerous crowd of women' was soon seen heading to Skaill from Stromness to reinforce their Sandwick sisters, and the nervous Presbytery decided to proceed to a hurried admission, without wasting time on a sermon.

Although now legally minister of Stromness and Sandwick, Tyrie still had to gain access to his churches and, for the next several Sundays, his congregation succeeded in barring the doors against him. One day, he attempted to preach in the fields at Skaill, but was:

by a crowd of women who had come the night before from Stromness ... in the time of prayer attacked by them and threatened to be tore in pieces if he did not desist which he was obliged to do and those who were with him for their own safety.

In a final act of defiance, the Stromness Furies went to Tyrie's peat bank and destroyed his peats 'as the next greatest injury they thought they could do him ...'[17] (By now, the destruction of peats will be recognised as a familiar weapon in ecclesiastical conflict!) Alas, the Presbytery records do not tell for how many Sundays Tyrie was barricaded out of his own churches, but he must have been made of stern stuff, because he evidently persevered until even the women of Stromness had run out of steam, and he remained in his charge for fully thirty-one years, until his death in 1778.

In his long ministry, James Tyrie would have seen his parish, and all Orkney, become a much more peaceful place. Episcopalianism had been suppressed and was no longer a political cause. The lairds trimmed their sails to the wind and became reconciled to their Presbyterian ministers. Resentment of patronage, however, was undiminished. By the time that Tyrie died, a number of Scottish congregations had already seceded from the Church of Scotland in protest against it. Within twenty years, Orcadians were joining the Seceders. Sixty-five years after Tyrie's death, patronage would be one of the main issues that split the Church from top to bottom, in the major schism known as the Disruption.

CHAPTER 8

Church-going may Seriously Endanger your Health

The materiall Kirk lyes lyk sheipe and nout [cattle] faulds rather than places for Christian congregationes to assemble into.

James Melville (1584)

There is a simple reason why virtually the only church buildings we see in Orkney are sturdy medieval ruins or the austere preaching barns of the nineteenth century: everything built in-between times was so shoddily constructed, for the minimum amount of money that could be extracted from grudging heritors, that it was soon in ruins. In the eighteenth century, most of the kirks were totally dilapidated, to the point of literally falling down around their congregations' ears, and the Presbytery records are a depressing catalogue of the miseries endured by ministers and people in hovels where the rain poured through the roof, and the wind howled through the glassless windows. To be fair to Orkney, this had been a widespread problem in Scotland since before the Reformation. In the mid-sixteenth century, few people in Scotland were going to church at all, due to the lack of kirks – especially in rural areas – or their state of disrepair.[1] An Act of 1563 ordering that ruinous kirks be 'reparit and upbigit' was not enforced,[2] and 200 years later the traveller, Pennant, commented acidly that 'in many parts of Scotland our Lord seems still to be worshipped in a stable, and often a very wretched one … the people appear to worship, as the Druids did of old, in open temples …'[3]

Even St Magnus Cathedral was literally a stable. By the early eighteenth century, the interior had lost all its medieval grandeur and was dark, damp and filthy. Only the choir was used for services, with the congregation seated in a ramshackle arrangement of home-made pews and galleries. Most of the windows in the nave were boarded up, and the walls were green with damp. The Rev. James Sands of Birsay and Harray led his horse through the building to pasture in the kirkyard, while another minister tethered his mount to one of the pillars while he delivered the sermon.[4] In 1756, the Kirk Session granted a lease of the Great Churchyard to Thomas Loutit, 'who delved it and sowed it with grass and corn';[5] and, in 1822, Sheriff Peterkin commented that it was only recently that cattle had been prevented from grazing among the graves.[6]

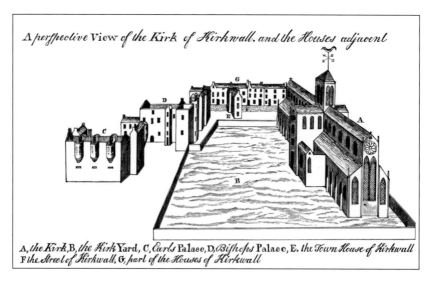

FIGURE 8.1

In George Low's drawing of Kirkwall in 1774, the cathedral looks a splendid building, but it was seriously dilapidated by this time and only the choir was used as a church. The nave was used at various times as a timber yard, and as a barracks for the Town Guard! (OLA)

St Magnus was even used as a guardhouse by the Town Guard during the Lammas Fair, much to the indignation of the Kirkwall Presbytery who complained of their

> most unchristian and more than barbarous practice … in shutting [shoot-ing] of guns, burning great fires on the graves of the dead, drinking, fiddling, piping, swearing and cursing night and day within the Church, by which means religion is scandalised and Presbytery most miserably

abused; particularly when they are at exercise in the said church, neither can the preacher open his mouth nor the hearers conveniently attend for smoke; yea, some of the members of the Presbytery have been stopped in their outgoing and incoming to their meetings, and most rudely pursued by the souldiers with their musquets and halberts, all of which are most grievous to the Presbytery and to any that have any sense of godliness.[7]

Eventually, the magistrates found the funds to put up another building for the Guard.

With St Magnus in such a state, one cannot expect to find the kirks in the country parishes faring any better. In 1744, the Orphir minister complained 'that the Breaches in the Roof of the Kirk occasioned so great cold especially when the wind was at the North that neither Minister nor people were able to Abide in it'.[8] At the end of the eighteenth century, the Rev. Hugh Ross of Evie and Rendall described his kirks as 'poor small houses, thatched annually with straw' which he had ruined his health by preaching in, long after they were derelict. Fortunately, he abandoned Evie shortly before the walls fell down one Sunday. The Rendall kirk becoming equally hazardous, he could only preach in the open air in the kirkyard.[9]

The problem, invariably, was the heritors, who were supposed to foot the bill for kirk buildings, but who evaded their responsibilities by simply refusing to reply to the Presbyteries' pleas and demands. Some of them were absentee landlords, administering their estates through factors, but even for the resident ones, attending kirk was obviously not a priority, and avoiding expense most certainly was. The Evie and Rendall heritors had promised that a new church would be built in the centre of the two parishes and the masonry finished by Lammas (August) 1797, but in November that year the minister reported:

it is certain that not a single stone is quarried for this purpose, and that the wood bought for said Church by Lord Armadale's late factor, having never been paid for, has by the Merchant been lately sold for some other purpose.[10]

Ross had to wait until 1799 for a new church, eighteen years after the old buildings had been condemned. Every meeting of the Kirkwall Presbytery lamented the state of their kirks; drew up plans; asked tradesmen for estimates; asked the heritors to pay their contribution; and eventually started the whole process over again because the estimates were out of date! Mr Watson of South Ronaldsay recalled his induction in St Peter's in 1786: 'On that day which was rainy, it is Notorious to the Presbytery that owing to the insufficiency of the Roof, the Presbytery, Your Petitioner and the Congregation were wet to the Skin.'[11] Presbytery remembered the miserable occasion all too well. The heritors were presumably absent. St Peter's remained roofless for fourteen years before it was finally rebuilt. At the same time, Mr Alison was stoically preaching in the leaking Deerness kirk until 'the roof was blown entirely off and the couples and walls were in danger of burying the Congregation in its ruins'.[12] Meanwhile, St Andrew's in Tankerness and St Laurence in Burray were in imminent danger of collapse, and St Mary's in Burwick urgently needing repairs.

To add to the ministers' discomforts, it was equally difficult to get any repairs done to their dark, damp manses, with their leaking walls and reeking fireplaces. Ross finally succeeded in persuading his heritors to build him a new manse, but it, he wrote, on a plaintively modern note: 'is exceedingly insufficient, receiving water at almost every part of the walls and roof, having been built by two contractors from Edinburgh, whose accounts are said to be unsettled to this day'.[13]

It was the same story in the North Isles. In 1707, Robert Baikie of Tankerness reported that the walls of the Eday kirk had fallen in and nothing remained of the roof, so that 'the minister is greatly endangered in his health by preaching in the open field'.[14] In Stronsay, in 1724:

> the whole three kirks are intirely demolished ... the Glory of God and the good of the Souls of the Inhabitants is what is denied, and our Minister hath been exposed these four years to the greatest hazard in preaching under the open heaven.

It was another twenty years before a new kirk was built in Stronsay; thirty years later, the new Eday kirk had still not been completed. The Westray kirks were in the same derelict state, and Walter Traill in Sanday lamented the dangerous condition of his kirk in Lady:

> The Heritors, to do them justice, were liberal enough in the Article of promise. But unfortunately for your Petitioner and the people of Lady parish, the time of performance never arrived ... without doors or windows it stands open to every shower and to every blast of wind. As the lofts are in danger of falling down ... in order to avoid danger from any fatal accident the Sacrament has been more than once administered in the fields. The churchyard dyke is also in so ruinous a condition that the swine are in the habit of rooting up the bodies of the dead ...[15]

FIGURE 8.2

Ladykirk in Sanday was semi-derelict even when it was in use, as the minister regularly complained. 'The lofts were so much decayed that he was obliged to prop them at his own expense, to prevent any accident befalling the people, the walls are not sufficient to defend the congregation from rain or snow ...'

The church of St Mary's at Burwick stands on the edge of the sea at the southernmost point of South Ronaldsay. An austere little nineteenth-century box, it has been rebuilt many times. In 1700, the walls stood roofless, 'yet the very Stones thereof [the people] reverence', their minister told John Brand, and 'so tenacious are they, that when in rough weather, he hath procured the conveniency of a Barn to Preach in, yet the People obliged him to come to this ruinous Fabrick'. The heritors wanted to rebuild St Mary's in a more central position, but the people insisted that they would rather re-roof the old church themselves than allow a new one to be built anywhere else.[16] It was the *place* that mattered. It had been the spiritual centre of the community long before the first kirk was built, and the kirkyard held the dust of the ancestors, who could not be abandoned merely for comfort or convenience.

The same story is repeated in parish after parish. Mr Clouston fought his parishioners to rebuild St Peter's in the centre of Sandwick, instead of at the edge of the parish and on the unstable sand above Skaill Bay. He lost the battle, and the kirk was built on the old foundations. The

FIGURE 8.3
St Mary's, Burwick.

gable walls promptly cracked again, but tradition remained unbroken and St Peter's still stands on its windy headland, a landmark for seamen, as the first kirk on the site was undoubtedly intended. Many a present-day minister who has had the temerity to suggest that his congregation move their place of worship may empathise with Clouston and the (chilled) minister of Burwick.

When the medieval kirks were finally rebuilt, they were redesigned internally to suit Presbyterian worship. The emphasis had shifted from the celebration of the Mass to preaching, so altars were removed and the focus of attention became the pulpit, where the minister thundered forth his message from a suitably elevated and dominating situation. The other essential item of kirk equipment was the 'repentance stool', on which Sinners were prominently placed to endure public rebuke and humiliation. At the beginning of the eighteenth century, there was rarely any other seating.

Gradually, it became customary to build a fixed seat for the minister, and the Sessions then allocated space in the church to the various heritors of the parish, according to the valuation of their property. It was up to the heritors to provide seats for their own family, servants and tenants – and to compete with one another for the most important and conspicuous places. Whatever the New Testament may have taught as to wealth and status being of no account in the eyes of God, they were vitally important issues as far as eighteenth-century Orkney lairds were concerned. They squabbled over their territories like gulls in a nesting colony. They quarrelled over the size and situation of their seats and they griped to the Session that another had encroached on their space or built a pew where he had no right. In Westray, John Stewart of Brough argued that 'Tuquoy had unjustly possessed two seats belonging to him'. William Balfour of Faray whined that 'he did not have that part in the West church which he should have and therefore craved that he should have his due proportion in the said church assigned him'.[17] In Orphir, the Taylor brothers had a fist-fight in the Orakirk pew for possession of the seat.[18] Clearly, the members of Presbytery were put to much work with valuation rolls, with measuring rods and with soothing the ruffled feathers of disgruntled gentry. They could not afford their discontent.

FIGURE 8.4

William Clouston lost the battle to build a new St Peter's in a more central position in Sandwick parish, and it was rebuilt on its old, unstable, foundations above Skaill Bay.

The heritors' arguments over space carried on beyond the grave. Burials were often made inside the church, under the earth floors of the family pew. Apart from a certain unpleasantness that this may have occasioned – it was not uncommon to find bones lying about the floor, and a smell arising from disturbed corpses[19] – it caused complications when property and, therefore, pew-rights, changed hands. George Sinclair in Waulkmill was given ground for a pew in the Orphir kirk, with the stipulation that he could not bury under it, 'it being the burial ground of Graemsay's family'.[20] People were sensitive about who trampled upon their deceased relatives, and so this became another cause of family feuds.

Even well into the nineteenth century, many of the parish kirks were grimly uncomfortable. In 1827, Mr Gerard wrote that some of the South Ronaldsay tenants had seats in the Burwick kirk, but there was no room for the growing population, for forty people from Swona, or for visitors. Even worse, there was no gate to the kirkyard, so pigs dug up the graves, and 'the bones of their fathers were tossed about as dung on the fields'.[21] William Tomison, who left the fortune he made as a Hudson's Bay agent to found a free school in his home parish, told Gerard that, having seen pigs snuffling around in the kirkyard, he would be buried in his own garden, and he built himself a pig-proof mausoleum.[22]

Since a rent had to be paid for a seat in the kirk, the arrangement of the pews faithfully reflected the earthly hierarchy. The eighteenth-century box-pews survived in the Papay kirk well into the twentieth century, and it was clear that, below the large panelled pews of the minister's and laird's families, the boxes decreased in size as the congregation grew poorer and thinner. Servants sat on benches, and were often tightly squeezed into lofts or galleries at the back of the church. 'Owing to the niggardliness of heritors such seating was often straightened in spacing and sometimes lofts were constructed with level floors, their seating being built upon an open framing in the most precarious manner like hen roosts'.[23]

One way of getting niggardly heritors to pay for church improvements was through fines for 'delinquency' – the usual euphemism for sexual immorality – which operated on a sliding scale, depending on the wealth, and obduracy, of the sinner. George Traill of Holland promised the Session that he would provide a loft with seats and a new pulpit in St Boniface Kirk, in lieu of a fine of £100 for his sin of fornication. (George would have been nearly 70 then, and shortly to marry his third wife.) Seventeen years later, the Session was still trying to persuade his son, Thomas, to provide the seats.[24] Fines were similarly exacted from Thomas and *his* sons for the family vice, which would have provided St Boniface with a

FIGURE 8.5
St Peter's, Eastside, South Ronaldsay.

handsome Fabric Fund, if the Session had ever found a means of making them pay.

When fixed seating was built, it was arranged around the pulpit which was placed in the centre of the south wall and flanked by windows, while the north wall was left blank, so that the minister was provided with the maximum light to see his text but his flock had no unnecessary distractions. The enormous pulpit dominated every Presbyterian kirk, elevating the minister to an impressive height so that there was no escape from his gaze, even in the gallery. 'This is the manner of architecture in the Church of Scotland, as though the minister is standing on the bridge of a great

FIGURE 8.6

St Peter's, Eastside, South Ronaldsay is one of the few kirks in which an eighteenth-century layout has survived, with long communion tables running down the centre of the kirk and the high pulpit in the middle of the side wall. The sounding board above the minister helped to project his voice; it was also useful in sheltering him from drips from leaking ceilings!

ship, directing its path through the sea.'[25] Below him sat the elders, backs to pulpit, so that they could keep an eye out for any signs of inattention in the pews. Here, the hard-working labourers, servants and apprentices spent much of their one day of rest enduring long extempore prayers and even longer sermons, while being cold, and frequently wet, and certainly uncomfortable. They attempted to restore their circulation by joining in loudly with the singing of the psalms – the only music that the Kirk permitted.

Before the Reformation, Scottish church music had grown very elaborate, but it was entirely performed by the choristers of the 'Sang Schools' and the congregation had no part in it. Calvin and Knox had been in favour of congregational singing (as long as only Biblical words were used), and there were several attempts to provide an acceptable translation of the psalms for singing in kirk. Music, however, fell on hard times in the seventeenth century. When James VI became king of England in 1603, many musicians and other artists followed the court from Edinburgh to London. Most insidious was: 'the invasion of Scotland, from south of the Border, by a pestilent type of Puritanism, inconceivably arrogant and intolerant, which ... sought to cast discredit on every form of art used in association with worship'.[26] The old music disappeared and, by mid-century, only a few simple tunes were known to which the 1650 Psalter could be sung. By the end of the seventeenth century, twelve tunes were the sum total of the Church of Scotland's tradition; most congregations used far fewer, and these had acquired the sanctity of the Sermon on the Mount. Anyone trying to vary the tunes could count on outraged opposition. As late as 1817, some of the Stromness Secession congregation were protesting against the introduction of tunes 'of a quick and giddy and light manner in their performance'. Even worse, their Session had chosen *an Englishman* to lead the music.[27]

This limited repertoire was sung, unaccompanied, line by line, after the precentor, who led the music from his desk in front of the pulpit. The custom of 'lining' the psalms was adopted in England in the seventeenth century, because so few people could read service-books. It was subsequently introduced into Scotland and, like the tunes, clung to, as a fundamental article of faith, long after it had been abandoned in the south. It was a practice guaranteed to mangle the sense of the text, sometimes with unfortunate results. The words of the psalm, 'The Lord will come and he will not be slow but hasten on', when 'lined' with a precentor, become:

The Lord will come and he will not.
The Lord will come and he will not
Be slow but hasten on.
Be slow but hasten on!

Nonetheless, 'lining' became so distinctive a feature of Scots worship 'that its disuse ... caused secessions of staunch Presbyterians from the Church'![28]

With a good, musical, precentor, the traditional singing of the psalms in a Highland kirk is a deeply moving and beautiful sound, totally unlike any other church music; but the only qualification for an eighteenth- or nineteenth-century precentor was that he should be someone with some standing in the community, such as the schoolmaster. Ambitious precentors 'could not resist the temptation to invent their own ornamentations and the people followed suit, garnishing the tunes with unauthorised shakes and quavers very much as their spirits moved them'.[29] Most visitors to Scotland found the noise horrible, and were amazed that the Scots thought that God could appreciate it. Elizabeth Grant, in her *Memoirs of a Highland Lady*, recalled the cacophony in her Rothiemurchus parish kirk in the early 1800s, when the precentor launched into praise.

FIGURE 8.7
In many kirks, the minister had a vestry immediately behind the pulpit where he could change out of his riding clothes and enter the kirk by a private door. In St Peter's, Sandwick, this room was directly below the enormous pulpit that elevated the minister to the level of the congregation in the galleries. There was no escape from his gaze!

The dogs seized this occasion to bark (for they always came to the Kirk with the family) and the babies to cry. When the minister could bear the din no longer he popped up again, again leaned over, touched the precentor's head, and instantly all sound ceased.[30]

When one stands in the redundant kirk at Skaill in Sandwick, for example, one should try to imagine the empty pews packed with people

FIGURE 8.8
Pews and gallery in the Old Kirk, North Ronaldsay, photographed. c. 1990. The astonishingly incongruous 'Gothic' pulpit was an early twentieth-century gift from the laird!

and the quiet space filled with a similarly enthusiastic noise. (There were probably dogs there as well; there are memories of the shepherds' dogs coming to the kirk – and of dog-fights during sermon – in many parts of the country.)

The mid-eighteenth century saw a considerable development in church music and the formation of church choirs in eastern Scotland, but Orkney congregations were struggling to have a roof on their kirks at that time, let alone a choir-loft, and it was at least another hundred years before 'lining' was abandoned in most kirks. At the Kirk Abune The Hill, in Birsay, the congregation were still 'lining' the psalms, while seated, in the mid-twentieth century.

Kirk interiors were far more colourful in the eighteenth century than they are today. The walls were always limewashed in ochre or white, and the woodwork of pews and galleries was usually painted in strong colours, according to the preference of the individual owner. Even in 1822, Sheriff Peterkin from Edinburgh was somewhat dismayed by the colour scheme in St Magnus Cathedral, and wished:

that the seating and interior accommodation were less incongruous, – that the good citizens of Kirkwall would spare their garish colours, red, blue and yellow, for carts and ploughs and not bedaub with these a set of boards which are fastened up to hide the chaste ornaments of Gothic columns in an antique cathedral.[31]

It is unlikely that the good citizens of Orkney would have understood Peterkin's Edinburgh prejudices. Nothing that we read about the state of their kirks in the eighteenth and early nineteenth centuries suggests that they were clean, well-ordered places, where people spoke in hushed whispers and behaved with quiet good manners. The kirks were the worn, often dilapidated, stage where the preoccupations of the congregations' weekday lives were enacted, Sunday after Sunday. The lairds asserted their social status by building their own pews, and defending their territories against their neighbours; women competed with one another in their best gowns and bonnets; young people hoped to cut a dash in the latest fashions; children giggled at the unfortunate sinners seated on the repentance stool; and everyone sang lustily the old and well-loved psalm tunes.

What was hallowed about the kirks was not their 'chaste ornaments', but the familiarity of the time-honoured words and music, spoken and sung within the framework of the time-honoured social hierarchy, and in the time-honoured place where their ancestors had gathered. Into this context, the hapless new minister 'fae sooth' had to make his entrance, burdened with a strange accent, unfamiliar habits and a weight of clerical education.

CHAPTER 9

Men of Enlightenment?

Came the minister, a black column of words.

George Mackay Brown (1971)

*A*s the stories of John Keith and James Tyrie testify, there were occupational hazards in being an Orkney minister. In the early eighteenth century especially, his life must often have been difficult and lonely. He was not usually a native of the islands, but came to Orkney as a very young man, after studying divinity in Edinburgh or Aberdeen. Often, he took a post as tutor in a laird's family while he waited, hopefully, for a parish to fall vacant. An exacting standard of scholarship was expected from him: he had to demonstrate his proficiency in Latin, Hebrew, Greek, Church History and Theology, as well as in delivering a Sermon, Lecture, Homily and Commentary – all part of the normal Sunday service! Freighted with this impressive amount of learning, the young minister took up residence in a leaking manse, and preached in a semi-derelict kirk to his mostly illiterate congregation. Presumably, their respective accents were often mutually unintelligible.

If he was lucky enough to be appointed to parishes on the Orkney Mainland, he could expect to be riding over appalling roads between his two kirks and his manse and his widely scattered people. His less fortunate colleagues had to face unpleasant, and often dangerous, journeys in small boats between two or three islands. John Brand left a graphic description of some of their adventures:

> The Ministers inform us, they are often in great danger in going to their churches from Isle to Isle, Sometimes pale death with its grim countenance

... staring them in the Face, as one drawn out by the hair of the Head, another escaping on the Keel of the overwhelmed Boat; sometimes they are arrested by a storm in the Isles, and kept from their own Families for some weeks, even when the passage will be scarce a Mile or half a mile over.[1]

These difficulties apart, he often faced the hostility of the local laird because of their political differences, as we have seen. A social gulf yawned between him and the rest of his parishioners, and he must have felt miserably isolated. Threatened by Lady Melsetter and her servants, John Keith lived for years in a state of anxiety for the safety of himself and his family. 'He lives in an inclosed Island ...', the Cairston Presbytery heard, 'and is cut off from converss by Letter, which makes him very melancholy ...'[2] As attendance at Sunday services was compulsory, and services were very long, the Kirk obviously played a large part in people's lives, but it does not follow that everyone was respectful, or even civil, to the clergy. In fact, there was a strongly independent streak in Orkney congregations, and woe to the minister who incurred their hostility!

Although the people did not have any right to 'call' a minister, as they do now, they had no hesitation in expressing their objection to an unpopular one. In 1661, a woman in Kirkwall called a minister who was not to her taste a thief, a vagabond, a renegade and – worst of all – a Ferry Looper,[3] still a term of contempt for an incomer today. Too much Hellfire and Brimstone in a Birsay sermon in 1730, and James Flett of Yeldavel addressed the minister in 'the most insolent and opprobrious language ... advising him to goe home to Birsay and sell Tobacco, for he was more fit to be a Packman than a minister'.[4] Too much fuss made about salvaging a shipwrecked cargo on the Sabbath, and the North Ronaldsay folk retaliated by refusing to send a boat to bring the minister, Mr Grant, over from Sanday.[5] The arrival of Mr Reid in Orphir in 1745 provoked violent riots, because 'they could not understand his tongue'[6] (strange accent?), and it was a year before he could take up his duties. Even in the mid-nineteenth century, when people, generally, were more polite, the new minister who arrived at the Walls kirk 'was accosted by a crowd of women who talked to him in a very unbecoming and insolent manner ...'[7]

The root of the problem was the system of patronage, and patronage survived, despite strong resentment and opposition, because it safe-guarded the political and social status quo. It ensured that the minister was dependent for his job – and hence for his home and status and stipend – upon the goodwill of his wealthy patron, and so he was bound to support the 'Establishment'. He who pays the piper calls the tune, and it would have been a brave minister who would have risked his livelihood by focusing too closely on Jesus' concern for the poor, or preaching on texts such as: 'It were easier for a camel to pass through the eye of a needle than for a rich man to enter the Kingdom of Heaven' (Matthew 19:24).

Even when the minister had no problems with his flock, he faced plenty of other potential pitfalls. If he was a compassionate man who took a lenient line with Sin, he was likely to be carpeted by Presbytery for not dealing out the appropriate fines and corporal punishment to 'delinquents'. He had to plead endlessly with his heritors to make repairs to his derelict manse or church, or to pay the schoolmaster of the parochial school, and he had the quite impossible task of bringing them to book for 'delinquency' when necessary, without upsetting them too much. If we read that the occasional minister took to drink, or succumbed to more serious temptations, it is little wonder, but the punishments were dire if he did. Mr Nisbet, minister of Stenness, was convicted of adultery in 1747, and spent two months on bread and water in the Inverness Tolbooth, before being banished to the plantations in Jamaica. (It turned out to be a lucky break for Nisbet: he made such a success of his new life that his whole family eventually moved from Kirkwall to join him.)[8]

However, by the late eighteenth century, the ministers were on a much more secure footing in a society that had become far less turbulent. People were no longer living in fear of civil war, and so politics ceased to dominate social life, and the ministers became more integrated with 'the gentry'. They were the only people in the community on the same social footing as the lairds, and so their family trees became heavily intertwined. The younger sons of landed families like the Baikies and the Traills entered the Church, and their sisters and cousins married ministers. Dinner parties in manse and mansion-house became an incestuous social round among a few close-knit families. They could expect Saturday night dinner-table conversation to be genial and entertaining – many ministers were typical offspring of the Scottish Enlightenment: widely read, cultured and intelligent – but sermon on Sunday was probably less than riveting. The Orkney clergy belonged to the Moderate, as opposed to Evangelical, wing of the Church, and moderation did not make for much excitement in the pulpit.

The Enlightenment was characterised by a zeal for acquiring and classifying knowledge which put Scots in the van of progress in almost every field of ideas or invention, but also produced an extraordinarily dull approach to religious belief. The urbane, and often sceptical, spirit of the age desiccated Christianity to a 'rational religion', shorn of miracle or mystery, and reduced to a dry catalogue of moral imperatives.[9] This unappealing package was delivered by ministers who carefully avoided anything that might inspire emotion or – perish the thought – 'Enthusiasm', that deadly sin of the Age of Reason. A contemporary commented that the Moderates talked of 'eternal concerns with a frigidity and languor which a good economist would be ashamed of, in bargaining for half a dozen haddocks'.[10] It is hard to imagine anything further from the spirit of John Knox, who would 'ding the pulpit to blads' as he got carried away with his own preaching. The Orkney clergy could quote from the pulpit in Latin, Greek and Hebrew, but their congregations of farm-labourers and fishermen rarely heard Jesus' words of compassion for the poor, or his indignation at those who oppressed them, in a language that they could understand.

If, on the whole, the eighteenth-century Church concerned itself little with social justice, there was a significant exception. In 1787, the campaign to abolish the slave trade was launched, and ministers of all parties joined forces in its support. In 1788, the first petitions reached the House of Commons, a high proportion of them coming from Scotland, and most of these from the Church courts, including the Presbytery of Kirkwall.[11] William Dickson of Moffat rode through Scotland from the Borders to Inverness distributing information describing the conditions on the slave-ships and in the plantations. Through his campaign literature, many people were made aware of the horrors of the trade for the first time. When the Orkney Presbyteries read the anti-slave trade pamphlets and saw the posters of the slave ships, they were probably genuinely shocked to realise that the huge fortunes which the tobacco and sugar plantations in the West Indies were bringing to many Scots, and Orcadians (one remembers the disgraced Mr Nisbet, who did so well for himself when exiled to Jamaica), were paid for by such unimaginable human misery. The North Isles Presbytery:

> took to their consideration the unhappy circumstances of the African natives, unjustly reduced to the state of slavery by the subjects of Great Britain, carrying on a cruel and unjustifiable trade to that coast. They unanimously agree to express in the strongest terms their abhorrence of such practices …[12]

They sent a petition to William Wilberforce in 1792, with many others from Scottish kirks, but it was not until 1807 that Parliament finally voted to abolish the trade.

The delay was partly due to vigorous counter-campaigning by the 'Tobacco Barons' and all those who had vested interests in the plantations, but partly also because the French Revolution had caused a reactionary backlash in Britain. In the government's hysterical terror that revolutionary ideas would spread across the Channel, panic legislation was passed forbidding public meetings, and any movement for change came under suspicion of fomenting revolution. Campaigning to extend the franchise was classed as sedition – the Moderator of the Glasgow Presbytery was imprisoned for three months in 1791 for preaching a sermon sympathetic to electoral reform[13] – and the anti-slavery campaigners were hampered in all directions by antiterrorist legislation which carried savage sentences. In the nervous Britain of the 1790s, it was dangerous to even use the word 'Liberty'.[14]

At that stage, the focus of the abolitionists was almost entirely on the slave *trade* and not on the even more controversial issue of emancipation. It took another thirty years of dedicated campaigning to free the slaves. Only after the Reform Act of 1832 extended the vote to include a middle class with a social conscience, but without huge vested interests in slave-worked plantations, did it became possible to force the Emancipation Act through Parliament. A huge part of the momentum for the campaign came from the Scots clergy and their congregations.

Apart from their involvement in the anti-slave trade campaign, the late eighteenth-century Kirk records paint a depressing picture of apathy or incompetence on the part of some Orkney clergy. Mr Leslie, in Rousay, hardly functioned in thirty years of claiming to be in a 'valetudinary state'; Mr Dennison, in Lady parish in Sanday, was quite mad, and his successor, Mr Traill, seems to have been mostly absorbed in getting his manse repaired. However, some ministers inspired affectionate memories: Mr Grant, of Cross and Burness, for praying for the safety of those at sea, but adding: 'Nevertheless if it please Thee to cause helpless ships to be cast on the shore, oh! Dinna forget the puir island of Sanday'!is

There were a few who worked hard for their parishioners and made a lasting contribution to Orkney scholarship as well. One of the most famous of these was George Low, minister of Birsay from 1774 to 1795 and a gifted natural historian. In 1772, the great naturalist, Sir Joseph Banks, stopped in Orkney on his way home from his travels in Iceland, and asked

Low to guide him on a tour of the islands' antiquities. It was as a result of the friendship and encouragement of Banks that Low undertook his fact-finding tours of Orkney and Shetland in 1774 and 1778 which resulted in such a wonderful fund of information about the islands. He constructed a water microscope and illustrated his studies with beautiful Indian-ink illustrations, but tragically, it was the long hours looking through a microscope that brought about his blindness. He continued to preach, and his congregation thought his sermons vastly improved! Low and several other Orkney ministers wrote superb articles for the *Statistical Account of Scotland* which John Sinclair compiled in the 1790s, demonstrating the breadth of their interests and knowledge of the geology, antiquities, economy and agriculture of their parishes. The influence that these men wielded in the course of their, often long, careers was enormous.

FIGURE 9.1

St Magnus Kirk, Birsay. A new kirk was built over the medieval one in 1664 and substantially restored and extended in the 1760s. Its most famous minister, the historian and naturalist George Low, was buried beneath the pulpit after his death in 1795.

One of the most meticulous accounts is that of William Clouston, minister in Sanday and North Ronaldsay for twenty-one years, and then in Stromness and Sandwick for another thirty-eight. Whatever talents or failings Clouston may have had as a minister, as a historian he is a delight. How much sharper is our picture of eighteenth-century Orkney for his summary of how modern and progressive the county had become in 1794, in comparison to 1700:

> In 1700 the use of tea was unknown, even in the families of gentlemen of the first landed property.
> In 1792, 860 pounds of tea were imported, and tea is drunk by tradesmen and mechanics ...
> In 1700, the wives and daughters of gentlemen of landed property, spun and manufactured their own wearing apparel.
> In 1794, the wives and daughters of tradesmen and mechanics dress in cottons and printed muslins ...
> In 1700, no dancing-school had ever been seen in these parishes.
> In 1793 a dancing-master opened a school, obtained 40 or 50 scholars, and drew £50 in four months.[16]

Ironically, it is also to the ministers that we owe the only descriptions we have of the pagan superstitions and festivities which they worked so hard to eradicate. Clouston left a magical picture of New Year celebrations in North Ronaldsay:

> There is a large stone, about 9 or 10 feet high, and 4 broad, placed upright in a plain ... The writer of this has seen 50 of the inhabitants assembled there on the first day of the year, and dancing with moon light, with no other music than their own singing.[17]

George Low wrote a description of the Johnsmass bonfires which were formerly lit in every parish on 24 June, the Feast of St John:

> They light up a large fire on every most conspicuous place facing the south and this is augmented by every person who attends, none of whom come empty. Likewise every person whose horses have been diseased or who have any of these gelded, brings them loaded with fuel to the fire, every beast is led round the same, always taking care to follow the course of the sun in their several turns, else they imagine their thanks for the recovery of the beast is not properly returned. The people go round in the same manner ... Sometimes great part of the parish assemble at this time and dance round and through the fire till late in the evening.[18]

Low was aware that the customs were fading out even in his lifetime. 'Formerly there were many more festivals in use ... Now these are laid aside and only a faint remembrance of them kept up.' One can sense a note of regret: it is not the minister but the historian and antiquarian who has watched the dancing around the standing stone and the Johnsmass fires, aware that he was seeing the dying embers of traditions that had originated in a time unfathomably remote. There is an evident nostalgia for all that was lost with the banished pagan past.

Many present-day ministers have chosen to abandon the traditional large manses and live among their parishioners, even when this has meant living in the poorest and most deprived of urban housing schemes. Such an idea would have appalled every eighteenth-century minister, who was deeply conscious of his status in life. They filled Presbytery meetings with moans at the wretched condition of their manses; the expense and danger of travelling between islands; and demands for an increase in stipend that would 'enable them to live in a Stile, in some degree suitable to the Station and rank in life which they have immemorially been considered as justly entitled to hold'.[19] In fact, they were very comfortably off in comparison to the rest of the population. Clouston valued his stipend at £76 per annum in 1794, while the maidservant at the manse could expect to earn twelve shillings to £1 a year, with board. Admittedly, his stipend was not exactly easy to come by, as it was paid mostly in kind, and from a variety of sources. Clouston said his was 'troublesome to collect as it is paid by nearly 100 heritors'![20] If these men could have imagined that their successors would be paid a regular salary, in money, from an office in Edinburgh, they would have been deeply envious. It was up to them to demand the agricultural products and services which every township in their parish was assessed to pay – hardly a task calculated to endear a minister to his flock.

To give a faint flavour of the complexity of his task, the following is a paraphrase of *just a portion* of the stipend that the Rev. John Scollay had to collect from his parishes of Cross and Burness and North Ronaldsay, in 1749:

> From Burness three merks [roughly one and a half kilos] of butter from each calved cow and one and a half merks from every calved heifer and farrow cow, one merk of wool out of each cowgild consisting of seven head about one year old, a lamb for every three cowgild, two cocks and two hens for each fishing boat in the parish together with teind eggs … From the glebe of Sandbeck twelve meils of bear [roughly 870 kilos], one meil of oat meal, five pounds of Scots money, one lispund of butter [roughly twelve kilos], the carriage of a big boat of peats from Eday requiring seven men, six poultry, three days tilth of a plough in labouring time together with the spinning of two merks yarn …[21]

It conveys an odd picture of the minister, shrewdly counting livestock as he rode past on his parish rounds, and one is not at all surprised to discover that his parishioners were reluctant to part with their precious animals. The Rev. James Izat found the Westray people 'disposed to take the most shameful advantage of their minister by concealing the number of their cattle and sheep and lambs'.[22]

Every minister was expected to add to his salary by farming his own glebe, which was often quite a substantial farm, and his manse included a steading with byres, barn, stable and corn-drying kiln. By the time that they were writing their articles for the *Statistical Account*, it is evident that many of them were extremely knowledgeable and practical farmers, and keen to encourage other landowners to try out the latest ideas for improving their lands through drainage, enclosure, crop rotation and the introduction of new fodder crops. The Rev. George Barry, for example, was one of the first to try out the new methods of modern farming on his glebelands in Shapinsay. Barry also published his monumental *History of the Orkney Islands* in 1805. It is a hugely informative volume, tinged with his self-conscious superiority. Here is his patronising summary of St Magnus Cathedral: 'Compared, indeed, with the magnificent ruins of the Abbey of Melrose, with the Cathedral of Durham, or the unparalleled Yorkminster, its grandeur and beauty suffer much', he drawled. 'But if the time in which it was built be considered, the people by whom, and the place where it was situated … it will strike us with wonder …'[23]

Barry and his contemporaries had plenty of time for both farming and scholarship. As long as they delivered a Sunday sermon, and presided over their Kirk Session, there was no great expectation that they would exert themselves unduly in caring for the spiritual or material needs of their parishioners. 'After the satisfactory discharge of his parish duties a minister may enjoy five days a week of uninterrupted leisure for the prosecution of any science in which his taste may dispose him to engage', wrote the young Thomas Chalmers, later a leading Evangelical, in 1803,[24] and this was certainly the attraction of the profession to scholarly, but impecunious, young men like George Low. To be given a church 'living' meant lifetime tenure, a good salary, a house, considerable social status and Time. It is worth registering just how valuable all this was, in order to appreciate what so many ministers would give up for their principles a few decades later.

Whatever the zeal or otherwise of the minister, the Kirk was pivotal in Orkney social life, and very few people in the eighteenth or nineteenth centuries would have considered existing outside its framework. Babies were brought to the kirk as soon as possible to be baptised, and accepted into the fold at the pulpit, literally and symbolically in the centre of the congregation. 'When the child was only a few days old it was carried to the church, attended by several females, who, of course, were plentifully primed for the ordeal with an unlimited quantity of home-brewed ale.'[25] Christenings were cheerful events, and celebrated with as much food and drink as the family could afford. In 1700, William Clouston informs us, this would consist of 'Orkney cheese, oat-cakes and ale brewed without hops', but by the end of the century one could expect the more sophisticated fare of 'English cheese, white bread, cinnamon-water and wine' to be presented at christenings.[26] This sounds as if Clouston is describing parties in lairds' houses: one cannot imagine anything as insipid as cinnamon-water being offered, or enjoyed, in most Orkney homes, where scones and cheese, washed down with ale and whisky, were much more likely to be provided.[27]

Marriages were also always performed by the minister, though not usually in the kirk. John Firth describes nineteenth-century wedding parties walking the four and a half miles from his district of Redland to the manse of Firth, where the minister performed the brief and perfunctory ceremony in the manse kitchen.[28] It was not until the mid- or even late-twentieth century that it became common practice to hold a marriage service in the kirk. In Papay, for example, the ceremony was always performed in the bride's house, and celebrated in the barn.

Death was the only rite of passage that ministers took no part in. Funeral rites were thought to smack of the dreaded 'popery', and so there was no service either in the kirk or at the grave, but the Kirk Session did insist that, for the sake of 'decency', all the men in a township should attend a burial and lend their neighbours assistance in carrying the dead to the grave.[29] This obligation seems to have been much resented – burials were presumably very frequent, and liable to interrupt a day's work – and, far from attending in a spirit of neighbourly support, people expected payment for their trouble, and graveside brawls sometimes occurred when they did not get it.

In 1722, Robert Inksetter complained to the Orphir Session that, at the burial of his son, some men had pulled off his coat, and he had been forced to pay them eighteen pence Scots each for attending.[30] In 1741, Thomas Loutit in Petertown complained that his neighbours would not attend his father's funeral. In their defence, William Halcro told the

Session that the dead man had been heavily in his debt, but as the family's only asset was a single cow, Halcro had refrained from taking the beast in payment, so that the son would have the means to bury his father.

> The people in the town did indeed convene but in regard the said Thomas would bestow nothing upon them, not so much as a mutchkine of ale or a piece of bread though he had the cow allowed him for that end, they declined to accompany his corps to the church and returned home to their houses.[31]

It sounds as if Thomas was mean, but the passage explains why people sometimes tried to avoid holding a funeral: it was an expensive business. By all accounts, people expected – and consumed – considerably more than a mutchkin, a mere three-quarters of a pint, of ale at funerals. (A century later, the Stromness Session was still trying, unavailingly, to limit the amount of liquor imbibed at the mourning-house.)[32] On the other hand, trying to sneak one's dead relative to the grave, without informing the township, was regarded by the Session as 'unbecoming indecent and scandalous' and a finable offence.

A SOUTH VIEW OF THE EARL'S PALACE IN THE PARISH OF BIRSAY, ORKNEY.

A. Front of the Palace.   B. Palace Garden.   C. Minister's House.   D. The Church.   E. Old Manse.   F. A Bridge.   G. The Brough of Birsay.   H. St Come's Church ; it is ruinous ; there is in the Churchyard here a Grave nine feet long.   The Sea runs between I and L.   K. are people busy at harvest.

FIGURE 9.2
George Low's drawing of his parish of Birsay. Interesting features which no longer exist are the enormous 'Old Manse' (lower right of the drawing) and the formal garden on the east side of the earl's palace. (OLA)

FIGURE 9.3
The Orphir kirk, rebuilt in 1829, dwarfs the remains of Earl Hakon's Round Church. The graveyard was the scene of frequent brawls at funerals. (Tom Kent/OLA)

By far the most important event, religiously and socially, in the kirk calendar was Communion, or the 'Lord's Supper'. For this event, people would flock from other parishes and other islands and camp in barns or outhouses for the several days that the celebration required. Usually it started on Thursday which was a 'Day of Fasting and Humiliation'; Saturday was a 'Day of Preparation', when there would be two or three sermons, to prepare for the solemn event on the Sabbath; and the congregation only dispersed after a service of Thanksgiving on Monday. On Sunday, there would be special services in the morning and afternoon, at which two or three ministers usually officiated, one preaching inside the kirk and the others by turns outside to the great majority who could not be squeezed indoors. At a Birsay Communion, for example, hundreds of people from all over Birsay and Harray gathered on the green beside the Old Palace.

The preacher outdoors might well be protected from the weather by a sort of wooden sentry box, a preaching tent, from the security of which he could thunder forth, at length, to his congregation seated on the ground and pulling their cloaks over their heads when it rained. The Communion itself was always celebrated seated at long tables, arranged down the centre of the kirk or taken outside if the kirk was too small.

In the Kirk records it all sounds very solemn, but this weekend was the only opportunity that many people had for taking a holiday, for meeting friends and relatives in distant parishes, and for assessing the local talent, who, of course, would be dressed to kill, and perhaps not entirely for the benefit of God. 'For many it does appear to have served the purpose that the County show does now, a festive occasion when long separated friends met and the young made merry.'[33] Even the ministers themselves sometimes sabotaged the solemnity of this occasion. James Paterson, minister in Rousay, was, on more than one occasion, accused of getting paralytically drunk on the Communion wine. When carpeted by Presbytery, he pleaded that he was a sick old man with not long to live, but he was still living, and drinking, twenty-six years later![34]

Although John Calvin had wanted the Lord's Supper celebrated every week, and the General Assembly recommended once a year, in many Orkney parishes it did not happen for years, or even decades, on end. Even the popular George Low managed to tear himself away from his microscope and organise a Communion only three times in twenty-one years of ministry, and in Sandwick in 1829, 'the Lords Supper had not been dispensed from time immemorial'![35]

FIGURE 9.4
A rare survival of a 'preaching tent' in Edderton kirkyard, Easter Ross. When large congregations met for communions, they had to gather in the open air as they could not fit into the kirk. The minister was sometimes sheltered from the rain in a wooden 'tent'; his flock were supposed to be stoical about getting cold and wet!

Walter Traill, minister in Sanday in the early nineteenth century, one day focused on the fact that there had been no Lord's Supper in Ladykirk for a considerable number of years and travelled to The Toon to buy the necessary bread and wine. While he was there, he visited his cousin and the two gentlemen agreed to return to Sanday in his smack. The wind dropped, the smack rocked becalmed somewhere between Kirkwall and Sanday, the gentlemen grew hungry and thirsty on their long journey, and when they finally reached their destination there was nothing left of their cargo but crumbs and empty bottles. Communion was postponed for another year.[36]

The ministers' excuses for failing to celebrate Communion sound a bit feeble: they claimed that they had none of the necessary equipment – tables, tablecloths, cups, money for bread and wine – and one sometimes suspects them of sheer laziness. It was true, however, that the event placed an enormous economic strain on the parish. The Orphir Session minutes for 1749 record payments made to the workmen who had cut the kirkyard grass, reinforced the lofts for the extra weight of people, mended the seats, put up the tent, and lengthened the Communion table, and to the Officer for carrying out the wine (nine bottles).[37] To defray expenses, collections were taken after each service, and the rest of the money was distributed to the poor. Also, the huge numbers of visitors staying for nearly a week – and, if they came from one of the remoter islands, there was always the risk that they would be storm-stayed for still longer – must have devoured the scant resources of a community often living precariously close to subsistence level. To feed so many extra mouths, and provide straw for their bedding, could leave a parish direly short of supplies needed to keep themselves, and their beasts, through the next winter.

There were even more serious issues. Mr Barry said that he did not administer Communion in the first year of his ministry in Shapinsay because his congregation were 'so ignorant of even the very essentials of Religion'.[38] This does seem a valid point, though it makes one wonder what on earth his predecessors had been doing. There was also an extreme dread of giving the Sacrament to anyone in 'a state of unworthiness' – in which state, presumably, most people were, most of the time.

CHAPTER 10

Sex and Sackcloth

In 1663 ... a meeting of the North Parish was convened to discuss the decay of religion, and the mushroom explosion of alleged thefts, malicious slanders, scandalous beddings, profanation of the Lords Day, playing at football ... sheep stealing, sitting in the reserved seats in church and crimes of assault.

Stuart Picken (1972)

When the kirks were so cold, damp, smelly and uncomfortable, one might well wonder why anyone attended Sunday service, but going to the kirk was not a matter of choice. Attendance was obligatory, and could be enforced by fines or much nastier punishments. In 1709, the Orphir Kirk Session found two youngsters in Hobbister to be 'ill kirk keepers', and sentenced one to pay thirty shillings or stand in the jougs – an unpleasant contraption consisting of an iron collar locked round the victim's neck and attached by a short chain to a post or wall. The other was to be 'whept about the kirk by the hand of the officer the first Court day, and his mother to pay half of the money for not correcting him as she ought when she found him going astray'.[1] Orkney society was dominated by the Kirk and, until the very end of the eighteenth century, that meant the Church of Scotland, established by law, and exercising its authority through the hierarchy of assemblies that spread down from the General Assembly, through the provincial Synods and local Presbyteries to the Kirk Session in every parish in the country. The minutes of the Orkney Sessions often read as a delightfully gossipy commentary on the squabbles and scandals, tragedies and triumphs of parish life, but they leave one in no doubt as to the enormous power these bodies had over ordinary people.

The Kirk Sessions, consisting of the minister and an elected body of elders, met regularly to discuss the business of the parish. One of their number was paid a meagre salary to be Session Clerk and write careful, verbatim minutes of their deliberations. The Sessions' concerns were extraordinarily wide-ranging. There were financial matters to be dealt with: money to be collected from parishioners owing fees for a marriage or a baptism, or fines for 'delinquent' behaviour, or payment for an impounded stray pig; and charity to be distributed to paupers, and a salary determined for the parish schoolmaster. Almost invariably, both kirk and manse were dilapidated, and the Session had to petition the heritors for money for repairs, and to referee arguments between them over the position or size of their pews, or rights to a burial plot. There were quarrels between neighbours to adjudicate, as when someone had tethered their cow too close to someone else's patch of grass; and rumours of ungodly activity to investigate, such as someone seen collecting sheaves from their stackyard on the Sabbath.

Something of the variety of activities the Sessions had to deal with is evident in the Acts that the Kirkwall Session laid down in the period 1618–59:

No. 13: That 'sik as gois in pilgrimage to Demsay, Bairnes of burgh [the Brough of Deerness] … or use foraine superstitions' to be punished …

No. 14: That all persons accompany the burial as occasion offers, under penalties.

No. 18: That women who come before the session with uncovered heads be 'shevin'.

No. 33: Anyone hewing timber in the kirk to be fined 20 shillings. [The cathedral nave was used as a timber yard at this time.]

No. 39: Fornicators to be fed on bread and water for 48 hours.

No. 40: Uncivil and rude people presuming to sit in the stalls [best pews], who will not rise up to give place unto their betters and superiors, to be fined 6 shillings.

No. 43: 'That any horses, calves, ky [cows] or the like, be found within the kirkyard, the owner theirof shall pay 2 shillings for every foote.'

No. 44: Anyone cross-dressing in the form of gysing to be fined, married people £10 and unmarried £5. [Guising, or dressing up in outrageous costumes, was a popular part of New Year and Hallowe'en festivities, and men often dressed as women.]

Despite Act No. 39, we read that, in 1627, 'my Lord Bishop – having considered how that the sin of fornication doth daily increase and abound in this land, but specially in this congregation', ordered that fornicators would stand on the pillar of repentance for several Sundays, as well as being fed on bread and water – the length of time to increase with each offence. On 2 November 1628, George Clouston and William Brown, tailor, 'were sharply rebuked for pissing against the kirk wall'.[2]

By no means all of the Sessions' concerns were narrowly parochial. Regular Edicts reached them from the General Assembly, asking for their congregations' pecuniary and spiritual support in all the wider affairs of the nation and the national Church. The number and variety of good causes that Orkney parishioners, most of them living in an almost cashless rural economy themselves, were expected to subscribe to is astonishing. In 1659, it was a fund for the persecuted Protestants in Bohemia; in 1697, one to build a church in Konigsborg in Prussia for the Scots Protestants there; and in 1719, one for those in Lithuania. Among many other things, Orkney folk contributed to a new church in Strathnaver in 1725, and also for one in New York;[3] to a bridge over the River Dee, in 1732 ('it may prevent many people going to Popish meetings which are much nearer than their own parish churches');[4] and to collections for the poor in a time of famine, in 1741. In 1799, they were subscribing large sums for the defence of the country during the war with France, and in 1815, they were collecting for the widows and orphans of the men who fell in the final battle at Waterloo.

The Assembly demanded that the congregations of Scotland not only contribute money towards building churches and defending the country, but also support the armies of the government with large contributions of prayer. Disasters were regarded as the just judgement of God upon sin, so it stood to reason that defeat could be averted as effectually by effusions of penitence as by action on the battlefield. Orkney congregations thus played their part in routing the Jacobites at Culloden, and foiling the invasion plans of the French Republic. Early in 1746, when the success of the Jacobite army was causing real panic throughout the country:

> Presbytery, considering the abounding sins of the Land, and the heavy judgements of God upon the same, being engaged both in a foreign and Intestine War, did Judge it proper to appoint a Day for solemn prayer, Fasting and Humiliation.

A few months later, the General Assembly was commanding a Day of Thanksgiving for the victory of His Majesty's army at Culloden, but, due to the length of time the edict took to reach the Northern Isles, Orkney congregations celebrated the day a month later than the rest of Scotland. It can have hardly been celebrated very wholeheartedly by those lairds whose sympathies were with the Jacobites, and who had implicated themselves by promising Prince Charles their support. 'Days', however, were not optional, and anyone who tried to avoid them was fined.[5]

Days of Fasting and Humiliation were ordained whenever calamity threatened, national or local. When disease of people or livestock, or the failure of the harvest, reduced the parish to destitution, as happened all too often, the wrath of God could only be appeased by a communal act of repentance. Everyone was expected to leave their work in mid-week and attend the kirk – a very long walk for many people. These Days must have been miserable occasions. One can picture families tramping through rain and wind to sit, wet through and hungry, in a bitterly cold kirk while being verbally lashed – at length – for their sins, and then tramping the long road home again. Probably, the laird and the minister were often the only individuals there not to have also fasted on all the other days of the week, from dire necessity.

Sometimes, however, the people were so desperate that they actually asked their minister to hold a Fast Day, as happened in Papay in 1718, when all the livestock were dying in an epidemic. The story of that Day is one of many episodes in the long-running feud between the Rev. William Blaw and the cantankerous Thomas Traill of Holland. Traill refused to allow his servants to attend the kirk, but had them all 'at work carrying dung and ware to the Land, but in the Just Judgement of God, when the Minister came by the said Holland's house going to the Church, his [corn-drying] kiln went on fire'. Seeing his own precious grain going up in smoke, Traill was so alarmed by the swift retribution of the Almighty that he immediately despatched his servants to the kirk, 'but came not himself'![6]

In February 1794, the entire country was ordered to their knees 'that Almighty God may be pleased to bless our arms both by sea and land against our enemies the French', and the Fast Day was an annual event for the duration of the war.[7] The news of national emergencies in the Session minutes reminds us what a very real fear there was that foreign invasion would bring bloodshed and the horrors of an occupying army even to the shores of remote Orkney parishes. In 1798, Mr Anderson read from the

Birsay pulpit a warning to his flock that only God stood between them and a French conquest of the United Kingdom. With considerable anxiety, the people gathered at a parish meeting to discuss how to protect 'the safety of our religion and liberty which we cannot expect to enjoy should the French Republic prevail and we made a French province'. Very similar fears must have been felt in Britain in the 1940s, at the threat of invasion and occupation by Nazi Germany.

Strife between nations and between neighbours all fell to the attention of the Session, but above all they acted as an Inquisition, controlling morality and conduct in the parish. The Session supervised all activity from the cradle to the grave – and from *before* the cradle, for suspicion of 'ante-nuptial fornication' fills more pages of minutes than all other kirk affairs put together. Failing to attend the kirk without good reason; 'breaching the Sabbath' by performing any work, or any unnecessary activity, on that day; 'slandering' one's neighbour by calling him rude names; drunkenness; and sexual immorality were all regarded as very serious offences. Anyone suspected of ungodly behaviour was ordered to present himself before the Session, which acted as a court of justice: interrogating, summoning witnesses, and handing out punishment.

If the culprit confessed and was suitably penitent, the Session might be content with 'exhorting and rebuking', especially if it was a first offence, but they could also exact fines or demand a public penance in front of the whole congregation. Unpleasant and humiliating as it must have been 'to submit to the discipline of the Session', the alternative was more frightening still. Without absolution, one was outside the pale of the Kirk, forbidden the sacraments, and risking unemployment and social ostracism in this life, and terrible consequences in the next.

While the members of the Session probably genuinely believed that they were simply encouraging Christian morality, it is hard to read these minutes without an unpleasant sense of a police state at work. By relying on an intelligence network of gossipy informers, they must have encouraged the worst aspects of human community, providing opportunities to settle old scores by reporting sins and backslidings to the elders. Often the gossip has an element of comedy, although this was certainly not appreciated by the sententious panel of elders at the time. In 1835, the Deerness Clerk solemnly recorded:

the evil reports spread abroad against Jannet Spence and Jane Horry respecting their behaviour at Mirkady during the fishing ... Margaret

> Russell saw Jannet Spence standing on the top of a barrel and the Master
> of one of the vessels lifted her down in a very unbecoming manner and
> they both went behind the barrel ... Also saw Jane Horry take four glasses
> of whisky at once.

There were, of course, Margaret Russells in every parish to spy on their
neighbours, and run to the Session with tittle-tattle.

When clandestine meetings behind fish-barrels or peatstacks had their
inevitable consequences, an unmarried girl had no hope of concealing
pregnancy from the eyes and ears of the elders, and could not escape the
command to appear before the Session, where she would be minutely
interrogated as to the when, and where, and, most importantly, with
whom, she fell into sin. If the man she named as the father was willing
to accept responsibility, the matter could be briskly dealt with. In 1795,
Helen Allen appeared before the Harray session,

> acknowledging herself with child and named Magnus Flett the father ...
> Compeared Magnus Flett and owned himself the father of said Child. The
> Session, considering that Helen Allen has now been guilty of fornication
> a second time, appoint her to pay a fine of Half a Crown and Magnus
> Flett to pay Six shillings ... which fines being paid down the Parties were
> suitably exhorted and absolved from the Scandal.

Magnus' misdemeanours had cost him a week's wages, but the fact that
similar cases were being dealt with in almost every meeting in every parish
suggests that the whole weighty machinery of Kirk Discipline failed to
alter human nature.

Of course, it was often more complicated than this; if the man was
absent at the fishing, or the Greenland whaling, or even in Hudson's Bay,
the case would have to be postponed until he reappeared. If he was still
in the parish, but tried to evade responsibility, he would be interrogated in
turn, and sometimes one wonders how the Clerk could write his minutes
with a straight face. George Mutch, the Birsay blacksmith, denied being
the father of Jean Sim's child, though he admitted 'he went to bed and
she went along with him. He could not say if his clothes were off or not
– part of them might be off, they twa lay on top of the blankets ...'[8] The
Session found Mutch guilty on the basis of having been 'in loco suspecto'!
At times, however, if the man persisted in his denial, things could take a
much more serious turn. Both parties would be referred to the Presbytery,
and if the woman continued to swear that X was the father, and X to swear

that he was not, the baby who had caused all the trouble might well be a strapping toddler long before the case were concluded.

A man had to feel very sure of his ground to withstand the threats of the terrible 'oath of purgation' which he had to swear before the whole congregation of the kirk if the woman persisted in her testimony.

> Protesting before the great God, and Jesus Christ, and the angels, wishing that all the curses of the law and the woes of the gospel should fall upon him, that he may never thrive in this world, and that his conscience may never give him rest, and torment him as it did Cain and that he may never hope for mercy, but die in desperation and in the great day be cast into hell if the oath he hath sworn be not true from the heart.[9]

No-one could doubt the sincerity of a man prepared to take such a dreadful oath, and this left the woman in a desperate situation, convicted of perjury as well as immorality. 'In consequence of Isobel Linklater's behaviour before the Congregation while Robert Tulloch was repeating the Oath the Session resolve to let her remain under the scandal until they are better satisfied of her sincere repentance', recorded the Harray Clerk in 1805. One wonders what kind of scene Isobel created, but her child was three years old before she was 'absolved from the scandal'.

The Session's determination to establish paternity had a practical as well as a punitive purpose: to ensure that someone took financial responsibility for the child of an unmarried mother, and she was not left without any support. If the father could not be traced, the child was likely to end up as a burden upon the slender resources of parish charity, which probably happened in the case of Barbara Muir in Eday, who 'was found in bed with a stranger seaman about eight or ten days after the ship was stranded, which answers most exactly to the time of the child's birth'.[10] Even when a child was born in wedlock, however, some Sessions would go to the lengths of making minute calculations of the days between the wedding and the birth, in case they could bring a charge of 'antenuptial fornication' against married couples. In the mid-nineteenth century, the North Ronaldsay elders were taking a tough line, 'owing to the increasing prevalence of that sinful conduct in this parish'.[11]

Every kirk was equipped with a 'repentance stool' on which the luckless culprit would sit – or stand – for as many Sabbaths as the Session saw fit. Between July and September 1701, John Brown stood on the Stromness stool for four Sundays between the two heavily pregnant girls for whose condition he was responsible. In October, they were allowed to

FIGURE 10.1

The Session House at St Nicholas Kirk, Holm. Rooms for the meetings of the Kirk Session were a standard part of the design of Presbyterian kirks: usually a single-storey extension, sometimes incorporating the main entrance, and often with a fireplace for the greater comfort of minister and elders while they deliberated the affairs of the parish.

pay fines and be absolved. In November, the Session paid Edward Irving for 'mending the repenting stooles'. In December, John Brown Junior was baptised.[12]

Repeat offenders, such as those accused of 'trelapse' or 'quadrilapse' (falling a third or fourth time into fornication!), or those convicted of the graver crime of adultery, could expect far longer sentences, and had to wear a sackcloth gown while they stood on the stool. In 1693, the Kirkwall Session considered the case of 'Adam Brebner, from Papa Westra, having on sundrie times appeared now in publick in sacco to the number of threttie [thirty] times ...'[13] In 1709, poor Henry Gray begged for absolution after having stood a 'year and day' before the Westray congregation in the wretched parish sack. Given the frequency with which wrongdoers were condemned to stand 'in sacco', it is surprising to read that the churches were inadequately supplied with these garments, and the penitent might have to wait his, or her, turn in a remorseful queue. In 1743, the Sanday

Session heard that Elspeth Corse was willing to appear in sackcloth, but her penance had to be deferred until the article was sent back from North Ronaldsay. Even at the cathedral, well stocked though it was with 'sacco', supply could not keep up with demand.[14]

When a woman had no hope of marrying her lover, she could be in a wretched position indeed, and it is not surprising that some were driven to desperate measures, but there was no crime that the Session regarded with such gravity as infanticide. When Christiana Stove in Deerness was suspected of having had a child secretly, and killed it, she was cornered in her home by no fewer than three elders and two midwives who

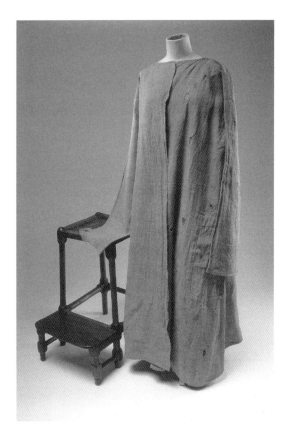

FIGURE 10.2
A late seventeenth-century 'parish sack' from West Calder Parish Church is a rare survival. The 'repentance stool' is from Old Greyfriars Church in Edinburgh, probably early eighteenth century.
(NMS)

examined the girl, and pronounced her lactating. Christiana claimed she could not account for this circumstance 'but in the miraculous way', but the Deerness elders were not disposed to believe in miracles of this nature, and sentenced her to be taken to Kirkwall and handed over to the magistrates for trial, to sternly discourage 'such monstrous Enormitis [sic] on human life ...' [15] Christiana managed to escape from prison, but her story ends with the Session interrogating her family, and one can be sure that they did not let the matter drop easily. Child murder was a frequent crime in Scotland, and 'the criminal records contain very many executions of poor creatures – several being hanged on occasions in batches – and the cause of their crime was too frequently the dread of facing the disgrace and terrible ordeals of the Church'.[16]

Even those suspected of far less serious offences sometimes found the inquisition of the Session so intolerable that they attempted to escape it by leaving Orkney altogether. In 1705, John Corner and his servant, Isabella Thomson, rumoured to have been seen kissing behind a peatstack, fled from Deerness to Caithness. We do not hear what happened to the fugitives, but it must have been impossible to remain in hiding when the network of Presbytery and Synod could alert ministers far and wide to 'enquire for them and return them to satisfy the discipline of the church'.[17] However long a sinner managed to evade discovery, and however respectable a life he led after his fall into sin, his case never lapsed and, sooner or later, his past would catch up with him. Robert Erskine, a notary public, moved from Edinburgh to Kirkwall to escape the consequences of his indiscretions, and established himself as a respected professional with a successful business. Four years after his flight from the Edinburgh Session, it tracked him down, and he was forced to submit to his penance.[18] In the last resort, the Kirk held the ultimate weapon: excommunication, or being thrown out of the Kirk altogether. No fines, or public humiliation, or imprisonment, or jougs, could compare with the awful threat of being damned for eternity. There would have been very few people in eighteenth-century Orkney who were sufficiently sceptical, or rash, to take such a dreadful risk.

The money that was collected in fines for 'delinquency' went into the parish Poor Box. Other sources of income included the sale of unmarked sheep found in the parish; fees for marriages and baptisms, and for hiring out the parish mortcloth which was used to cover the bodies of those too poor to pay for a coffin. In 1799, the Birsay Session 'collected 1sh 11½d this day the marriage money of Peter Spence and Andrew Anderson ...'

19. The North Kirk (centre) and former St Peter's, Stromness

20, 21. Stained glass windows in St Mary's Episcopal Church, Stromness

22. St Laurence, the old Rendall parish kirk

23. The kirkyard at St Nicholas, Holm, on Scapa Flow

24. The chapel in the grounds of Westness House, Rousay

25. The kirkyard at Warbeth, Stromness, and the Hoy hills

26. The Old Hackland Kirk, Rendall

27. The parish kirk in Eday and the ruined Secession kirk in the background

28. The Free kirk, Sourin, Rousay

29. St Margaret tramples the dragon of evil: detail of window in Graemeshall chapel, Holm

30. St Peter's, Skaill, Sandwick

31. The Italian Chapel, Lamb Holm

32. Memorial to the Longhope lifeboat disaster, Osmundwall, Walls

33. Celebrations in Papa Stronsay, 2003. Monks perform a Maori 'haka'

34. The Moncur Memorial Church, Stronsay

35. St John's, North Walls

36. The old parish church at the Bu', North Hoy

The Sessions showed their more compassionate face by adjusting their charges according to their parishioners' means. 'William Isbister paid 6d for a mortcloth to his wife and Agnes paid 9d for the mortcloth to her daughter, which the Session accepted as they are both very poor'.[19] As the small sums accumulated in the Box, the Session distributed this money in charity to widows, unmarried mothers, fathers of twins, orphans and 'lunatics': the only welfare benefit that the poor could hope for. We read that money was given

> to a poor child to buy him clothes ... to three poor English prisoners ... to John Ewenson by reason he had his corne burnt ... to buy a bible to a fatherless boy that the Session had put to school ... to William Byar, a blind boy, 1 sh ... in charity to Marjory Gaudie 1sh 6d ...

Marjory was on the Poor Roll for six years and, in that time, by far the largest disbursement that the parish made on her behalf was the three shillings and four pence paid for her burial in 1802. The annual hand-outs would not have stocked her larder for long. Her last years saw poor harvests when the price of grain was high, and one and sixpence might have bought her just half a stone of oatmeal, or perhaps three hens for sixpence each, so she could have eggs to sell for a penny halfpenny or twopence a dozen.[20]

With their very slender resources, the Sessions did what they could for the destitute of the parish. In 1801, when famine threatened, the Birsay Session bought a boatload of grain from Kirkwall. When calamity overwhelmed a family, as happened often when a barn burned down, or sickness or shipwreck took away the breadwinner, a special collection was taken up for the victims. In 1798, a Birsay fishing boat was wrecked in a tragic accident with the loss of four men and '11 fatherless children was left, seven of which belonged to William Johnston who are orphans and no substance left to bestow on them and their poor mother Janet Folster unable to provide for them'.[21] A collection of £2 was raised and given to Janet, but one can only wonder how the widow provided for her seven children when that was spent. The following year, she received five shillings from the Session, a generous amount on account of her large family, but school fees alone could cost her two shillings to four shillings a year for each child, more if she wanted them to learn arithmetic as well as reading and writing.[22]

While sexual immorality absorbed by far the greatest amount of Session time in any parish, other sins were also dealt with severely. Slander was a far more serious offence than we think of it today: to damage or take away someone's good name with evil words was to cause real harm to that person, and it is interesting that, when quarrels between neighbours are reported to the Session, it is not the rights and wrongs of who *did* what that they are interested in, but what was *said*. In 1697, Janet Brown was before the Stromness Session for calling Besse Sutherland 'a blabing Bitch'. Perhaps she was, but Janet was ordered to do repentance before the pulpit on the next sermon day.[23] For the poor, and for poor women especially, their good name was their only asset, their only passport to employment, or a tenancy, or marriage, and their only redress for the theft of their name was in the Church courts. The slandered person had to be protected from damage, but so had the soul of the slanderer. Ursula Gunn in Orphir was fined for swearing at her neighbour for stealing her corn, and 'exhorted to repent and amend and behave herself otherwise she would ruin both her soul and body'.

Slandering one's neighbour's name remained a far more serious offence than damaging his crops, his livestock, or even his person, well into the nineteenth century. In 1841, the Deerness Session investigated several quarrels of the kind that must have erupted frequently when there were no dykes or fences between the little farms, and animals were tethered, or herded, in the summer months to keep them out of the crops. The Session was not concerned with the rights or wrongs behind the quarrels: the issue was not if it was true that Andrew Skea's sheep were in Mary Leask's corn, or if her dog had torn one of his lambs, or if he had beaten her dog ... but that Mary had 'scandalised' Andrew by calling him 'a common thief'. Andrew's provocations were ignored. Mary was found guilty and punished. The Sessions' judgements seem harsh, but once it had absolved a sinner, the case was considered totally closed. Anyone who tried to continue the quarrel, or reproached a neighbour for sins for which they had done penance, was liable to be severely rebuked and fined themselves.

The breaking of the Fourth Commandment by performing any work on the Sabbath was a punishable offence, and in a community where so much work was necessarily out of doors, and in full view of one's neighbours, it was quite impossible to break it undetected. In November 1784, the Birsay Session heard how several of their parishioners had been harvesting on the Sabbath 'until late of the night which was a grief to their neighbours and such an offence against the Law of God that it is wondered at in other Parishes ...' Even talking of workaday matters was forbidden: John

Redland was charged for 'speaking about the price of a horse'. Far more tragic is the story of the widow, Anna Hestwall, in Stromness, who was found 'at the ebb' on a Sunday in 1702. Anna confessed that she had been looking for some seaweed for her children to eat 'not having anything to give them'. The minister ordered her to appear before the pulpit the next sermon day and acknowledge her fault.[24] There is no record of the Session concerning themselves with the desperate situation of the widow or her famished children, and this short entry speaks volumes about the hideous gulf between the practice of the eighteenth-century Kirk and the teaching of the gospels.

Not only was any form of work a 'Sabbath Breach', but so too was playing games, travelling anywhere other than the road to the kirk, or just 'vageing', going for a walk. To prevent anyone from loitering with intent to enjoy themselves, the elders patrolled Kirkwall on a Sunday afternoon, with orders to 'apprehend and imprison all idle vageing persons' who could not produce a good enough excuse for being found out of doors.[25] Given the long hours that most people worked every other day of the week, a summer Sunday must have been particularly miserable. In Sabbath School, the children were taught to repeat endlessly the first article of the Shorter Catechism: 'Man's chief end is to glorify God and enjoy Him forever', but the Kirk ensured that there were scant opportunities for enjoyment.

What is interesting is the fact that, despite the inevitable retribution, the rebuking and the fines, some did kick against the traces and reap their corn, or dry it in the kiln, or take their ponies to the peatbank on a Sunday, suggesting that the Session could not always intimidate people into toeing the line. It seems to have been quite impossible to stop boys from playing football, and absolutely no amount of threats, admonitions, fines or punishments could stop men from hunting whales on the seventh day. In Compton Mackenzie's novel, *Whisky Galore*, the men of the island of Toddy gaze miserably at the sinking SS *Cabinet Minister* with her cargo of whisky for twenty-four anguished hours, from the moment the clock strikes twelve on Saturday night. This was apparently not the case when a pod of pilot whales was sighted off the Orkney coast on the Sabbath. The prospect of laying in a store of meat and lighting oil for the dark and hungry winter overrode all other considerations – even for a Kirk Officer, like Stromness man, John Loutitt, who was 'charged with Sabbath profanation in going out with several others on the Lord's day in a boat after whales', in 1814.[26] His case was only one of many.

It was, of course, much easier to defy the Session when there were numbers of sinners involved. In 1842, the Deerness elders were busy trying to punish a mass Sabbath-breaking, after a shipwreck on the island of Copinsay brought most of the able-bodied of the parish running to the shore, or to their boats, to see if anything could be salvaged – just as it would today. Eventually, the Session decided to let off with a rebuke those who had merely *looked* at the wreck, but to demand a public penance from anyone who had actually laid hand on anything – thus breaking the Eighth Commandment as well as the Fourth! If only one or two men had been carpeted by the Session, they would probably have submitted, but this time there were over twenty of them, well outnumbering the elders, and 'they positively declared that they would not submit to such discipline'.

Other sins that the Sessions had to deal with concerned 'superstitious practices', such as visiting holy wells or shrines in the hope of cures, or simply resorting to magic. In one intriguing story, Thomas Loutit in Orphir was interrogated because 'as they were laying his wife in her coffin he took corn and put some in her mouth as well as laid some in the chest'. Loutit explained that he had the best of motives: it was to stop his wife coming back and bothering her stepdaughter who she had quarrelled with during her life, but the Session were unimpressed with the explanation, and demanded a public profession of repentance in the kirk. Loutit was defiant. (The parish of Orphir seems to have had plenty of rebellious souls who refused to be in the least penitent for their misdeeds.) However, the Session had the trump card: those who 'proved contumacious' were handed over to the Civil Magistrate. Loutit was made to pay two pounds Scots into the Box.[27]

Fines were an important source of income for cash-strapped kirks, and the sums were flexible, adjusted according to the wealth of the sinner. 'Persones of more abilitie are to pay conformitie to ther qualitie'. The more acute the Sessions' financial problems, the more ready they were to give absolution in return for ready money. In 1692, the St Magnus Session considered the great expense of maintaining the fabric of the cathedral and the relatively small sums in the Box, and imposed a hefty fine on a 'delinquent', Arthur Rendall, instead of a public penance. It was not politic, however, to inflate the scale of fines too steeply. According to Hossack, one parish increased its tariff and, as a result, the number of fineable sins dropped, with such drastic effect on its finances that it had to quickly revert to its previous rates. There was very little cash circulating in the Orkney economy, but, when money was not available, the Session was prepared to take payment in kind, such as the 'brown-rigged, white-horned three-year-old cow' paid by Elspeth Linkletter. The cow bought Elspeth's escape from imprisonment in the dreaded Marwick's Hole, a nasty cell within the cathedral where impoverished sinners who had no means of paying their fines were incarcerated, but she still had to make a public appearance on the repentance stool for the next six months.[28]

St Magnus not only levied higher fines than the country kirks, but it was also far more terrifyingly well-equipped to deal with backsliders among its parishioners. 'Outside of the Cathedral were the Cuckstool, the Jougs, and the Stocks, while inside were the White Stone of Repentance, the Stool of Repentance, Sackcloth, the Prison and the Minister – the last worst of all.'[29] The Cuckstool was similar to stocks, in which the offender sat with his legs locked in holes in a wooden board. The jougs (or gogs) was the common punishment for slanderers, and sinners imprisoned in either of these unpleasant devices wore a placard round their necks stating the nature of their 'crime'.

What is most obvious and unattractive about the way that the Sessions operated is that it was far from impartial. The offenders were almost invariably of low social class: farm-labourers or apprentices or domestic servants. Many of them were young girls. The men sitting in judgement were the older and socially dominant members of the community. Elders were drawn from the merchant class in the towns, and from the lairds and substantial farmers in the rural parishes. For them, the Session must have had the convenient function of acting as a means of social control over their inferiors. Fornication seems to have been just as common a vice among people 'of quality' as among everyone else, but, while labourers and servant-maids had to do public penance in sackcloth for their sins, 'antenuptial delinquents of quality' were often allowed to make 'private satisfaction' to the Session, paying large fines into the Box that the poor could not afford.[30] Poor people had to make a public apology for calling their neighbour a 'knave' or a 'bitch', despite considerable provocation, but Thomas Traill of Holland could call the minister 'a witless villain', and many worse things, with impunity. Occasionally, a Session did try to bring a laird to book, but they had little authority if he simply refused to cooperate. A free-thinking laird like Traill might refuse to pay his fines, and defy the possibility of eternal retribution, but, for the lower classes, such independence of mind could cost them their job or home.

Inevitably, the Kirk was seen as another arm of the lairds and the magistrates, enforcing their authority with its own power of punishment. In 1742, for example, Peter Fea was found guilty of inciting the kelp riots in Stronsay, and sentenced to pay a fine, and to stand at five different kirk doors for an hour before the service, bareheaded (in midwinter), and with an extract of the verdict on his chest. In 1760, a time of famine in Orkney, one of the Stronsay lairds ordered his factor to put a notice on the kirk door forbidding people from taking peats from Rothiesholm Head.[31] The Established Kirk had no scruples about serving the interests of the Establishment, rather than those of the poor.

However, once The Kirk had ceased to be The One and Only Kirk, its authority inevitably diminished. With mass defection, first to the Secession Church at the end of the eighteenth century, and then, in a tidal wave of dissent, to the Free Church in 1843, the Church of Scotland lost its monopoly on salvation. All the breakaway Churches adopted the same structure of Kirk Sessions and Discipline, and had their own stools of repentance, but errant members were able to play off one against the other. If they were too harshly disciplined in one Church, they could transfer allegiance to its rival, without losing their place in the Christian flock. While the wealthy and powerful of Orkney society tended to remain 'Establishment men', their employees and tenants often defected to Churches which, both in their evangelical message and their social structure, were more egalitarian.

CHAPTER 11

Dissent and Disruption

Any country in the hands of an undivided church must be subject to priestly tyranny ... This was the condition of Kirkwall down to the last decade of the eighteenth century, when, with dissent, came the dawn of freedom.

Buckham Hugh Hossack (1900)

W hen the Orkney ministers wrote their entries for the *Statistical Account* in the 1790s, they described with some satisfaction the progress that their flocks had made, both in moral improvement and material prosperity, under their benevolent supervision. They had some reason for feeling smug: their authority was still unchallenged, while in many other parts of Scotland the parishes had been torn apart in the course of the eighteenth century. It was patronage, and the people's opposition to it, that was the chief cause of schisms that fractured the Church of Scotland – and, eventually, the social fabric of every parish in the country. The 'Original Secession' had been the first to break away, in 1733, followed by the 'Relief Church' (relief, that is, from the oppression of patronage) in 1761. We have seen how fiercely some Orkney congregations objected to their 'patron', the Earl of Morton, appointing the Rev. James Tyrie to their kirks against their wishes. However, there is no suggestion that they thought of leaving the Established Church in protest. Schism and Secession appeared to have passed Orkney by altogether. As the South Ronaldsay minister claimed, with some complacency, in the 1790s: 'There are no dissenters or sectaries of any kind in these parishes. No mischief is dreaded here, either from the flame of fanaticism or the fire of sedition.'[1]

The islands were, apparently, equally untouched by political dissent. News of the terrible events of the French Revolution produced shudders of horror, but there was no anxiety that inflammatory ideas might disturb the immutable hierarchy of Orkney society. Lairds and ministers entertained one another and their much interrelated families, and supported one another in maintaining their dual authority over the parish. There is not a breath of awareness in their writing that their flock was becoming so restless that two-thirds of it would soon defect from the Kirk altogether.

When we look at the eighteenth-century Church of Scotland, it is less surprising that so many people abandoned the Kirk than that so many remained in it. The shortage of ministers that left pulpits empty on a Sabbath; the huge social gulf that yawned between ministers and people; the too-cosy alliance between manse and mansion-house; the dull, moralistic sermons endured in damp and draughty buildings; the almost total lack of connection between the teaching of the New Testament and the practice of the Kirk – it was hardly an appealing package. One might have expected these shortcomings to put people off religion altogether, but, on the contrary, as soon as an evangelical preacher appeared on the scene, the response was overwhelming.

In 1785 and 1786, an American Quaker, John Pemberton, toured Orkney, and enormous crowds gathered wherever he preached, 1,500 people squeezing into the cathedral to hear him.[2] Pemberton was presumably an eloquent preacher, but some of his companions mystified the Orcadians with their silent services.

> The parishioners assembled at the Kirk of Firth to hear the Quakers; who, not beginning their worship or exhortation immediately, were entreated by an old man to make haste, if they were to say anything, as the day was short, and several of the people had far to return home.[3]

A decade later, people flocked to hear James Haldane and John Aikman when they arrived on the eighteenth-century equivalent of a Billy Graham crusade. The unsuspecting Orkney ministers hospitably opened their manses and their kirks to the visitors, and were knocked sideways by a tidal wave of religious 'Enthusiasm'. It was exactly the sort of emotional response that the 'Moderates' had tried so hard to keep the lid on.

'The islands of Orkney ... have been for a period beyond the memory of any man living as much in need of the true Gospel of Jesus Christ ... as any of the islands of the Pacific Ocean', reported Haldane. He was appalled at what he found in Orkney: the lack of schools, and the lack of even the most basic idea of what Christianity was about in some parishes. No sermon had been preached in Evie for eight or nine years; church service in Rousay consisted of the proprietor, when he was at home, reading a sermon.

> Owing to the want of churches, or rather to the churches being in want of repair, as well as to the occasional trouble and difficulty of crossing the Friths [*sic*] … to say nothing of the want of zeal, many of the people see their pastor but seldom in the course of the year.[4]

The evangelical preaching of Haldane and Aikman must have been electrifying to people whose only church experience had been of a dour morality and the dreaded Discipline. For the first time, they heard a gospel that had much to say about, and for, the poor, and a 'good news' message about salvation and love. On their first day, Aikman preached to 800 people in the Palace Close, on the next Sunday to crowds of 1,200 and 3,000 people. Haldane went to Shapinsay 'and preached twice by the sea-side to congregations comprising the greatest part of the island'. Even at the Lammas Fair, as many as 6,000 people at a time left their horse-dealing and drinking-booths to gather to hear the preachers.[5] Haldane and Aikman's stamina was impressive: they preached fifty-five times in the course of ten days!

Although the ministers of the *Statistical Account* had not noticed it, society was shifting under their feet, and people were ready for a message that challenged the old structures. The Bible-based preaching of Haldane and his successors had an enormous influence in creating not only a hunger for a more emotionally fulfilling religion, but also a new sense of individual responsibility and individual worth. People no longer saw the earthly social hierarchy as something sanctioned by the Almighty, or the ministers and the 'gentry' as having a monopoly on religious truth. This new self-confidence was also driven by economic change. Even the poorest labourers and apprentices were much better off by the end of the eighteenth century than they had been fifty years before. There was more diversity of employment, and emigration had created a labour shortage which pushed up wages. Servants were no longer in terror of being jobless if they did not have a character reference from their minister. Now they could find work easily, so they were altogether more confident, and independent, than they had been. Tradesmen were growing more prosperous, and more articulate.

This was the social context in the early 1790s, when a tailor called John Rusland went to Newcastle on his holiday, and came back fired with the evangelical preaching he had heard in the Secession church there.

With a small group of other tradesmen, he started a prayer meeting in Kirkwall, but their number soon outgrew a private house, and they began to collect funds to build a Secession kirk of their own. Then they had to choose which of the breakaway Kirks to apply to for a minister, and they were advised that they could obtain one from the 'Antiburgher' Church for half the price of one from the Relief Church. The Antiburghers were the more radical wing of the Original Secession, which had split in two over the perennially vexed question of the powers of the State versus the Church. It was, significantly, congregations of this persuasion that came to proliferate across Orkney, from the last years of the eighteenth century onwards.

Much of the impetus, and money, for the new church had come from the Freemasons, and the foundation stone was laid with solemn Masonic rituals after a procession from St Paul's Lodge. Unfortunately, when the new minister arrived, it was discovered that Antiburghers did not approve of Masons, and the first Kirk Session dealt punishments to those who had taken the Masonic oath![6]

Despite this setback, the new Secession Church grew rapidly. The church that was built in Kirkwall in 1796 to seat 800 folk was soon so overcrowded that it had to be enlarged in 1800. A second congregation formed in Stronsay in 1799, and others rapidly followed. Until they got their own Secession kirks, people walked from the outlying parishes, over the appallingly rough and muddy tracks, and through the often appalling Orkney weather, to reach the service in Kirkwall. (Until the Orkney Roads Act of 1857, roads were almost non-existent even on Mainland.) Inner Isles folk came by sea, despite a disaster in 1822 when the overloaded boat from Shapinsay swamped, and twelve people were drowned.

> By three o'clock on a Sabbath morning families were astir and wending their way over the Rousay hills to the boats by which they crossed to Evie. On reaching mainland they travelled on foot, fully 16 miles, over very rough hill-country to Kirkwall.[7]

Church of Scotland congregations had waited for decades for the ponderous machinery of Presbytery to extract funds from unwilling heritors to build new kirks. The Seceders, with no-one but themselves to provide funds and labour, immediately set about building with their own hands. By 1801, they had their own 'Kirk Abune the Hill' on top of the steep brae that dips down to Birsay. Much of the work was done by the women, who worked at night, when their day's labour was over, carrying stones to the site from the quarry.

The story is eloquent of how earnest was the desire to hear Biblical preaching, but the tragic side-effect of Secession was the souring of relationships within the parish. Sunday mornings in Birsay saw one procession of folk walking down the brae to the parish kirk in Birsay village, and another walking up the brae to the Kirk Abune the Hill, passing each other silently on opposite sides of the road. The image is one that characterises too much of Scottish parish life in the nineteenth century, and even into the twentieth. Once the authority of the One National Kirk had been undermined, there was nothing to hold together the endless variety of human opinion, and religious schism became a way of life in Orkney, as it had been in the rest of Scotland since the first Secession in 1733. Around 1805, the first Independent, or Congregationalist, meeting broke away from the Orkney Secession; in 1820, a group of Protestors

FIGURE 11.1

The Kirk Abune the Hill, Birsay, the last kirk of the 'Original Secession' to survive in Orkney. Today its position appears quite isolated, but Swannayside was well populated until the mid-nineteenth century, when a number of the crofters were evicted in the course of agricultural 'Improvements'. Resentment against landlords fuelled opposition to the Established Church, which generally supported 'the gentry'.

took the huff over the appointment of a new minister. Over the next decades, Orkney's landscape became peppered with the kirks and chapels and meeting-houses of all those who had agreed it was time to walk *out* of the Church of Scotland, but could by no means agree as to what they would walk *into*. It was a busy time of construction, that was desperately socially destructive.

Something of the divisive effect of Secession can be seen by following the progress of one of James Haldane's recruits, the North Ronaldsay cabinetmaker, William Tulloch, who was dispatched into the mission field of Westray. Tulloch was at first welcomed as a preacher, but the decision made by him and some of his followers to break from the Kirk and form an independent congregation caused considerable rancour in the community. All doors were closed against them, so they met in the open air, and then in the dark and damp of the cavernous kitchen of Noltland Castle. After much difficulty, they eventually obtained a building site, and Westray's first Dissenting church was built at Rackwick in 1804.[8]

After only five years, however, the congregation was thrown into disarray by the discovery that Haldane had become a Baptist. To Tulloch's dismay, many of his followers chose to leave him, and the church they had laboured so hard to build, to join the new movement. Separation was averted only at the last minute. When everyone gathered in the church for a final service together, their voices were drowned by the ferocity of an exceptionally violent storm, 'such as had never before been experienced in the island'. When it abated, Tulloch's mind had changed. He and most of the congregation became Baptist together, ten of them being baptised in Burness loch in the summer of 1810.[9]

Differences of opinion were not often resolved so amicably. Under the next Westray pastor, Henry Harcus, the Baptist movement flourished and spread to other islands. In 1867, however, missionaries from the Plymouth Brethren persuaded most of the Westray congregation to leave their new church[10] and found a meeting-house a short distance away. Harcus was so heartbroken that he emigrated to Canada, and another legacy of bitterness was wedged into the social fabric of the island.

Although the divisions were unfortunate, the overwhelming impression is one of a genuine searching after religious truth; there is a much more earnest 'buzz' about the nineteenth century than about the eighteenth. In February 1843, eleven Westray converts to the Baptist Church wanted to be baptised, but the total immersion practised by the Baptists was impossible, as all the lochs in the isle were frozen solid at the time. Rather than delay, they volunteered to cut their own baptistery out of the ice: a memorable image of serious commitment.[11]

The number of redundant churches in every Orkney parish today (some smartly converted into houses, some decaying as barns) is the visible legacy of the kirk-building boom at the time when the population was at its height, but the largest congregations have left no trace on the landscape at all. The diaries of visiting ministers reveal an almost desperate urgency to hear the gospel message that is quite hard to imagine in the twenty-first century. A popular preacher would draw people from all denominations to attend huge open-air gatherings, with the same enthusiasm that draws people today to travel vast distances and camp in wet fields in order to hear their favourite bands. An Orkney minister described seeing:

> upwards of 1,000 people assembled in a country barnyard by 9 o'clock on a Sabbath morning and some of them from a distance of 8 and 10 miles, to hear the gospel ... the whole country apparently in motion as far as the eye could sweep the horizon.[12]

Often, these itinerant preachers came from southern Scotland and were astonished, equally, at the dreadful roads, frightening sea journeys and the lengths that Orkney folk would go to in order to hear them. Despite the long hours that most people worked, crowds of 300, or even 500, would turn out on weekday evenings to hear a favourite preacher.[13] Families from Rousay and Wyre would travel by boat to Rendall and walk over the hills to the Congregational chapel in Harray, and return the same evening, a day's walk of nearly forty miles.[14]

> With indomitable perseverance, in the midst of the inclement weather which prevails so much in the islands, and in perils by sea and land [the minister] was accustomed to travel from 50 to 70 miles a week to preach ... in the winter season, when no barn could be found sufficiently large to hold the numbers who came to hear, he would address them in the rain and snow, so anxious was he to preach and so willing were they to listen to the words of life.[15]

The words paint a moving image of these remarkable preachers who toured the islands, often wet through and frozen, but unflagging. Some of their journeys must have been truly frightful. Poor Mr Masson tried to get to the island of Stroma in 1839, but his boat was carried past by the fierce tides, and he had to spend *twelve hours* tossing in the Pentland Firth. When he finally reached the island, 'a boat came out full of rough men armed, who tried by threats to deter them from landing, supposing Mr Masson to be a revenue officer'.[16] I hope that the unfortunate minister was able to convince the illicit distillers of Stroma that his visit concerned an altogether different Spirit. A rapprochement between ministers and the folk of Stroma must have been reached, if reports of contraband hidden in the Baptist kirk are true.[17]

With their congregations melting away into the Secession kirks, the Church of Scotland ministers must have felt despair, but far worse was to come. In Edinburgh and Glasgow, argument was raging over the issue of Parliament's right to interfere in Church affairs. Finally, at the General Assembly in May 1843, this came to a head with the massive walk-out led by Dr Thomas Chalmers, which came to be known as the 'Disruption'. In disgust at legislation which, effectively, made the Kirk subservient to the State, 474 ministers, 192 probationers, all the missionaries in foreign fields, and thousands of ordinary people left the Church of Scotland to found the Church of Scotland Free. For their stand on principle, the ministers gave up a respected position, a large house, a substantial salary and all security for themselves and their families – a considerable social and financial sacrifice that won them widespread admiration. (Perhaps the most courageous thing that they did was to go home and tell their wives that they could start packing!) Overall, the Kirk lost about one-third of its members, but in parts of the West Highlands almost the entire community abandoned the parish churches.

The conflicts that led up to the Disruption were followed anxiously all over Scotland. In the parishes of Birsay and Harray in Orkney, a young man called John Garson who had studied in Edinburgh under Thomas Chalmers, came home, full of evangelical zeal, to be an assistant to the elderly Rev. Thomas Blyth. News of the Disruption reached Orkney within a few days of the event, and Garson immediately 'came out' to join the Free Kirk. As a result, Presbytery excluded him from preaching and appointed the Sandwick minister, Charles Clouston, to officiate in Harray on the following Sunday. While Clouston preached inside the kirk, Garson preached outside to a much larger and very excited crowd.

St Michael's Kirk was just a few years old at that time, but the kirkyard was ancient, tumbling over a prominent mound where a broch had once dominated the fertile lands that sweep to the Harray loch. That day, the roads to the kirk had buzzed with the news from Edinburgh; the women's summer dresses made bright splashes of colour against the gravestones; everyone's eyes were fixed on the young minister who was speaking with

FIGURE 11.2
The kirk of St Michael's in Harray where John Garson, excluded from the kirk, preached the first sermon after the Disruption in the open air in May 1843.

such passion from the top of the mound. The door of the kirk opened. Clouston emerged, torn between desire to appear calm and dignified, and the urgency to get to his horse as quickly as possible. It was saddled and waiting; so was Garson's. Did the ministers exchange looks before they leapt on their horses and raced each other to get to the Birsay kirk? They were followed by cheering from their congregations, who were laying bets on who would win.

> The distance between Harray and Birsay is eight miles and the great question was – Who would reach Birsay first? Mr Clouston had got a start and was known to be a fast rider but [Mr Garson] mounting his steed he set off at full gallop … and passing by on the other side of the road his priestly brother he soon outdistanced him. The Free Kirk preacher arrived on the scene somewhat heated and flustered and was eagerly welcomed by some of his 'shrewd lieutenants' who were waiting for him and had the people assembled in the old church at the Old Palace ready for action when the word of command should be given. In the meantime the other preacher had arrived and said to some of the men standing by 'As soon as I get the horse put up I'll arrange for the service in the church'. But no sooner had the minister and the horse turned the corner than Magnus Flett whispered 'Weel, he can 'range awa' as he pleases!' On hearing this, one of the elders, Peter Johnston, marched right into the church and faced the congregation with mingled feelings of solemnity and responsibility. There was a hush and a silence that was only broken by the homely words uttered by Mr Johnston – 'Ye're a' bidden tae come oot!' At once the

people rose up en masse and made for the outside as fast as possible and many of them never again entered within those walls. One old woman, a few years ago, when asked by someone if she had been to the Auld Kirk, replied in these laconic words – 'I hae never been in fae I came oot.' Outside in the open air and under the blue canopy of heaven, Mr Garson conducted the first Free Church service in Birsay![18]

Garson became the first Free Kirk minister in Birsay, and stayed there for thirty-eight years, apparently much loved. At one stage, he wanted to leave to become a missionary overseas, but he was dissuaded by Magnus Spence of Hundland's caustic reminder: 'He needna gang tae the heathen, he'll find heathen enough hame.'[19] He stayed hame.

FIGURE 11.3

A plaque inside the Twatt kirk commemorates John Garson, the first Free Kirk minister of Birsay and Harray. His congregation had soon outgrown their first building, hastily erected in 1843, and built this large galleried kirk in 1874.

All over Orkney, the news spread like wildfire, and congregations 'came out' with the rush of a spring tide. Six out of twenty-one ministers joined the Free Kirk immediately in 1843, most of them taking the majority of their flock with them, and many of the other kirks were half-emptied. In the Highlands and Islands, the heritors were almost universally hostile to the Free Kirk, and there are many stories of the suffering of congregations which had to meet, in all weathers, in the open air, because they were not allowed a site to build a kirk. In Orkney, although the gentry tended to remain 'Establishment', there does not seem to have been the same overt hostility.

There was even one laird who gave a church to the Free Kirk: Thomas Traill of Holland. His father, George Traill, had sympathised with the Westray Seceders and allowed them to worship in the barn at his farm of Brough, until they could build their own church. When Thomas built a new kirk for Papay at his own expense, in 1842, Presbytery were absolutely delighted. However, when the minister arrived to take a service, he found that the building was firmly locked, and no amount of threats or persuasion would release the key. Traill had himself 'joined the new sect of Dissenters commonly denominated the Free Church'[20] and taken the whole island with him. He gave St Ann's to the Free Church at its first General Assembly, on 23 May 1843.[21]

That first summer, there was an absolute frenzy of kirk-building in Orkney. Both men and women laboured, in every hour of their spare time, quarrying and carting stones so as to speed the masons on their way and have a kirk roofed before winter. Birsay, Orphir, Firth and Stenness had new kirks in 1843; Evie, Rendall and Stromness by 1844. As soon as the kirks were built, work started on the manses, and then the schools. The speed with which an entire alternative parish structure was erected is astounding. The Old Kirk had endured derelict buildings for centuries, with an almost inconceivable inability to raise the cash, or the will, to mend a window or a broken slate, but in almost every parish the New Kirk folk were worshipping in their own kirks within months of the Disruption.

Without any doubt, part of the attraction of the Dissenting Kirks was simply their practical ability to provide new churches where they were needed. It is not difficult to imagine that attending a waterproof building, within reasonable walking distance, was a more attractive option than trudging for miles to shiver in a dilapidated one, quite apart from the theological issues involved. Gradually, even many of the well-to-do in Kirkwall defected from the miserable discomfort of St Magnus to the Secession kirk, where they could at least be more certain of obtaining a seat, and less certain of catching pneumonia. The Dissenters were also able to provide regular preachers in the country parishes where the Establishment minister had divided his time between two or more churches, leaving his parishioners for half the year 'exposed to the arts and snares of sectaries',[22] as the Old Kirk recognised, woefully late in the day.

Where the Establishment minister was unpopular, Dissent gave the people the opportunity to vote with their feet, but it made no headway where he was loved. There was no Free kirk in South Ronaldsay until twenty years after the death of the Rev. John Gerard, an eccentric, down-to-earth Aberdonian, with a direct line to the Almighty that no-one could compete with. Who would have wanted to leave a minister who could tell God in harvest time to:

> send us a guid soughing wind that will ripen the strae an' winna hairm the heid. But if Ye send us a rantin' reivin' roarin' wind as Ye sent us last time, Ye'll play the verra mischeif wi' the aits an' clean spoil a'.[23]

Gerard was sympathetic to the Evangelicals, and no-one could ever accuse him of the arid preaching of the 'Moderates', but he was blunt about his reluctance to leave the security of his stipend and his manse. When the Disruption was discussed at Presbytery, Gerard told his colleagues:

> Weel boys, if I was a young man, I wad come out too; but whaur I am, I am sure o' me meal, I am sure o' me milk, I get me peats pitten hame tae me door, and if I was to leave nobody wad gae me half-a-croon a year for my preaching, so I think I may as weel stop whaur I am.[24]

FIGURE 11.4

The austere interior of North Ronaldsay's New Kirk. Almost the whole island followed their minister, Adam White, into the Free Kirk in 1843, but because of the opposition of the laird and factor they did not have their own building for another nine years.

The scale of defection to the Free Church left the remaining Church of Scotland ministers in Orkney in total disarray. Of the fourteen who were left, three were over seventy years old, one was sympathetic to the Free Church and had only stayed in because of his ill-health, and one, Charles Barry of Shapinsay, was insane and in a lunatic asylum in Edinburgh. The situation in the North Isles was particularly acute, only one minister was left sufficiently sound in body and mind to do his job.[25] Things got rapidly worse: assistant ministers, elders and schoolmasters defected, one after another, and Presbytery meetings started to resemble a shipwreck: as soon as a leak was plugged in one place, water poured in through another. They were frantic.

FIGURE 11.5

The legacy of religious dissent: at least two, if not three or four, kirks in every parish. The derelict Secession (later United Presbyterian) and Church of Scotland kirks side by side at Brinian in Rousay.

In North Ronaldsay, Adam White led almost the entire population into the Free Church. In small islands like North Ronaldsay or Papay, which only saw their Establishment minister occasionally, the Free Kirk had no effective opposition and became all-powerful, but this was not possible in the larger parishes, where there were now several kirks competing for the congregation.

In more recent times, the Free Kirk has gained the reputation of being much more stern and puritanical than the Church of Scotland. There is no evidence that this was so in the mid-nineteenth century. Victorian clergy (with the exception of the genial Mr Gerard) tended to be more prim than their fathers, especially with regard to the vulgar habit of *dancing*. Charles Clouston, who took stern measures against 'promiscuous dancing' (i.e. men with women) in Sandwick, was a minister in the Established Church, as was William Grant, who congratulated himself on banning merriment from North Ronaldsay. 'During the winter season, it was customary to carry on a perpetual succession of merry-makings, called balls ... Their moral effect was decidedly pernicious ... but the Kirk Session having interfered, little or no excess of this kind takes place.'[26]

FIGURE 11.6

The 'Sheepy Kirk' in Westray, even in ruin an impressive monument to the commitment of dissenting congregations who built their kirks with their own hands and out of their own pockets. When it was built in 1823, with seats for 300 people, it must have seemed enormous, but after a few years the galleries were enlarged so it could seat 450 and in 1867 the congregation abandoned it for the even larger and more magnificent New Kirk nearby. The building was later used as a sheepfold.

Although all the Kirks maintained the same apparatus of Kirk Sessions and punishments to discipline offenders, in practice, it was much more difficult to administer Discipline when the guilty party could evade it by moving to another kirk. When the Sandwick Kirk Session summoned George Wishart to answer charges of being habitually drunk, he replied, not very politely, that it was nothing to do with them, as he was now an elder in the Free kirk,[27] and when the Rousay Free kirk tried to discipline John Kirkness for going fishing on the Saturday of a Communion weekend, he refused point-blank to admit the error of his ways, and said he would return to the Established kirk.[28] The number of cases of antenuptial fornication brought before the Sessions of both Kirks remained distressingly high, and we find young women begging for readmission to one Kirk, when the dreaded sackcloth and stool of repentance threatened in the other.

Dissent stamped every parish in Scotland with its characteristic proliferation of churches. At Brinian in Rousay, the gaunt grey hulks of two empty kirks slouch into ruin by the shore. By the time the new parish kirk was built here, in 1815, religious schism had already been unstitching Orkney's social fabric for nearly twenty years, but it was 1837 before the Rousay Seceders managed to build their own kirk, next door. Did the rival congregations acknowledge one another as they met on the road? Six years later, the crofters of Sourin built their Free kirk a couple of miles away. For the rest of the century, one island was divided among three factions: neighbours who worked together all week were divided on Sundays; their children walked to different schools.

The divisions between the Kirks bit deep into island life, but Dissent was not all about rivalry. It also had far-reaching and positive effects. At the end of the eighteenth century, the great majority of people in Orkney had no voice in the important issues of their day at all. Only a handful of large landowners in the whole county had the right to vote. The Established Church saw its own interests bound up with the political status quo, and used its authority to enforce conformity and obedience. Dissent, however, gave even the poorest the right of choice, and, for the first time, people saw themselves as able and entitled to make their own voice heard.

Buckham Hugh Hossack, whose 1900 history of Kirkwall bristles with anticlerical prejudice, saw Dissent as a liberating influence, freeing people from the 'priestly tyranny' of a single, authoritarian Church backed by the power of the State. It was not that any of the Dissenting Churches were less strict than the Established Church, 'but with a choice of churches, ministers were bound to be civil lest they should lose their customers'.[29] Here, Hossack does less than justice to the contribution and achievements of the Secession and Free Church ministers. The Dissenting movement started with their protests against the muzzling of the Church by the State, and the Gospel by the Church, and, by the second half of the nineteenth century, they were the leading radicals in the islands, championing justice, political freedoms and social improvement. By the end of the century, the Orkney crofter voted in General Elections and had security of tenure of the land he farmed. These things, which would have been unimaginable a hundred years earlier, had been brought about largely by the campaigning of ministers of the Dissenting Churches.

CHAPTER 12

A Holy War

> *On Sunday, the bibled elders*
> *Lead douce families, this way and that*
> *To the three kirks.*
>
> George Mackay Brown (1996)

*T*he Free Kirk minister in Sanday, that colourful character
Matthew Armour, was at the centre of the extraordinary Revival
movement which swept through Orkney for a fevered year
from the late summer of 1860 and vanished again as abruptly as it came.
The 'Great Awakening' was an emotional whirlwind that moved swiftly
across countries and continents, sweeping everyone in its path into a
temporary frenzy before moving on. It started in America in 1857, crossed
the Atlantic, and by 1859 was spreading across Northern Ireland and
the west coast of Scotland. Early in 1860, huge open-air religious revival
meetings were held in Glasgow and Edinburgh, Dundee and Aberdeen,
and the wave of enthusiasm was being carried by the fishing fleets
up the east coast as far as Wick. In June 1860, *The Orkney Herald* was
reporting, with some disappointment, that 'in churches in Orkney there
does not seem to have been any movements like the revivals which have
visited other parts of the country', but, by October, the whirlwind had
hit Sanday.

People of all ages and all religious denominations flocked to the
churches, demanding services many times their usual length and frequency,
and gathering in prayer meetings in-between services. Mass conversions
were frequently accompanied by hysteria. *The Orkney Herald* described
the scene:

> Some were on their knees praying, and others lying on their faces
> groaning in agony. Some running about apparently wild with joy, and
> others in groups singing hymns and psalms of praise … the session house
> was crowded with praying people, and so were the porches … and many
> were found prostrate on the floor of the church; between the seats and
> in out-of-the-way corners in great mental agony.[1]

The Rev. Matthew Armour was an impassioned preacher. In fact, his
eccentric style in the pulpit had so annoyed some of his congregation that
almost half of them walked out and built a rival 'Free Church Station' just
a few minutes' walk from his kirk. However, many others were deeply
moved by his sermons, and, when he undertook a preaching round of the
isles, Revival enthusiasm erupted wherever he went. In the first months
of 1861, the newspapers reported on its spread to new parishes every
week: they described people flocking to the kirks, and then refusing to
go home, and claimed that 'even young men in bothies read and pray
together'.[2] For once, the ministers of the different kirks, overwhelmed
by the sudden demand to preach for hours on end and then listen to
confessions all night, sank their differences and worked side by side.
Those whose congregation had not yet been smitten felt it as a personal
failure and prayed mightily for the 'outpouring of the spirit' on their
own kirk.

By January 1861, normal life in North Ronaldsay had ground to a
halt: 'during ten days all work was suspended except what was absolutely
necessary for the preservation of their own animals', while virtually the
entire population spent the time on their knees.[3] Mr Peddie's prayers for
the backward people of Papay were at last answered in March 1861, when
he was able to report that: 'last week young men and women have
commenced prayer meetings … some of the children on their way home
from School have prayed together in boats on the beach and by dyke
sides'.[4]

The newspaper reports show that there were mixed reactions to
the Revival. Many witnesses were favourably impressed, but there was
considerable criticism of the 'unseemly' hysteria that Matthew Armour
aroused. 'The desire for physical manifestations we regard as an un-
healthy symptom', commented *The Orkney Herald* primly, 'which could
easily be traced to the same source as the passion for balls and the
theatre'. The Roman Catholic missionary, Dr Stephan, was even more
caustic: 'In Orkney the protestants begin to be mad from revival
humbug', he wrote to his superior. 'A man of their kind was put to the

lunatic asylum at Edinburgh ... Many other people have lost their senses, amongst them a minister of the Free Church and the medical man told me yesterday that this minister will be sent probably to the same lunatic asylum.'[5]

New Year 1861 was an extraordinarily sombre occasion. In Westray, Christmas and Hogmanay (still observed according to the old calendar on 7 and 14 January), had always been celebrated by the men and boys with games of football and visits to the pub, but that year 'none of the antiquated follies to which youth clings so tenaciously made their appearance during the day. The village of Pierowall was perfectly quiet, and some said the day was just like a Sabbath'.[6] However, references to the Revivals in the newspapers thin out in the summer of 1861, and then cease altogether. Matthew Armour was not sent to the asylum, and the whirlwind passed over Orkney. The mirthless New Year was never repeated, and 1862 was brought in with the traditional celebrations.

One of the interesting side effects of the Revivals was that the clergy were so pressurised by the immense demands made on them that – for a time – the traditional prohibition on women preaching was lifted. Early in the next century, Thomas Groat reported that: 'in byegone days, consecrated women were wont to conduct revival meetings in the island [of Hoy]'.[7] Even more surprisingly, in 1869, the attention of the Free Church Presbytery of Orkney was 'called to the fact that a female member of the Society of Friends had been permitted to address meetings in two of the churches within their bounds'.[8] The Presbytery 'generally agreed' (this does not sound unanimous) that this practice was unscriptural, and should not be allowed again, but it is significant that at least two Free Church ministers had not seen anything amiss with women in their pulpits. This is astonishing at this date: long before there were women teachers in the Orkney parochial schools and a hundred years before women would be accepted for ordination by the Church of Scotland.

A lasting effect of those hours in which exhausted ministers laboured side by side with their brethren of different denominations was that their rivalry died down, and most of them saw that what they had in common was far more important than their differences. The United Secession and Relief Churches had already unified as the United Presbyterian Church (UP) in 1847, and the gap between it and the Old Kirk narrowed, as the latter was shaken out of its complacency and transformed by the growing tide of evangelicalism that characterised the time. In 1874, Parliament finally abolished patronage (the most obvious symbol of the Kirk being under the thumb of secular power, and the issue which had caused most of the rifts in the first place) and a major stumbling block in the way of further reunions was removed.

At first sight, it seems odd that the UPs and the Free Church should have remained separate for so long when they obviously had so much in common. The major stumbling block was the political issue that had haunted the Scottish Kirk since the time of Columba: its relationship with the State. The Free Church had severed its connection with the State on a question of principle, but it believed that the State *should* support and fund a national Church, while the United Presbyterians believed that the Church should be entirely 'Voluntary', independent of State funding and control. Obviously, this line of thought leads to the conclusion that the State can be an entirely secular institution, a view that is unremarkable in the twenty-first century, but horrified most people in the nineteenth.[9]

It was not ideas and theories that filled the Dissenting kirks in Orkney, however, but the devout and dynamic men who preached in their pulpits on Sundays, and filled the rest of their days with their energetic efforts to improve, reform and transform the world around them. The Kirkwall United Presbyterian kirk was fortunate in being led by a succession of remarkable ministers who were not only eloquent speakers, but had an organisational gift for *doing* things, and who lived very long lives in which they got a great deal done. William Broadfoot was followed by Robert Paterson, minister for fifty years, and Paterson by David Webster, minister for another thirty-six. Under them, the UP congregation grew so huge that they built, and filled, a new kirk with room for 1,500 people.[10]

Photographs of Paterson show a tall, spare man, with an intelligent

FIGURE 12.1
The Rev. Robert Paterson, minister of the Kirkwall United Presbyterian Kirk 1820–70 and an energetic campaigner for justice and social improvement. (OLA)

face and a commanding presence that one can imagine dominating pulpit or meeting. He was totally committed to working for the reunion of Scotland's sundered Kirks and to campaigning for social justice, and was, unquestionably, one of the most influential figures of nineteenth-century Orkney. For a portrait of Webster, we have a wonderful pen-picture drawn by Edwin Muir, though he admits to being so overawed by the minister's appearance that he could not remember a word he said!

> He was handsome and majestic beyond all expectation and … might have stepped from a fresco of Michelangelo into the bare and austere Orkney landscape. I recall his dark eyes, which actually flashed as his prophetic voice rose, I remember his unusual height … His majestic carriage and his sweeping white Mosaic beard.[11]

Webster preached twice every Sunday, regretting that his hearers were unable to concentrate for more than a mere hour-and-a-half to two hours at a time.

From the outset, the Dissenting kirks led the demand for justice and social reform. In the 1820s and 1830s, for example, the Secession kirks were prominent in the second phase of the anti-slavery campaign, which eventually overcame the huge opposition from vested interests and achieved full emancipation in 1838. 'It is but justice to notice that the United Synod of the Scottish Secession church, representing upwards of 300 congregations, led the way, as a religious body, in this work of justice and mercy.'[12] As a result of the long campaign, people were made aware both of the need to make some amends for Britain's frightful part in the slave trade, and also of the appalling conditions in the West African countries which had supplied the slaves for the traders. When, in 1845, the Jamaican Church looked for support from Scotland for a mission to West Africa, Provost Baikie of Kirkwall presented it with a brand new sloop.[13]

A small but incredibly courageous number of Scots sailed, for example, to Nigeria, where the climate was often fatal to European people, and war, slavery and cannibalism were endemic. Against all the odds, they spread a network of schools, agricultural colleges, hospitals and leprosy clinics across the country. Among them were people like the Rev. W. and Mrs Marwick, who originated from Rousay,[14] and Margaret Manson Graham, a nurse from Orphir who died in Arochuku, aged 73, after a lifetime of service to the community. 'Often Miss Graham … bound up cut throats and slashed stomachs, arms well-nigh severed, skulls splintered, and bodies mutilated in the fierce quarrels which flared up continually in a heathen community.'[15]

Something of the pride that Orkney took in those of her sons who carried their strong Presbyterian convictions with them to the ends of the earth can be seen in the huge tomb erected for William Balfour Baikie in St Magnus Cathedral. Baikie was not a missionary but a naval surgeon and explorer who surveyed the Niger river in the 1850s, an anti-slavery campaigner, and a classic indefatigable Victorian Hero.

> Stranded for two years when his river steamer failed to reach him with supplies … although racked with bouts of fever and frequently on starvation rations he continued surveying and mapping new territory.[16]

To fill up the time, he translated chunks of the Bible into Arabic and Hausa and 'devoted life, means and talents to make the heathen, savage and slave … a free and Christian man'.[17] One cannot help feeling that Heroes are just not made like that any more.

Nineteenth-century Britons, of all religious persuasions, were enthusiastic about their obligation to make the Heathen a Christian man, and Sunday pennies were gathered in every corner of Orkney for the work of, among others, the Jewish Mission, the India Mission and the Colonial Mission. By the end of the century, the United Presbyterian and Free Kirks were, between them, funding 2,500 missionaries and teachers in seventeen foreign mission fields. Both Kirks believed passionately in their duty to improve this world, not just to save souls for the next, and 'Mission' meant practical aid, not just evangelisation. The congregation of the Kirkwall UP kirk, for example, raised funds to educate a number of Indian orphans and to support a travelling medical mission to Indian women.[18]

The UP and Free Kirks were also vigorous campaigners on behalf of the poor and the oppressed at home. As everywhere else in the country, there were huge disparities in wealth in Orkney. Take, for example, the living conditions of some of the inhabitants of the parish of Sandwick, around 1840. The chief heritor, William Watts, was living in his mansion, Skaill House, on the considerable income of his mercantile and business interests, as well as of his huge landed estate in the West Mainland. The parish minister, Charles Clouston, had a newly built kirk and manse in which to enjoy his stipend of £150 a year, which, by this time, was paid in cash. Below them on the social scale were a few other landowners, but the great majority of their parishioners were tenants, living, without security of tenure, in 'wretched hovels, with holes in the roof instead of chimneys ... and cows, calves, pigs, geese and fowls [sharing] the benefit of the peat fire, placed on the middle of the floor for the accommodation of all'.[19]

In such a house we can imagine James Irvine and his family. He had six children under the age of ten, but the two oldest were out at work as herds (the elder had 'a promise of 7 shillings a year beside his maintenance'), so only four were living with him. We know exactly what furniture they had, from an inventory in the Kirk Session minutes. There was:

> a wooden press, 3 clothes chests and a meal chest, 3 chairs, 1 creepie, 2 small chairs, a spinning wheel, one pot, a pair of tongs, ... 2 tubs, a small kirn [churn], an old keg, 2 collars, [some items indecipherable] ... the staves of an old Barrel and ditto of a cog, a small part of an old gridiron, an old coffer without the bottom, 2 water pails, a small keg for weighing meal ...

James's annual income as a farm servant was around £5, but in 1841 he was in debt to that amount and penniless.

In another Sandwick house lived Seaman David Robertson and his wife and grown-up son. After eleven years' service in Hudson's Bay, he owned: 'a bed and bedding, a table and 4 chairs, a chest and a Hammock, ½ doz plates, 5 spoons and a pot, the ¼ part of a tea kettle, one hen and a cat'.[20]

Irvine and Robertson petitioned their Kirk Session to be taken on the Poor Roll: the register of those who were incapable, usually because of age or infirmity, of supporting themselves or their dependants, and so were eligible for support from the parish. The Established Kirk had always accepted its obligation to give charity to the needy, but it had rarely taken up political cudgels to address the causes of need. The United Presbyterian and Free Kirk ministers, on the other hand, actively engaged in politics, and were not afraid to rock political boats by championing liberal and progressive ideas. They had the advantage of being neither 'established' by the State nor dependent on wealthy landowners for patronage and salary. They were supported solely by the contributions of their own congregation, and so had much more freedom to speak and act according to their conscience.

The UPs were great encouragers of education, lobbying for State-funded education instead of the old system of parochial schools controlled by the Church. Since the 1696 Act for Settling Schools, every parish in

Scotland had been obliged to support a schoolmaster and provide him with a house and school; occasionally, these were supplemented in rural areas by teachers paid by the Society for the Propagation of Christian Knowledge. These teachers, theoretically, supplied at least basic education for all children, but it is evident from the Orkney Presbytery records that, frequently, there was no school at all. Even Stromness and Sandwick, with a combined population of 4,000 people, 'were destitute of parochial schools' in 1822.[21] There was the usual problem of extracting the teacher's salary from the close-fisted heritors, and even when a school and schoolhouse were provided, the teachers were usually poorly qualified and miserably paid. In large country parishes, many children lived too far away from the only school to attend it regularly, even if their parents could afford the fees and did not keep them at home to help with the

FIGURE 12.2
The Paterson Kirk or East Kirk in Kirkwall, opened by the United Presbyterian congregation in 1849. (Wilfred Marr/OLA)

FIGURE 12.3
*The interior of the East Kirk, the largest church ever built in Orkney. In 2001 the kirk
was sold to the Orkney Islands Council and converted into offices.* (OLA)

farm-work. As well as lobbying for the State to provide free education,
the UP Kirk ran its own Sabbath schools which taught the Three Rs as
well as the Bible, to both children and young people who had missed out
on basic schooling. In Robert Paterson's time, there were 500 scholars in
the Kirkwall Sabbath school alone, and there were eight other schools in
the country parishes.

The Kirks also had considerable social influence through their encouragement of the Temperance Movement. This was growing in popularity
in response to Scotland's serious drink problem: it was estimated that
the quantity of spirits consumed per head of population in the mid-
nineteenth century was seven pints a year in England, thirteen in Ireland
and twenty-three in Scotland![22] Orkney had its share of inns: 'tippling
houses that do not contribute to the improvement of morals'.[23] In 1841,
there were three in Orphir, four in Sandwick, and no fewer than thirty-
four in Stromness! Tippling – usually home-brewed ale – was an essential
part of all social occasions. According to John Firth, who was a Free Kirk
elder when he wrote his *Reminiscences* and, perhaps, exaggerated the
depravity of his parish, one could expect most, or all, of the participants
at a birth, baptism, marriage or funeral to be intoxicated.

In general there was little joy in life apart from the exhilaration imparted by the ale cog ... the farmer's ... entrance into life and his exit from it were alike marked by that conviviality which comes from the free use of the social glass.[24]

In 1872, the first lodge of the International Order of Good Templars was founded in Orkney: the *Star of Pomona* in Kirkwall, and soon there was at least one in every parish. Good Templars followed the Freemasons in adopting a distinctive ritual, regalia and passwords, but every member was pledged to abstain from alcohol and to work for the banning of the production and sale of strong liquor. A great strength of the movement was that, unlike the Church and almost every other institution of that time, women were admitted on equal terms, and the lodges' weekly meetings provided social events that were a welcome opportunity for gathering in mixed company. They were extremely popular. Even lectures on Temperance and Total Abstinence drew far more people from their firesides than any entertainment would do today! The success of the

THE EXCELSIOR LODGE,
A group of the office-bearers taken many years ago. The late Brother John Mooney is seen in the centre.

FIGURE 12.4
The Excelsior Lodge of Good Templars, photographed in the early twentieth century. (OLA)

Temperance societies became most evident in the plebiscites on local prohibition that were held in 1920. Astonishingly, the people voted for *No Licence* for selling liquor in Stromness.[25]

However, it was in the cause of land reform that the Dissenting Kirks made their most dramatic and lasting impact in Scotland.

> In rural areas like Orkney, crofters had always harboured grievances but they lived in a society where the laird was liable to construe any open expression of discontent as a crime, supported by the church which called it a sin.[26]

Bible in hand, the Free Kirk ministers overturned that assumption, immediately becoming the champions of the poor and the oppressed. (It is no coincidence that the Free Kirk's greatest support came from the West Highlands and Islands, where poverty and eviction were far more serious problems than in Orkney.) When the potato famine, which would kill around two million people in Ireland, broke out in 1846, it was the Free Kirk population in the cities and the Lowlands which immediately raised the then enormous sum of £15,000 for famine relief, and prevented a similar tragedy in Scotland. The ministers of the Established Kirk had witnessed the Highland Clearances passively, merely telling their congregations to accept their eviction as God's punishment for their sins, but the Free Kirk ministers actively encouraged and helped their people to fight for land reform.

In Orkney, the main stage for that battle was set in Rousay, the only island to experience evictions on a large scale, and the central characters of that story were three generations of Free Kirk ministers who championed the crofters' cause. Far from supporting the laird, the Rev. George Ritchie denounced George Traill for evicting his tenants from Quandale and Westness in the 1840s, and when Traill countered that he had a right to do what he liked with his own land, Ritchie trumped him with: 'No! "The Earth is the Lord's and the fullness thereof".' The clearance went ahead, but the people of Rousay credited Ritchie with laying a curse on Traill when, about a year later, the laird died of a heart attack in the lavatory of his London club.[27] The heirs of laird and minister continued the war. Traill was succeeded by Frederick William Burroughs, 'The Little General', who became notorious for his treatment of his tenants. Ritchie was followed by the Rev. Neil Rose and, after him, by the Rev. Archibald MacCallum, who made Crofters Rights into a Holy War waged from his headquarters, the Sourin Free kirk.

At the time of the Quandale evictions, a change in the law to protect tenants was unthinkable because the vote was still, despite the first Reform Bill of 1832, confined to a handful of the wealthy and land-owning. The first step to land reform was the reform of the franchise, and both issues were debated heatedly in Parliament, ale-house and pulpit. In Orkney, it was Free Kirk ministers with radical views: Matthew Armour in Sanday, Alexander Goodfellow in South Ronaldsay and Neil Rose in Rousay, who vigorously campaigned at political elections for a Liberal candidate who would support reform.

The Second Reform Act of 1867 extended the franchise (though still only to people with a property qualification), and for the first time, would-be MPs had to court votes at a hustings. As there was no secret ballot, elections were turbulent and often violent occasions. There was an uproar in Rousay in 1868, when Neil Rose lambasted the Tories for trying to browbeat the crofters into voting for their candidate, his oratory leaving the Tory chairman with a face 'blanched like a cabbage stalk'! Finding that some of the Rousay men were not at the polls in Kirkwall, the minister made the round trip of twenty miles by boat to fetch them there.[28]

In 1884, there were demonstrations all over the country when the House of Lords attempted to block a bill to extend the franchise further. In Thurso, the slate-workers were out in the streets with banners proclaiming: 'Down with Tyranny', and Archibald MacCallum delivered an impassioned speech at a Land Reform and Franchise conference in Dingwall 'in the cause of ... right against wrong ... of liberty against systematic and cruel oppression'. His speeches are a world apart from the self-satisfied complacency that lurked around eighteenth-century pulpits. For MacCallum, there was not the slightest doubt that political agitation on behalf of the poor was his Christian duty: 'the voice of the Church ought not to be silent, but should be clearly heard in the pleading of this righteous cause'.[29] When the bill was passed, the number of voters in the Orkney and Shetland constituency had more than doubled, and most of these new voters had everything to gain from land reform. In the next election, MPs were elected all over the Highlands and Islands specifically on a land-reform ticket.

It was through the Free Kirk that the Rousay crofters – who would normally have had no contact with events in the Gaelic-speaking Highlands – were brought into contact with the mainstream of the crofting movement.[30] However, this was not a campaign fought only in the crofting areas. There was considerable leadership from the Free Kirk in the cities, especially from the professors in the divinity colleges in Edinburgh and Glasgow.

In 1884, the government appointed a Royal Commission to investigate the conditions of crofters and cottars in the Highlands and Islands. When it reached Kirkwall, most of the Orkney crofters were quite unprepared, but the Rousay tenants, encouraged by Archibald MacCallum, were ready with the evidence of their grievances: rack-renting, the loss of their common grazing, summary evictions. One of the Sourin tenants, James Leonard of Digro, bravely gave evidence against General Burroughs to the Commission. In revenge, an angry and bitter Burroughs evicted Leonard and his family from their home. Through the Free Kirk network, the vindictive treatment of Leonard became a cause célèbre, and aroused widespread sympathy for the plight of tenants who had no security of tenure, and could be rack-rented or evicted by a landlord at will.

In Sanday, Matthew Armour was as impassioned in his championship of the crofters' political rights as he was about their salvation. At an election meeting held by the Tory candidate before the 1885 election, Armour was shouted down and interrupted by the Tory henchman, who was all too aware of Armour's ability to ask awkward political questions. The result was a minor riot among Armour's supporters, and the minister was charged with disorderly conduct and breach of the peace. At his trial in Kirkwall, the Sheriff made no secret of his Tory sympathies and sentenced Armour to four days' imprisonment.

A hasty telegram to the Lord Advocate in Edinburgh, however, brought his release in a matter of hours, and the minister – now a hero – emerged from gaol into a huge crowd that had gathered near the prison and escorted him to the Free Church manse, amid deafening cheers![31] The case attracted widespread publicity in the national press, most of it sympathetic to Armour and severely critical of Sheriff Mellis. 'The story reads as if the Sheriff's sentence were an Act of political retaliation.'[32]

In the following year, 1886, the Crofters Act was finally passed, guaranteeing security from eviction, fair rents and the right to pass on a tenancy to one's heirs. The Sourin kirk was packed with worshippers celebrating with a service of Thanksgiving. 'The effect of the Act will be not unlike the Redemption of Israel out of Egypt', claimed Archibald MacCallum, who gave a lecture explaining the workings of the Act and – in flights of passionate oratory – pledging himself to continue to fight till death for all the things it had failed to achieve.[33] He had been the only minister, he pointed out, who had lifted a finger 'towards delivering the people of this land, long groaning under oppression, out of the cruel and merciless hands of the instruments of a system wet with tears and reeking with the blood of the Lord's poor'.[34]

And where indeed, one might well ask, were the ministers of the other Rousay kirks when all this was going on? We may conjure up, for a moment, a vision of Mr Spark of the Established Church, who politely declined an invitation to the Sourin meeting. He was far too busy arguing with Presbytery about his manse, insisting on extra bedrooms, zinc sash-chains and marble fireplaces.[35] In fact, despite all that was provided for his greater comfort, he declined to exile himself to Rousay at all and removed to Kirkwall, promising that he would deliver a sermon in his parish once a month.

Following on from the Act, a Crofters Commission was appointed to visit all the estates in the crofting counties and adjudicate fair rents. The Commission reached Orkney in the summer of 1888, and it was Matthew Armour again, always in the political thick of things, who spoke up for the crofters in Sanday. Ten years later, the people of Sanday celebrated their minister's Golden Jubilee with celebrations that lasted for three months! Even then, he still had five years to go, becoming the first Moderator of the Orkney United Free Church Presbytery in 1900, and achieving the remarkable record of being kept from his pulpit by illness only once in fifty-five years of eventful ministry.

Archibald MacCallum's subsequent career was far stranger and, sadly, inglorious. In 1888, he left Rousay under a considerable cloud: not only had his drinking bouts become a scandal, but also he had made a girl pregnant: Hannah Leonard, the daughter of his Session Clerk, co-campaigner for land reform, and assiduous advocate of the Temperance Movement. A few years later he reappeared – astonishingly – as a minister in the Established Church in Lewis, a career move which his alcoholism brought to an end in a blaze of publicity, in 1895. When MacCallum was heard of again, he was in a Turkish prison, having been arrested under suspicion of fomenting revolution under the guise of distributing Relief. The British ambassador in Constantinople succeeded in securing his release, and the last rumour of this strange, sad man who had achieved so much for the Orkney crofters was that he had emigrated to America.[36]

Erected
by the people of Rousay
in memory of
James Leonard
of Digro
1835 - 1918

CHAPTER 13

Redesigning the Ark

Some do not go to church because there is no organ in the church; some because there is one.

James Whyte (1902)

*A*t Warbeth, the Stromness dead crowd into the cemetery opposite the Hoy hills. 'Merchant', 'Ship's Captain', 'Ships' Agent' lie under these stones by the shore, as close as possible to the sea which provided their livelihood. In the oldest part of the kirkyard, stands a remnant of wall that was once the parish kirk, St Peter's. Its tower was still a landmark to sailors at the turn of the twentieth century. Nearby, the simple headstones of the earlier graves lean at haphazard angles, and paint long shadows on the grass in morning sunlight. In the early 1800s, Stromness was a growing port: fishermen, whalers, explorers and merchants sheltered in her harbour. Ships making for the trading posts on Hudson's Bay collected fresh water and Orkney crewmen, before sailing for the 'Nor'Wast'. St Peter's was moved from rural Warbeth to the bustling town, and the new kirk built high on a brae, so that it dominated the straggle of houses and shops growing along the waterfront, and its spire could still be a landmark for those at sea.

By the late nineteenth century, the Merchants and Ships' Agents were enjoying the kind of comfortable prosperity that likes to be recognised. They lie as closely packed in Warbeth as their houses still are in the town: granite obelisks and draped urns jostle one another for space and prominence. These were not people to be levelled, even in death, and certainly not in the kirks to which they would walk on Sundays, dressed in their best, to sit conspicuously in the most expensive pews. They were not isolated either, from ideas and fashions that were in vogue further south. It is evident that, just as the good citizens wanted something more emotionally fulfilling in their religion than the dour and legalistic package which had been delivered to them in the past, they wanted more from their kirk buildings than just a barn-like shelter from the elements. Late Victorian Stromnessians could afford a little style in their lives, and they wanted their kirk to be stylish too – preferably a little more so than the one belonging to the rival congregation down the road. Not only was there more money around than in the past, but also the Calvinist assumption that beauty, or comfort, was inconsistent with godliness was evaporating in a more affluent and more tolerant age. 'Christianity … is essentially a religion of progress', Dr Robert Paterson had stated, and that applied to architecture as well. After being suppressed for so long, spires, finials and Gothic windows burst out of Presbyterian kirks in a positively flamboyant fashion.

Walk a few paces from the harbour in Stromness, and you are at the bottom of Church Road. When St Peter's was built at the top in 1814, its builders would hardly have expected it to be so crowded by the competition. At the foot of the brae stands the former Free kirk, rebuilt

FIGURE 13.1

Building the new UP kirk in Sanday, 1881. The architect and chief mason are in the right foreground, holding the plans. It is obvious that the kirk has been designed to be a grand, eye-catching building. (Tom Kent/OLA)

180

in 1892 and boasting miniature turrets. The Episcopal church of St Mary takes a much more modest place, halfway down the terrace of houses. A little further along Victoria Street, a steep flight of steps leads up to the large and imposing façade of the former United Presbyterian church, rebuilt in 1862 and clearly intended to impress. A kirk was no longer a plain little box built by local tradesmen, but required an *Architect*, and skilled stonemasons to execute his plans. It is clear that, by this time, Orcadians had finished with ecclesiastical austerity.

Kirk interiors were different too, transformed by the need to keep up with fashion. St Peter's in Sandwick and St Michael's in Harray were built in 1836 in the traditional 'sideways on' design, with the pews centred on the pulpit in the centre of the long south wall. By the second half of the century, this was regarded as very old-fashioned, and kirks were designed 'end on' (like English or Episcopal churches), with the pulpit in the gable wall and windows in both side walls. Heritors were evidently so anxious not to be seen as being behind the times that they often (as in the Papay Free kirk) ripped out the fittings of kirks they had built only twenty or thirty years earlier, in order to 'recast' them in the modern design! Wherever congregations could afford it, furnishings became more elaborate and interiors less plain. Features like stained glass, which would certainly have been denounced as 'popish' in a more puritanical age, occasionally brightened windows. The Victoria

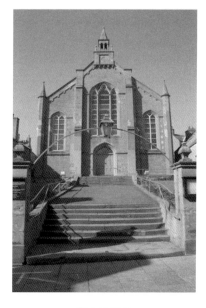

FIGURE 13.2
Victoria Street Church (formerly UP), Stromness, 1862. By this time, Orkney congregations wanted their kirks to be much more grand than the simple 'preaching barns' of the past.

Street and North kirks in Stromness had large horseshoe galleries facing – and this must have made many past members of the congregations birl in their graves – *an organ*.

Any innovation to church music could – and still can – be guaranteed to cause dissension in the pews. Singing anything in kirk, other than unaccompanied psalms, was unthinkable to most Presbyterians for generations. The Relief Church, the most liberal body, published a hymn book in 1794, but this would not have been known in Orkney. It was not until 1852 that the United Presbyterians followed suit, and 1870 before the Church of Scotland published its first hymnal. It was fiercely resisted in some quarters. The Rev. Matthew Armour of Sanday once took a service in Thurso, and announced a hymn, at which a number of the old people got up and walked out, rather than submit to the singing of 'a human hymn'.[1] It would be well into the twentieth century before instruments and hymn-singing found their way into many Orkney kirks, and some still regarded them as quite diabolical. In the late 1940s, Winnie Breck of Swannayside attended the Kirk Abune The Hill in Birsay, which resisted all innovations and unions and survived as the last Original Secession congregation until 1957. 'We sang psalms and a few paraphrases but we never sang hymns', she remembered. 'My Granny ... said they were the work of the devil.'[2]

However, when the American evangelist duo, Moody and Sankey, arrived in Britain in 1873, their hymn-singing rallies were enormously popular. Sankey's hymns were 'as close to the musical and emotional taste of his time as any pop singer today', and his *Sacred Songs and Solos* was by far the bestselling book of the century, after the Bible.[3] It cannot have been long before they were being sung in Orkney. Singing was an important part of the Evangelical Revivals of the late nineteenth and twentieth centuries, and is especially associated with memories of the fisher-folk who thronged to the fishing ports during the herring season. In the early 1900s, 'Sunday was a red-letter day in Stromness during the fishing-season', recalled Thomas Groat, a colporteur, or distributor of religious literature.

> There was a large open-air service at the pier in the forenoon, conducted by the fishermen themselves ... The singing at the evening service could not fail to inspire any speaker; hundreds of voices would join lustily in pouring forth the simple old melodies.[4]

Another busy fishing port was Whitehall in Stronsay. In Thomas Groat's day, there were as many as eighteen curers and 1,800 fisher-girls working there during the herring season, and he contrasted their fervour for buying Bibles and attending his services with that of the men on the English steam drifters, who cold-shouldered him and went out fishing on Sundays.[5]

NEW USE FOR DOG

❖◆❖ ◆◆❖ ❖◆❖ ◆◆◈

Carries Cable Through Pipe 60 Feet Long

KIRKWALL, Scotland, June, 1926.
WHILE erecting an organ in a church here, electricians were con-
fronted with the problem of getting an electric cable through a
twelve-inch pipe. sixty feet long and bent at right angles in the middle.
A small dog was placed at one end of the pipe, with a string attached
to his collar. His master went to the other end and called to him
through the tube, and along came the dog. the string and finally the
cable.

FIGURE 13.3
Installing organs in churches involved technical problems – and ingenious solutions.
(Tom Kent/OLA)

In 1866, the General Assembly of the Church of Scotland had made
the controversial decision that organs could be permitted in kirks, but
the cost – and the difficulty of finding somewhere to put them – placed
them out of reach of most country kirks. In 1888, St Olaf's Episcopal
Church acquired 'a fine organ … the first introduced into any church in
Orkney'.[6] This must have caused a considerable stir, for it would have
been the first time any instrumental music had been heard in an Orkney
kirk for 300 years. Gradually, organs appeared in the larger town kirks:
one was built for the Victoria Street kirk in Stromness in 1906, with half
the cost donated by the famous philanthropist, Andrew Carnegie. Until
mains electricity reached the town in the late 1940s, the power for organs
was usually supplied by a small boy, wielding a pair of bellows, but the
organs in the North and Victoria Street kirks were powered by large water-
driven engines:

> In the North Church, the engine was under the pulpit … When ships
> came into the harbour to take on water, the water pressure was sometimes

FIGURE 13.4
St Magnus in the early nineteenth century, with the short pyramid spire that replaced the original steeple, burnt in 1671. (OLA)

reduced so much that there was not enough pressure to drive the organ-motors, which struggled and then wheezed into silence.[7]

In Kirkwall, St Magnus Cathedral also underwent drastic changes in the course of the nineteenth century. When Alexander Peterkin had arrived in Orkney to take up the post of County Sheriff in 1814, he thought that the cathedral was the only beacon of civilisation to be found in a bleak and benighted landscape.

> The islands are in general flat and partially cultivated; and a dark brown hue over the whole surface, without a tree, or green hedgerow, or a smiling cottage, with its garden shrubs, to enliven the aspect, – the rude and antique huts … the primeval aspect and costume of the peasantry … produce … a sort of chilling consciousness of being in the midst of dreariness and desolation. In the bosom of all this apparent barbarism, however, the stately pile of St Magnus cathedral is to be found, a Christian temple which has stood during nearly the half of the Christian era.[8]

Although St Magnus may have appeared a stately pile to Peterkin, those who actually sat in it, Sunday after Sunday, found it 'damp, cold and unwholesome as any cellar or icehouse'.[9] This was probably an understatement. Not only had generations of burials in the kirkyard accumulated to such a depth against the east and south walls that the congregation must have felt as if they were underground, but the floor inside was also an overcrowded and unsavoury graveyard. The General Assembly of 1588 had forbidden burials inside kirks, but the well-to-do of Kirkwall had always ignored this and staked their claim to their family burial plot. Even the choir was dug up for those who could afford the premium rate, despite the inconvenience of temporarily dismantling someone's pew in order to inter a new corpse underneath it.

As we have seen, in the eighteenth century the cathedral was in a ghastly state, the nave windows boarded up and only the choir in use, where the congregation perched on a ramshackle collection of homemade pews and galleries. By the early nineteenth century, not only were these seats far too few for the growing population of Kirkwall and St Ola, but, crammed between the large pillars, it was quite impossible for most people to either see or hear the minister,

> while many of them are likewise so exposed to currents of cold air, as well as to excessive damp or moisture, occasioned by the state of the roof, the walls, or the windows, that attendance on public worship is rendered not only very uncomfortable, but even highly prejudicial to health.[10]

The cathedral ministers, William Logie and Peter Petrie, implored Presbytery and the heritors to abandon St Magnus, as only suitable for a mausoleum, and build a new church. Not only was it a major health hazard, but also the lack of seats, and the discomfort of the available seats, was keeping many away from Sunday service. 'Is it any wonder that, in these circumstances, Juvenile delinquency should be on the increase in Kirkwall?'[11]

Although the ministers were seriously concerned that some of their congregation were deprived of the opportunity to hear or see the preacher, evidently some of their flock thought it would be better still if no-one could see *them*. In 1823, the Rev. John Dunn complained that: 'one of his parishioners Mr Baikie of Tankerness' – the most important family in the parish – 'clandestinely put up a rail and green curtain around his seat in the cathedral church of St Magnus so as entirely to conceal those within from the view of the minister in the pulpit'. It must have caused immense speculation as to what was going on behind the green curtain during divine service. Mr Dunn, 'considering this an innovation of a very pernicious kind and one which many will be inclined to follow, immediately wrote to Mr Baikie advising him to take it down, but received from him a very unsatisfactory answer'.[12]

In 1841, a new parish kirk, with sittings for 1,000 people, was built next to the cathedral with funds raised by public subscription. Some of the heritors, however, were outraged at the idea of abandoning St Magnus (seeing that this would lead to its falling into complete ruin), and so the congregation divided. The comfort-loving half defected with Mr Petrie (minister and congregation would soon join the Free Kirk), while the hardy traditionalists loyally continued to occupy their unwholesome seats along with Mr Logie.[13] However, in a rather odd turn of events, they soon found themselves ejected.

The Crown, represented by the Office of Woods and Forests, had inherited the Orkney estates which had formerly belonged to the bishopric, and assumed, not unreasonably, that these would include the cathedral. The Office of Woods and Forests eyed the malodorous building with horror and, in 1845, expelled the congregation, so they could get on with restoring the building to the status of a respectable historic monument. The walls and floor were excavated and the dilapidated pews and galleries swept to the bonfire, but no sooner had the government expended over £3,000 on the restoration than its claim to ownership was contested by the Royal Burgh of Kirkwall. After a legal battle, the Crown acknowledged the Charter of 1486, in which James III had given St Magnus to the city, and withdrew its claim. The citizens repossessed their stripped and sanitised cathedral in 1851, and got busy re-erecting their family pews. Architectural purists were scandalised.

'The choir, which is used as the parish church, has been rendered hideous by pews, galleries, whitewashed, pinkwashed, or yellow-ochred pillars, and a tawdry deal screen which shuts off the choir from the nave', expostulated the historian, John Tudor in 1883.[14] The ecclesiologist, T. S. Muir, could write of St Magnus only five words: 'outraged, internally, of late years'.[15] However, if some found the refurnishing unaesthetic, at least the cathedral had been saved from an even worse fate: that of ending up as a scraped and empty museum.

Victorian restoration was often uncompromising. The superbly carved seventeenth-century Bishop's seat and Graham gallery were swept out with the old pews, though fortunately some of the woodwork was later recycled in St Olaf's church in Kirkwall. (Some still survives in the cathedral triforium.) In the course of excavation, discoveries were made, such as the long-lost grave of Bishop William the Old, who had accompanied Earl

Rognvald to the Holy Land in 1151 and returned to die in Orkney, after an episcopate of sixty-six eventful years. To make sure his identity would be recognised, an inscribed lead plate had been placed in the cist with his body: 'Here lies William the Old of happy memory, the first bishop.'

If the gentry and merchant lairds who bought their burial plots inside St Magnus hoped for a peaceful last resting place, they made a very bad investment, as their bones were disturbed three times over in the repairs of 1847–9, 1855–6 and 1913–30. The nineteenth-century work did not halt the serious deterioration of parts of the building, but one man who did notice the problems and was in a position to do something about them was George Hunter Thoms, Sheriff of Orkney, Caithness and Zetland between 1870 and 1899. An eccentric and generous bachelor, Thoms left an estate of £80,000 to charities when he died, the bulk of it for the restoration of St Magnus. His two disappointed nephews, who were left nothing but a pair of screens and a gong, attempted to contest the will on the grounds of their uncle's unsoundness of mind. Thoms had decided he was Chief of the Clan MacThomas of Glenshee, and insisted on being thus addressed; he had also left a legal document stating he was to be buried in St Giles' Cathedral in Edinburgh, 'in a wicker or other slight coffin, so as to have a chance to begin early at the general scramble at the resurrection'. A very public legal case found these peculiarities did not constitute insanity, and

FIGURE 13.5
Workmen with the weather-cock from the top of the spire, during restoration work.
(Tom Kent/OLA)

St Magnus won the means for the major restoration that was undertaken in the early twentieth century.[16]

Between 1913 and 1930, the cathedral was given a radical face-lift. From the outside, the major change was the new spire which was seventeen feet higher than the former dumpy pyramid, and covered in copper rather than slates. It was now 150 feet high, a similar height to the original steeple that was burnt down in 1671. As before, the steeple was 'furnished with a good Clock, to remind the good Citizens of their

FIGURE 13.6
Carvings on the ends of the choirstalls in the cathedral, installed during the early twentieth-century restoration.

latter end, and point out to them the divisions of time'.[17] The roofs of nave and aisles were re-slated and the churchyard wall facing Broad Street was rebuilt to incorporate a gateway commemorating those who fell in the First World War. Inside, the transformation must have been far more dramatic, as the windows were filled with stained glass, and the walls and pillars steam-cleaned so that people saw for the first time the lovely rose-coloured stone that had originally been painted with formal patterns in red and black, and then hidden under layers of whitewash. With new timbers, new heating, new electric lighting, new floor, new furniture and much more, St Magnus was in good form for the celebrations of the octocentenary of its foundation, in 1937.

When the hideous partition and pews were removed, and until the organ was sited, amid much controversy, between the pillars of the choir, and the new pulpit and choirstalls built, for a short while one must have been able to appreciate the cathedral as a unified space, with a continuous vista from west end to east. The east end is dominated by the huge tombs to two of Orkney's great explorers: John Rae, peacefully asleep in his Arctic hunting gear, in one corner, and Dr William Balfour Baikie, who explored the Niger, in the other. Above them a four-light memorial window was erected to the glory of God and the memory of Sheriff Thoms, whose eccentricities had so mercifully included a love of St Magnus.

Despite the huge amount of repair and reconstruction that took place as the result of Thoms' bequest, only forty years later it was realised that St Magnus was in a critical state, its 800-year-old foundations sinking and the west gable threatening to collapse into Broad Street. However, an urgent Appeal raised £300,000 to save Rognvald's Ark from shipwreck. By 1974, it was securely lashed together by an invisible network of steel girders, and ready to sail into new centuries.

CHAPTER 14

The Mission to the North Pole

The Spirit moves on the deep always.
It crosses the hills of Orkney on shining feet.

George Mackay Brown (1996)

Despite all the differences of political and religious opinion, life in late nineteenth-century Orkney was generally much more stable and sedate than in the previous centuries. Political elections were accompanied by a great deal of noise and excitement, church factions sniped at one another in a sometimes uncharitable fashion, but on the whole conflicts were bloodless. Scenes such as the wild women of Stromness and Sandwick trying to tear Mr Tyrie in pieces were not a feature of Victorian social life. With more people travelling out of the islands and immigrating into them, Orkney society was also becoming a little more multicultural. The memories of civil war had been left far behind, Britain had settled into the self-confidence of its role as a major World Power, and the hysteria of religious intolerance that had scarred the previous centuries finally started to fade. Presbyterians and Dissenters of all kinds buried hatchets, and the Roman Catholics and the Episcopalians, who had disappeared almost entirely out of sight in the previous hundred years, at last re-emerged into the light.

In the eighteenth century, a few leading Orkney families such as the Traills of Elsness and Westness and the Balfours of Trenaby, who had retained their old loyalties to the Episcopal Church, were forced to meet secretly in what survived of the old St Olaf's Church in Kirkwall, or in one another's houses. After the 1745 Rebellion, they suffered under savage penal laws but, gradually, with the Jacobite cause completely crushed, the Episcopal Church ceased to be seen as a political threat. Its adherents were

FIGURE 14.1
St Olaf's Episcopal Church, Kirkwall.

no longer regarded as potential terrorists and they were finally granted freedom of worship in 1792, on condition that worship included prayers for King George III and his family.

A congregation does not seem to have been re-established in Orkney, however, for another eighty years. Only in the late nineteenth century does an Episcopal Church reappear in Kirkwall, and by then it was a very different institution, much more closely resembling the Church of England. It drew much of its support from the landed gentry, both members of Orkney landowning families such as the Balfours of Balfour Castle, Hebdens of Evie and Sutherland Graemes of Graemeshall, and wealthy incomers like Frederick William Traill-Burroughs who had bought, or inherited, Orkney estates. Both groups had always found Presbyterianism uncomfortably democratic, as well as dour.

They held their first public service in the Volunteer Drill Hall in Kirkwall in August 1871. Three years later, the foundation stone of a new St Olaf's Church, designed by the Inverness architect Alexander Ross,[1] was laid by Colonel Burroughs, and the new kirk was dedicated on St Olaf's day, 29 July 1876. The 'neo-Gothic' architecture is typical of Ross's Episcopal churches, and makes a deliberate statement about their continuity with the medieval, pre-Reformation, past. The carved stonework, the handsome wooden furnishings and the stained glass windows belong to a tradition that had never seen any religious merit in banning art and fine craftsmanship from churches, but the most spectacular feature of the interior is the roof of Swedish redwood, an extravagantly beautiful use of timber that might have been designed to make expatriate English feel at home, and forgetful of their treeless surroundings.

However, the real delight of St Olaf's is finding here, used and treasured, rare survivals from medieval churches that were long ago swept out by Presbyterian brooms. The oldest is the font, which once stood in the kirk of St Mary's in Rousay.

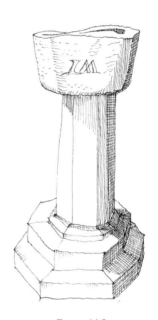

A lovely carved stone 'sacrament house' (for storing the bread and wine for communion), which was carved for the old St Olaf's Kirk in the sixteenth century, somehow survived its demolition and was built into the new church.[2] The wooden chancel screen, erected in memory of Mr Sutherland Graeme of Graemeshall in 1897, was made from parts of the gallery and bishop's throne that his ancestor, Bishop George Graham, commissioned for the cathedral in about 1620, and that were discarded in the nineteenth-century restoration.

There are contemporary treasures too, especially the wooden statue of St Olaf, carved by the sculptor, Frances Pelly. The helmeted saint conceals his drawn sword behind his back, in readiness for anyone who would not accept baptism on demand.

FIGURE 14.2
Medieval font from Rousay's old parish kirk, now in St Olaf's Church.

At first sight, the saintly credentials of St Olaf are a little opaque. A Norwegian aristocrat born in AD 995, he pursued a conventional career in piracy until he was converted to Christianity and elected king of Norway, aged only 20. Olaf pursued the same robust conversion methods as his ancestor Olaf Tryggvason, demolishing heathen temples, building churches and harrying reluctant pagans into them at the point of the sword. He introduced English clergy who eventually succeeded in making Norway Christian, but his conservative subjects rebelled against his harsh methods, and Olaf was forced into exile. When he returned to Norway and attempted a counter-coup to regain his throne, he was defeated and killed at the Battle of Stiklestad, in AD 1030.

Like St Magnus, Olaf's violent death at the hands of his own people was soon followed by reports of miracles performed at his grave. Olaf was rehabilitated as the champion of his country's independence and their patron saint. Pilgrimages to his shrine became so popular that, in the later twelfth century, a new cathedral was being built in his name at Nidaros, and there were over forty churches dedicated to him in Britain alone. In Orkney, not only St Olaf's in Kirkwall but also the parish church in North Ronaldsay and chapels in Stronsay and South Ronaldsay carried his name.

By 1888, Stromness also had its own Episcopal church: St Mary's. An unpretentious building that had been a school, a Drill Hall and a Masonic Lodge, the exterior in no way prepares you for the wonderful burst of colour inside. Paintwork, furnishings and textiles are bright blue – the colour always associated with Mary. Best of all, are the glorious stained glass windows by Shona McInnes. When the sun shines through them, they glow with brilliant blues, reds, purples and yellows, and throw swirls of vibrant colour on to the walls. The eagle of St John and the ox of St Luke triumphantly straddle landscapes which are both real scenes of Stromness (the tall grey houses, the purple hills of Hoy in the distance), and symbolic. The windows were donated by Dr Petrie, a retired Stromness GP. St Luke is the patron saint of physicians, and the doctor's bag and stethoscope and the healing hands at the base of the 'ox' window celebrate his profession. In the 'eagle' window are symbols of the Virgin Mary: the lily and thornless rose of purity, the crescent moon and stars, the wine jar for the miracle at the wedding feast in Cana, where Christ turned water into wine.

FIGURE 14.3
The lovely sixteenth-century carved 'sacrament house' in St Olaf's Church, originally in the old St Olaf's in Kirkwall.

The congregations of St Olaf's and St Mary's tended to be thinly scattered about the islands, and the Mainland was not always within easy reach. However, there were a number of wealthy Episcopalian families with the means to build private chapels beside, or inside, their own mansions. The Sutherland Graeme family created a chapel in Graemeshall, in 1898; the Balfours, one in Balfour Castle in 1903; and a chapel in Nisthouse, Harray was dedicated to St Michael and All Angels in 1904.[3] Thomas Middlemore, who had made his fortune manufacturing bicycles in the Midlands, bought the old Moodie property of Melsetter on Hoy and commissioned the Arts and Crafts architect, William Lethaby, to rebuild the house. In 1900, Lethaby added the chapel of St Margaret and St Colm, one of the loveliest church buildings, of any age, in Orkney.

May Morris described Melsetter as 'a sort of fairy palace on the edge of the great northern seas', but there is nothing flimsy or whimsical about either the house or the chapel beside it, that seems to grow out of the rubble walls of the old kitchen garden. It looks as if it has stood there for ever. Nowhere is the metaphor of the church as a ship, 'the ship of salvation', more clearly expressed in architecture than at Melsetter. Both the vault of the roof and the little bell-tower have the unmistakable shape of an upturned boat, such as Lethaby would have often seen used as a shelter in the islands. The cross

FIGURE 14.4

The sixteenth-century font in St Mary's, Stromness, was found in the Boardhouse Loch in Birsay parish. The shield bears the Craigie arms.

on the east gable is carved as an anchor. With its stoutly buttressed wall, and its hull braced with the massive chancel arch, the small building has a reassuring solidity. This is no fragile craft but a ship securely anchored, which will withstand any shocks of wave or storm.

All the artists of the Arts and Crafts movement were anxious to see their work as the continuation of a tradition, not as something new and coming out of nowhere. Lethaby gave the chapel an arched doorway modelled on the mausoleum of the Moodies of Melsetter, and carved into the wall a copy of St Colm's cross that was found near the mausoleum.[4] The chapel's red sandstone walls and slate roof blend effortlessly with the older estate buildings, and the interior is full of treasures, old and

FIGURE 14.5
The Chapel at Melsetter House, designed by William Lethaby.

contemporary. Originally, the walls were hung with William Morris fabrics.

Melsetter is exceptional in being designed as a chapel by an eminent architect. All the other Episcopal or Catholic chapels were converted from existing rooms or outhouses. In the garden of Westness House in Rousay, a little building which was once the engine-house for heating the Middlemores' enormous hothouse was converted into a chapel by the Grant family, who bought the Trumland estate from General Burroughs. A stone's throw from the sea and sheltered by a grove of sycamore trees, a chapel could not have a more peaceful site. Just below it is a jetty, where the mailboat that used to run from Evie to Hullion on Rousay would sometimes divert to drop off the minister of St Olaf's, as he travelled around the isles visiting his small and scattered congregations.

On the other side of Eynhallow Sound is probably the smallest ecclesiastical building in Orkney. The dovecote at Woodwick House was repaired and converted into an oratory by Hugh and Jill Birley in the late 1970s, the ivy-clad walls of the little building recalling the obligatory Gothic Hermitage of an eighteenth-century landscape park!

If life was grim for Episcopalians in the eighteenth century, the situation of the Roman Catholics in Scotland was far worse. They were finally granted toleration in 1793, and the fact that there were any left to be tolerated is a miracle of faith and endurance. They had suffered two centuries of persecution designed to exterminate them altogether. After the Reformation, Scottish Catholics were made outlaws who could be killed, or have their property robbed, without any right of redress. Their churches were plundered, their priests were put to death, and anyone caught harbouring a priest or his 'gear', the utensils, books and wine essential for celebrating Mass, suffered imprisonment or death as well. In the seventeenth century, a few brave Irish Catholic priests travelled in disguise to the West Highlands and the Hebrides, where the Reformation had never been fully accepted or, sometimes, even heard of![5] Their lives were constantly in danger and usually ended on the gallows. After 1745, the penal laws made it almost impossible for ordinary Catholics to exist. Many families were ruined by the huge fines imposed on them; they were forbidden to take employment, or to employ others; their marriages were not recognised, unless performed by

FIGURE 14.6
The font in Melsetter Chapel.

FIGURE 14.7
The interior of Westness Chapel, Rousay, furnished by the Grant family and used for occasional services since 1925.

197

a Protestant minister; and they could not educate their children, except in Protestant schools.

Despite the savagery of the legislation, the General Assembly remained convinced that there was a priest lurking behind every bush, and the whole country teetering on the brink of relapse into 'popery'. At regular intervals, the Orkney Presbyteries received hysterical circulars about 'Trafficing Papists', which read rather like articles on asylum seekers in today's tabloids. In 1734, the ministers were commanded to 'make exact enquiry into the state of Popery in their several Parishes, and take notice of the Persons who are active in promoting Popery, time and Place, parties and witnesses, Names and designations …'[6] In England, the Catholic Relief Act granted freedom of worship in 1778, but when the same Bill was introduced in Scotland there was uproar in the General Assembly. In Edinburgh and Glasgow there were street riots, with mobs threatening to murder educated Protestants who were known to support the Bill. The Catholic Bishop, George Hay, returned from London to find his home in Edinburgh being sacked and his library of 10,000 books destroyed. The Bill was hastily withdrawn, and it was not until 1793 that Scottish Catholics gained a measure of toleration, although they would still have no civic rights until 1829, and even then only in the teeth of vigorous opposition. There were three times as many petitions to the House of Commons *against* Catholic Emancipation as *for* it, and many of them came from the same churches that had petitioned for the abolition of slavery![7]

In these circumstances, it is not surprising that we know very little about Orkney Catholics. There is a tradition that the last Mass was said in Rapness in Westray, a remote district that was often cut off from the rest of the island by impassable bog, and which seems to have remained a Catholic stronghold for some time after the Reformation. After that, they apparently disappear, but Alison Gray has shown that a few Catholic families did survive, and there were even converts to Catholicism. In 1790, Bishop John Geddes visited Savil in Sanday at the invitation of Ann Traill and her sister Christina Chapman, who had both become Catholics the previous year, but it was so dangerous to have Catholic contacts that all mention of the visit was removed from journals and correspondence. Ann's brother-in-law was Walter Traill, the Presbyterian minister of Lady parish in Sanday, so her situation must have been particularly delicate![8] 'My duty as a Wife and Christian fixes my residence here', she wrote to Geddes, 'but we are without a Sacrement [*sic*], a priest or a church …'[9] It is sad that we do not know more about the visit: Geddes was scholarly, charming and sociable, and described by Robert Burns as the finest Christian minister he had ever known.[10]

Despite the Catholic Relief Act only three years later, the young women would still have had no priest in Orkney. It was not until 1854 that Rome made provision for northern Roman Catholic souls, with the founding of the romantically named 'Prefecture of the Arctic' by Pope Pius IX. Orkney started to receive occasional visits from itinerant Polish

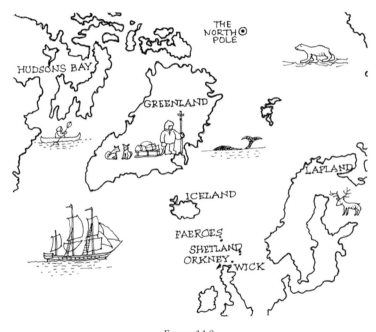

FIGURE 14.8

The territory of the North Pole Mission. One priest, based in Wick, had responsibility for the Catholics in Caithness, Orkney, Shetland, Lapland, the Faeroes, Iceland, Greenland and Hudson's Bay ...

and Belgian priests who had been given the lonely and difficult task of overcoming all the barriers of language, and immense maritime distance, to establish the North Pole Mission. The Prefect Apostolic of the North Pole was Dr Stephan de Djunkowski, to whom the Vatican had entrusted the spiritual welfare of Caithness, Orkney, Shetland, the Faeroe Islands, Iceland, Greenland, Lapland and the British dominions in Hudson's Bay.

From the viewpoint of Rome, these places presumably appeared sufficiently contiguous to all be supervised by one man with a base in Wick.

Dr Stephan's letters to his superior, Bishop Kyle, at Preshome in Banffshire, give fascinating glimpses of his extraordinary job. He rejoices in good news from Lapland: '22 conversions in Tromsoe', and in a historic occasion in Orkney. 'This morning I baptised two children and celebrated Holy Mass which some people suppose was the first since 300 years at Orkney', he wrote to Bishop Kyle from Kirkwall, in August 1860. He is surprised himself at the number of Catholics in Orkney, partly the result of immigration from Ireland, but it is a measure of the continuing intolerance that, sixty years after they were granted freedom of worship, they were still keeping their religion secret.

> During my stay in Kirkwall I have had the satisfaction to administer the sacraments to a far greater number of Catholics than I would expect. Some from town and others that came from the surrounding country where many of them had remained for years and been obliged by the social intolerance of the Presbyterians to conceal that they were Catholics.[11]

That Dr Stephan does not exaggerate the intolerance is evident from a quick dip into the newspapers of 1860, when Orkney celebrated the Tercentenary of the Reformation with a round of lectures and sermons condemning the 'soul-deluding nature of popery', delivered to packed houses and to great applause.[12] The anniversary of the first General Assembly on 20 December brought all the Protestant churches together in a day of uncharacteristic concord. 'There was one pervading spirit of Christian tolerance and love', reported *The Orkney Herald*, quite without irony, as everyone pledged themselves to stand together 'in every assault upon the one great common foe'.[13] The year 1888 produced more outbursts of Protestant jingoism in the celebration of the anniversaries of the defeat of the Spanish Armada in 1588 and the Revolution of 1688, when Mr Melville denounced the 'blighted mildew and poisonous plague' of Roman Catholicism from the East Kirk pulpit in Kirkwall. The invention of the notion of political correctness, or legislation banning incitement to religious hatred, was still a very long way off.

Against this background, the difficulties and dangers of the North Pole mission can be imagined, and it is no surprise to read that there were riots in Wick when it opened a chapel there. Without a church, the itinerant priests had to carry portable altars, in order to celebrate Mass in private houses, but in 1870 the Orkney Catholics were meeting in 'a poor room at the top of a house in the poorest locality of Kirkwall'. Father Capron, Apostolic Missionary of the North Pole, raised money to build a chapel in Kirkwall, and his letter in an Irish newspaper, requesting donations, is quoted sneeringly in *The Orcadian* 'for the amusement of our readers'.[14] However, the money was raised, and the chapel was built in 1877, the first in Orkney since the Reformation. 'In Groat's Garden, Bishop McDonald erected his church and manse', wrote Hossack, 'the modest buildings contrasting most markedly with the cathedral and Palace of Rome's palmy days.'[15] The following year, the Roman Catholic Church was officially re-established in Scotland. Orkney, Shetland and Caithness were transferred from the wilds of the Prefecture of the Arctic to the far more prosaic location of the Bishopric of Aberdeen.

The church of St Joseph and St Mary may be modest in comparison with the cathedral, but it marked a social milestone. Despite the sneering of *The Orcadian*, it was coming to be accepted that different churches – even the Roman Catholic! – could, and would, peacefully coexist. By slow degrees, the concept of toleration was making a nervous beginning. Nonetheless, everyone who was around in 1877 would have been astonished if they could have foreseen that, less than a century later, Orkney would be proudly cherishing and preserving a Roman Catholic chapel that vied with Maeshowe and Skara Brae as its most famous and visited tourist attraction!

CHAPTER 15

Postcards from the Voyage

We may note, page by page, the new
And the old works of time; how all
*   Fall into ruins, or go dancing*
*   Towards green April harps*
*   Forever, somewhere, are joy and dancing.*

George Mackay Brown (1996)

*A*fter the kirk-building boom of the 1800s, the Orkney 'arks' sailed into the next century in a large and confident fleet. In 1900, Queen Victoria was still on the throne, the sun still did not set on the British Empire, and the majority of people still attended one kirk or another. Even those who rarely did still thought of themselves as part of a Christian nation, and expected their government to support Christian values. No-one anticipated the tempestuous voyage that lay ahead. Through two world wars, a long period of economic decline and drastic depopulation and, finally, the scepticism and materialism of a much more affluent age, the Orkney arks were storm-tossed, battered and often abandoned. Astonishingly, by the end of the century, there was a loud sound of building and rebuilding in almost every parish. So, what happened on the way? The stages of the voyage through the twentieth century to the third millennium can be imagined as a series of postcards from ports of call.

The first postcard has to be not from Orkney but from Edinburgh, where a momentous event was celebrated on 31 October 1900. The Free Church Assembly marched from their Assembly Hall, the United Presbyterian Synod from their Synod Hall, the two bands of frock-coated gentlemen met at the Mound and solemnly proceeded to the great hall of Waverley Market, where the banners of the Covenanters and swords which had been used at the battles of Drumclog and Bothwell Bridge were hanging on the walls. Among these emotive reminders of the violent religious conflicts of the past, some 1,500 ministers and elders 'lifted up their right hands before God and the church and the world and said: We are no longer twain, we are one, we are the United Free Church of Scotland'. In Orkney, the event was celebrated with a triathlon of praying and feasting and toasting. The speeches at the dinner in the Masonic Hall, and at the soirée in the Paterson kirk afterwards, filled the densely packed columns of two entire pages of *The Orkney Herald.* Poor Mr Aitken, who was scheduled to give the last after-dinner speech, admitted himself totally exhausted after nine and a half hours of united dinner-eating, united soirées and united oratory![1]

If the First World War had not broken out in 1914, the United Free Church would undoubtedly have reunited with the Church of Scotland much sooner than it did, but the war, and the exhaustion that followed it, protracted negotiations until 1929. To become acceptable to the 'Voluntary' UFs, the Church of Scotland had to give up many of the privileges and endowments that went with being a State-established institution. Its congregations now had the obligation to support their own kirks, but they had gained much of the social commitment of the Dissenters. In Orkney, there were some misgivings but eventually every congregation agreed to the union, with the exception of that of Westray which voted against it by a large majority. (On the whole, the kirks that remained outside the unions were almost entirely confined to the West Highlands and Western Isles, where the Free Presbyterian Church had already fiercely rejected 'modernist' tendencies to stray from rigid adherence to extreme Calvinist doctrines.)[2]

The 1929 Union was marked in church services, but there is no mention of dinners and communal celebration. If they happened, the readers of *The Orkney Herald* were no longer interested. The gentlemen who had celebrated the 1900 Union with lengthy speeches, soirées and euphoria had been full of optimism about the future: they had believed that they were celebrating another milestone on the inevitable march of Progress. However, their confident vision of humanity on an upward spiral of material and moral improvement was soon shattered. In the face of the trauma and dislocation caused by the First World War, and the disillusionment and economic depression that followed, their faith in the future evaporated. When one reads the newspapers of the interwar years, one is aware of a cultural shift. The note of self-assurance has gone, and the readership is more interested in tips for economical housekeeping than in matters of morality and religion, which had been of such absorbing interest a generation or two earlier.

The 1929 'postcard' is not of ministers toasting one another, but of the housewives of Firth parish frantically baking and running cake-stalls. They were raising money to install a water supply in the manse before their new minister, Mr Anderson, arrived. The shortage of ministers was a chronic problem throughout the country, but it was particularly difficult to persuade men to accept a charge in Orkney, which must have appeared to many clergy, and their wives, to demand as much heroism and self-sacrifice as venturing into the mission field of darkest Africa. First, there was the ghastly reputation of the Pentland Firth, which had to be recrossed every time the minister wanted to be reunited with family or friends, or attend the General Assembly. Second, there was almost equally ghastly reputation of the Orkney Manse, still a stranger to the modern plumbing and conveniences that, by this time, were taken for granted south of that dreaded stretch of sea. Orkney was poor between the wars, and its standard of living lagged behind that of mainland Scotland. It must have been difficult for its hard-working congregations, who had so little spare cash themselves, to provide a manse that came up to the exacting standards of ministers trained in the relative luxury of Edinburgh or Aberdeen. In 1929, the newly united Presbytery of Orkney was struggling to fill as many as twenty-two vacant pulpits.[3]

When the population was at its height in the mid-nineteenth century, it could fill three kirks in every parish every Sunday, but, by the time the congregations reunited, their numbers had been considerably thinned by emigration. There is no lack of ruined buildings in the landscape evoking the disappearance of the people from the land. The derelict Hackland kirk in Rendall appears to have wandered off-course and then been forgotten, to sink into a quiet meadow above the farms and the old school. In early summer, it is a lovely place, the grey walls washed by a sea of buttercups, the brown-purple Rendall hills framed in the glassless windows. When it was opened in 1845, the Agricultural Revolution was about to transform the traditional landscape of unfenced, undrained plots of arable land and bog into a neat patchwork of enclosed fields, producing crops in orderly and labour-intensive rotation. Orkney's export trade in livestock suddenly took off, the economy boomed, and crofters benefited from the steeply rising prices for their stock. However, within a few decades, the 'Golden

Age' of agricultural improvement was over; landlord and tenant were both suffering from the recession, and the people for whom the kirk was built were turning their backs on the grinding poverty of the little farms, and looking for opportunities elsewhere. For those who were left, the world was a changing place. The lonely position of Old Hackland seems a metaphor for the social relocation of the churches, which had lost their pivotal role in the centre of the community, and were being pushed out to the margins.

In every island, kirk buildings were made redundant by depopulation and church unions. In Rousay, the doors were locked for the last time on the former Church of Scotland and United Presbyterian kirks. United in dereliction, they crumble side by side at Brinian; their windows boarded; their view across Wyre Sound the blank gaze of eyeless sockets. Weeds choke the padlocked doorways, and decay is made even more forlorn by the neatly mown patch of graveyard behind the old parish kirk. A few miles away, Sourin kirk also stands an empty shell. Pigeons perch on the pulpit where the Rev. Archibald MacCallum once thundered his passionate oratory, and the pews sag under dung and damp. There is always a sadness about abandoned buildings; the silence of an empty space where so many people gathered, and sang, and argued, and mourned, and celebrated, hangs heavy in the dust. Yet, it

FIGURE 15.1
The locked door of the parish kirk at Brinian, Rousay. A symbol of hope, rather than decay?

is also possible to see a symbol of hope in the locked door. The doors have been shut forever on the absurdity of a situation in which a rapidly dwindling population was supporting at least three ministers and three large buildings in every parish. A legacy of dissension and conflict locked inside: the people liberated to gather under one roof, rather than being divided among several.

This was the ideal outcome, but congregations did not always abandon the habits of dissension so easily. Twentieth-century people were as reluctant to leave the kirk built by their parents or grandparents as their eighteenth-century forebears had been to abandon the places sacred to their remote ancestors, and the 'unions' agreed on paper were often furiously resented by the congregations, even when the union was between two kirks of the same denomination. The parish of Holm was put on a war footing when the two United Free congregations were joined in 1913, and Presbytery decided that only one building could be maintained. The protagonists of Holm East and Holm West refused to attend one another's kirks, reinforcing their point by smashing the rival's windows. When the final decision was made that the East kirk would be the sole place of worship, an enraged West kirk arsonist set fire to the building in the night. It was totally gutted. 'It is an old, old feud, and I fear that the spirit of the feud has been handed down from one generation to another', wrote a parishioner.[4] Kirk affiliations had provided convenient camps for fostering ancient enmities, which people were not going to be deprived of lightly.

While there was never a repeat of 'Revivalism' on the scale of the movement which swept through every island in Orkney between 1859 and 1861, local Revivals recurred frequently, and one of them led to the forming of a branch of the Apostolic Church in the 1930s. This was a Pentecostal movement that had its British beginnings in a mass Revival that took place in Wales in 1904, and spread rapidly around the world. It did not have a professional clergy, but its spiritual leaders, its Pastors and Prophets, were marked by their 'gifts', such as speaking in tongues. A photograph taken around 1930 shows a group of eleven 'Apostles' outside their wooden church on the Back Road in Stromness. They are bearing placards with imperative texts: 'Ye Must Be Born Again', and the imagery of their preaching was vivid and uncompromising on what happened to you if you were not. It is no accident that it was in the economic depression and insecurity of the interwar years that people turned to a charismatic Church with its highly emotional services. Nor is it surprising that, while Pentecostalism continues to flourish in Africa and in Latin America, it did not enjoy a lasting popularity among the traditionally reticent Orcadians.

During the Second World War, the Orkney coastline sprouted air-raid shelters and gun-emplacements, and Scapa Flow filled with aircraft-carriers and battleships. In this unlikely setting, Italian prisoners-of-war built the chapel that has become, after St Magnus Cathedral, Orkney's most loved and visited building.

FIGURE 15.2
A group of 'Apostles' outside the Apostolic Church in Stromness, 1930s. (OLA)

We must thank the warmen
(Late enemies in a tank-strewn desert)

That here, out of rubbish and tinsel of war
On another shore
They have built this pastoral

Where all the world's peoples
May gather at an altar of peace.[5]

The story of the Italian Chapel begins with the humiliating disaster suffered by the British Navy in 1939, when a German U-boat penetrated the defences of Scapa Flow and sank the *Royal Oak*, with the loss of over 800 lives. The 'Churchill Barriers' were designed to prevent repetition of such a tragedy: solid causeways which would link the South Isles and block the eastern approaches to the Flow altogether. The construction and transport of 66,000 5- and 10-ton blocks of concrete on a foundation of a quarter of a million tons of rock laid on the sea-bed required a massive amount of manpower. The solution was to utilise Italian prisoners as a labour force.

For the Italians, captured after their defeat in North Africa and interned in hastily erected camps in Orkney, their situation and surroundings must have seemed bleak in the extreme. With great resilience, they gradually transformed them. The men of Camp 60 on Lamb Holm made gardens between the Nissen huts, constructed a theatre with painted scenery, and sculpted a statue of St George on horseback out of concrete and barbed wire. A splendidly moustachioed George transfixes the evil dragon with his spear and tramples it beneath his horse's hooves. In the base of the statue is a roll with the names of all the prisoners in the camp, whose own triumph was over defeat, captivity and exile. In 1943, they began to create a chapel out of two Nissen huts joined end to end.

FIGURE 15.3

The prisoners of 'Camp 60' who created the chapel. Domenico Chiocchetti, who painted the interior, is standing, extreme left. Palumbo, the smith, stands in front of the left pillar. (OLA)

The name most associated with the chapel is that of Domenico Chiocchetti, who came from Moena in the Dolomites, a town with a tradition of fresco painting that is still evident in the decorated gables of old houses. Chiocchetti was the chief artist, but there were other skilled tradesmen among the prisoners who recycled scrap materials discarded from the camp, or salvaged from the old ships that had been sunk to block access to the Flow. Bruttapasta, a cement worker, moulded concrete into

FIGURE 15.4

The interior of the Italian Chapel. The altarpiece is based on the The Madonna of the Olives *by Barabina, copied by Chiocchetti from a card he carried in his pocket throughout the war. The altar and altar-rails were made out of concrete, the wrought-iron screen and the candlesticks out of scrap metal, and the tabernacle on the altar of wood from a wrecked ship.*

tracery for altar and altar-rails, and totally disguised the unlovely façade of the Nissen hut with a red-and-white gable in which a Romanesque belfry, Gothic pinnacles and a classical portico are cheerfully blended. Pennisi, an electrician, carved a head of Christ in red clay for the pediment. Palumbo, a smith, wrought scrap metal into candelabra for the altar and a chancel screen of astonishing delicacy. Floor tiles to surround the altar were salvaged from the toilets of the block ship, *Ilsenstein*.

Chiocchetti was responsible for painting the chancel to resemble an Italian church: a Madonna and Child above the altar, angels and the symbols of the evangelists on the 'vault'. He and his assistants then gave the entire corrugated-iron interior a sense of solidity and permanence with a trompe l'oeil of brickwork above carved stone. Their achievement is remarkable, but it is not so much the artistry of the human hand that is inspirational as the alchemy of the human spirit: its miraculous power to transmute the base metals of war and defeat into precious symbols of peace and hope.

> These were men whose love of God and of neighbour had triumphantly survived the brutalising effects of Fascist materialism and of modern warfare. The space they created says more about the human – and the Holy – spirit than almost any other in Scotland.[6]

The chapel was barely finished before war ended, but Patrick Sutherland Graeme, then Lord Lieutenant of Orkney and the owner of Lamb Holm, promised the prisoners that their chapel would be preserved and cherished. (Another Italian chapel at Camp 34 on Burray was dismantled with the rest of the camp.) In fact, Chiocchetti was still working on the font at the time of the armistice, and stayed behind to complete it when all his comrades were repatriated in 1945. Fifteen years later, he returned to help the Preservation Committee with the chapel's restoration, and a long-lasting friendship has been established between the people of Orkney and those of Moena. From that little town in the spectacular Dolomite mountains, so far from the sea, and so very different from the flat and gale-swept island to which Chiocchetti was exiled, came the gift of the carved crucifix that stands outside the chapel. In 1992, eight of the men who had come to Orkney as prisoners fifty years earlier, returned to the islands as guests. Members of the Chapel Preservation Committee welcomed them back to 'this little bit of Italy and of the Catholic Church implanted in our hearts in Orkney'.[7]

When the bus tours have left the chapel to silence, it is still a poignant memorial to the loneliness and sadness and dislocation of war. In 1999, the London Sinfonietta performed in the chapel, in near darkness, Messiaen's haunting music, *Quartet for the End of Time*, which he wrote in a prisoner-of-war camp in Saxony. It was first performed there, in the dark and bitter cold and hopelessness of January 1941, before an audience of 5,000 prisoners. Messiaen described the movements of the Quartet in words which perfectly capture the spirit that built the Italian Chapel. The third movement is: 'Abyss of the Birds … the abyss is Time, with its sorrows and lassitudes. The birds are the opposite of Time: our desire for light, for stars, for rainbows and for jubilant songs.'[8]

FIGURE 15.5

Another Italian Chapel was built in the Burray POW camp, but only the 'chancel' of the Nissen hut was decorated, and the chapel was demolished at the end of the war. (OLA)

The Churchill Barriers made a lasting difference to the South Isles, linking them for the first time to the Mainland by causeway, instead of by boat, but all over Orkney the pace of change was greatly accelerated by the war. The huge numbers of service personnel stationed on the islands created a ready market for farm produce, which brought a brief period of affluence, and social life was enlivened by the cinemas and dance-halls constructed for the troops. In the postwar years, electricity and radios arrived, roads and houses were improved and, on the farms, the horse was replaced by the tractor. When articles were being gathered in preparation for a *Third Statistical Account* in the 1950s, the contributors were enthusiastic about the innovations. Some of them were even confident that their parish was on an upward spiral of moral improvement as well: 'It is gratifying to note that in Sandwick the people are God-fearing and law-abiding.' Drunkenness was apparently unknown, and the people more refined in their conversation than they were forty years previously.[9] (The capacity of the people of Sandwick for improvement had already been noted in the *New Statistical Account* of 1842, when they were reckoned by their minister to be equal to those of other parishes in civilisation, although lagging half a century behind them only twenty years earlier.)[10]

The influence of the outside world, imported in such a large and sudden quantity during the Second World War, had its effect on the old habits of strict observance of the Sabbath, and the ministers' attempts to keep their flock on the straight and narrow path often went unappreciated. In Rousay, the young Ernest Marwick 'came to regard ministers as clouds on the face of the sun'[11] but, despite their efforts, the old sombre Sunday was changing.

> Sunday observance in Kirkwall is by no means as strict as it is in the Highlands or Western isles. Golf can be played on Sunday; it is a favourite day for excursions by car in summer, and many people wear sports clothes, rather than the sober black suit and bowler hat.[12]

The writers of the *Third Statistical Account* were also unanimous about the declining numbers who attended a kirk of any kind, often attributing this to the lack of ministers: 'There is a marked tendency for young boys to stop attending church when they leave school … Many of them are seldom in church again until a baby is to be baptised.'[13] Many pulpits were vacant; the kirks themselves were too large and, invariably, in need of repair; the number of kirkgoers was falling as unrelentingly as the rain on leaking kirk roofs.

Depopulation was especially drastic in the North Isles. At the end of the nineteenth century, there had been over 1,200 people living in Stronsay, for example, one of the most fertile and productive islands. By the time of the 1951 census, there was only half that number. It comes as all the more of a surprise, therefore, to see an impressive church, built in 1955, soaring out of the barley fields in the middle of this island. The astonishing Moncur Memorial Church was the result of a bequest by a rich Dundee jute manufacturer, Alexander Moncur, who left part of his fortune to build a church in memory of his mother, Eliza Moncur, and his grandfather, the Rev. James Mudie, who had been the United Presbyterian minister in Stronsay. Moncur's memorial, designed by Leslie Grahame MacDougall, would have been grand even in a city, and is far more sophisticated than any other kirk built in the islands since the Reformation. Yet this is still an island church, built of its own stones with local labour; austere and solid rather than ornate.

It surprises by its sheer scale, its height emphasised by the slenderness of the tall windows and the narrow buttresses that run the full height of the walls. The severity is broken by the Italianate belfry and the attractive contrast of red freestone bordering bluestone walls. Internally, seeing the impressive timberwork of the roof and the flight of steps leading to a raised chancel, it is hard to believe that one is in an Orkney church. If the Moncur church is far too spacious for the normal Sunday congregation, and the lofty roof space swallows the heating, it is a handsome and solidly-built landmark that generations of Stronsay ministers, lamenting the dilapidated condition of their three churches – or even holding services in the open air because there was not one that was safe to enter – would have greatly envied.

More often, it is not in kirk buildings but in kirkyards that one must look for 'postcards' that represent the twentieth century, and there must be few places where one is so conscious of the mingling of the recent and the remote past as in Osmundwall in Walls. A chapel stood here in the ninth century, and the dead are still brought to the shores of Kirk Hope, the bay where Earl Sigurd was baptised – at the point of the sword – in AD 995. It is a lovely place, but resonates with tragedy. The two World Wars, in which the deep waters of Scapa Flow served as an anchorage for the British fleet, have left behind a sad ebb of white gravestones.

FIGURE 15.6
War-graves at Osmundwall on the site of the old parish church. The Moodie Mausoleum is in the background.

Even more poignant is the bronze figure of a lifeboatman gazing out to sea, surrounded by the graves of the eight men who lost their lives in the Longhope lifeboat disaster on 17 March 1969. The boat set out in appalling conditions in response to a distress call from the *Irene*, a Liberian tanker which had gone aground off Halcro Head on South Ronaldsay. The *Irene*'s crew of seventeen were all saved from the land by the St Margaret's Hope Lifesaving Company, but the Longhope boat overturned in sixty-foot waves, and all its crew were drowned. They left behind them seven widows and ten orphans, and a devastated community. Two women lost both their husband and two sons in the disaster.

In the decades after the Second World War, emigration slowed down considerably. By the 1970s, immigration to Mainland Orkney was even reversing the overall population decline, but it did not fill the hard and uninviting nineteenth-century pews. Yet, behind the apparently depressing signs of leaking roofs and redundant buildings, a reviving wind of change was beginning to blow through the Kirk. The most obvious sign of it was the entry of women into the ministry: in 1968 the Church of Scotland finally – after lengthy debate – agreed to ordain women. The Congregationalist kirks had already done so for nearly forty years, and provided Orkney with its first woman minister, Joyce Collie. By the 1980s, most of the vacant Orkney pulpits were filled, about half of them by women. Of course, it was not uncontroversial; many female ministers and elders faced considerable opposition, but their presence in Presbytery is generally agreed to have led to a much happier and 'less macho' atmosphere, and considerably speeded up meetings! Perhaps it was the high proportion of women at the helm, that helped the different kirks to shrug off their denominational straitjackets and get on with the business of serving the community.

The role of women in reconciliation and in revitalising the life of the Kirk is very evident in the small private chapels in Orkney, which have all provided spaces where people have discovered that what unites them is far more important than what divides. In a nice twist of history, Savil in Sanday, where Bishop Geddes visited in such secrecy in 1790 for fear of anti-Catholic reprisals, became a Catholic home again 200 years later, when Maurice and Jean Soord bought the old house. Their drawing-room became the Chapel of the Sacred Heart, and Mass is said there whenever a priest comes to Sanday, but the door is open to all. In 1983, Bishop Mario Conti of Aberdeen blessed the chapel of 'Our Lady, Star of the Sea, and St Magnus' which Charles and Audrey Wilkinson had created out of a little byre at their home at Breck in Rousay. Originally conceived as a thanksgiving for Charles Wilkinson's recovery from serious illness, it was a place of open welcome, the family's hospitality extending far beyond the small Catholic congregation.

It is not the buildings themselves or their furnishings that make the Savil or Breck chapels special, but a sense of the outgoing spirit of warmth and generous sharing that went into their making, and of a refreshing view of faith, not as a closed box but as an opportunity for cheerful celebration with friends and neighbours. An appreciative Bishop Conti wrote, after his visit to Breck: 'I will long remember the Mass and the Buffet'!

FIGURE 15.7
The Chapel of Our Lady, Star of the Sea, and St Magnus at Breck in Rousay, created by Charles and Audrey Wilkinson from an outhouse at Breck in Rousay.

In 1996, Conti became the first Roman Catholic bishop to preach in St Magnus Cathedral since the Reformation, when he officiated at the funeral of George Mackay Brown. In 1998, he blessed the chapel of St Ninian which Pat Gray had created from a byre even smaller than that at Breck, at her home, the Howe of Hoxa, in South Ronaldsay. The mangers and chains for binding two cows are still there; at the other end, a simple stone slab forms an altar below a window looking out on fields and the sea. Benches run along the whitewashed walls; with a dozen people they feel comfortably crowded. Roman Catholic, Episcopalian, Church of Scotland and Methodist ministers have all celebrated the faith that began in a stable in this beautiful small space.[14]

While most Orkney communities were welcoming the blasts of fresh air that were blowing through the Kirk in the late twentieth century, one was fighting vigorously against them. In the late 1990s, a small group of monks wearing distinctive long black robes were seen on the islands. They were looking for a site to establish a new monastery that would be the headquarters of their order, the Transalpine Redemptorists. In 1999, they bought the island and farm of Papa Stronsay, and as they added buildings to the old steading and herring station, monks and novices gravitated to Golgotha Monastery from all over the world. Father Michael Mary is himself a New Zealander of Orcadian descent; his brothers gather from Scotland, America, Australia, Samoa, Singapore, Zimbabwe and many places besides, to live under a strictly observed Rule. They hold all property in common, and rise at 4am to sing the first office of the day. Followers of the ultra-conservative Pope Pius X, who rejected all modernising tendencies in the Roman Catholic Church, they were separated from it until a reconciliation in 2008.[15]

FIGURE 15.8
The first monks of the new Golgotha Monastery on Papa Stronsay pray in the excavated foundations of the medieval chapel of St Nicholas, 2000. (Orkney Photographic)

It seemed a romantic completion of the circle that there should be a monastery on Papa Stronsay so many centuries after its original *papar* left it. In July 2000, the Mayfield Singers sang a William Byrd Mass in the old fish-curing station that the monks were using for a chapel, celebrating the return of the Latin Mass to the music of the island, but Golgotha was soon the centre of controversy. The monastery dress-code, which stipulated that women under the age of 30 must wear ankle-length skirts and cover their heads, and their arms to the wrists, provoked indignation when a party of archaeologists came to work on the island. The younger women, compelled to dig in long skirts, and the older ones, whose legs were apparently past disturbing monastic susceptibilities, were equally outraged. Father Michael Mary's explanation, that 'modest clothing as worn by our ancestors even to 1950 nurtured virtue and innocence', provoked an angry reaction in *The Orcadian* to this revision of history, both costume and social.[16]

The row died down; the monks continued to add to their flock of sheep and herd of Jersey and Highland cows, make cheese, dig boreholes for water, and build additions to the monastery. In 2000, they raised an eight-foot granite cross as a memorial to all the monks who had lived around Orkney in the first or second millennium, but if the first *papar* of Papa Stronsay could return, would they recognise a great deal of common ground? The Latin of the daily offices would be familiar, but they would have been shocked at the idea of separation from the rest of the Church, and the spreading tide of concrete on the little island – conspicuous from afar – suggests a very different attitude to nature and the environment.

In contrast, the little hermitage at Hamarfiold in Rousay brings the story full circle, back to those Irish monks of over a thousand years ago, whose poetry describes their 'little oratories' in the woods, and their contentment with a simple life lived close to the natural world. One can imagine them feeling entirely at home in David Rawling's hermitage in the Wasbuster moorland, a place as close to them in spirit as the twentieth century could get. David was an Anglican priest from Teesside who, after many years in a busy inner-city parish, came to Rousay in 1982 to find a place where he could live the life of a solitary. 'David's life of prayer and work ... was forever troubled by the tension between his calling to be a solitary and his natural friendliness.'[17] At Hamarfiold, he grew his own vegetables, and planted trees in defiance of the Orkney wind, and shut out the world behind walls of drystone and flowering bushes, yet he touched all who knew him with his kindliness and sense of humour, and a deep spirituality that was (and is) felt to pervade the place long after his sudden death in 1991.

The hermitage – a caravan in an overgrown quarry, invisible until you almost fall into it – is a reminder that the Kirk is not always a prominent feature of the physical landscape. One stumbles into it in unexpected places and – although at times it causes one to almost despair – it always has the capacity to surprise, and even delight.

There must have been many times when people wondered if kirks would feature in the Orkney landscape in the third millennium at all, other than as decaying monuments to half-remembered beliefs. By the mid-twentieth century, they were no longer leading social change (as they certainly had in the previous century) but lagging behind, and not only physically crumbling but metaphorically drifting to the margins of parish life. Yet, in the 1990s and the first decade of the twenty-first century, the rebuilding or renovation of kirks and parish centres has already happened, or is in progress, in almost every parish in Orkney. Probably nowhere in the country is so much confidence in the future being demonstrated so tangibly in bricks and mortar. It would appear that the Ark has neither sunk, nor been scrapped, nor shipwrecked, but only docked for a refit. Although this is the final chapter, it is certainly not the end of the voyage.

A vital part of the 'refitting' has been the creating of buildings designed to serve the whole community all week, not just one kirk congregation on Sundays. In 1999, the Rousay manse was converted into a Parish Centre, housing the Senior Citizens' club, as well as the kirk. In the following few years, the new St Magnus Centre opened next to the cathedral, and the churches at King Street, Kirkwall, and in Firth, in Papay and in Westray were totally renovated and transformed. More plans are afoot in other parishes for the revitalising of their kirks. A common factor of these new buildings is the enormous effort made by their congregations to raise the funds. (Could anyone quantify the sheer tonnage of home-baking that has rebuilt Firth or Westray parish kirks? Forget the gopher-wood: these Arks were built of fatty-cutties.)[18]

The remodelled interiors suggest that people no longer think that the kirk experience should be a penitential one, endured sitting bolt upright on a narrow board. Along with the old pews, the damp and the draughts, they are also discarding the narrow sectarianism that disfigured past history. Thomas Baikie may be shuddering in his Presbyterian grave at the thought of an Episcopalian minister serving in his cathedral and a Roman Catholic congregation saying Mass within its walls (while their own church was being renovated after flood-damage), but such situations are commonplace. It is hard to remember that they would have been inconceivable only a few decades ago. Those who meet together in manse, or kirk, or chapel come from a much wider variety of religious traditions than the islanders of the nineteenth century did. They do not all think alike, but they now meet in one place, on the common ground of one faith, rather than one opinion.

Their beliefs are the same as those brought by the first missionaries whose curraghs beached on Orkney some 1,300 years ago, but attitudes and priorities have changed continually. If the Pillars of the Kirk of 100, or 200 years ago, could revisit their own kirks in the early twenty-first century, they would be appalled. In 1836, for example, dancing at weddings, balls, or any occasion at all was strictly forbidden by the Stromness Victoria Street kirk. One hundred and seventy years later, its minister was telling her congregation that 'the one thing [she] would love to see was dancing in the church'.[19]

Even fifty years ago, there was no awareness of the global problems threatening the planet, but today many Churches recognise that they

FIGURE 15.9

Westray's parish kirk, its energy provided by a ground-source heat pump and a wind turbine. In 2003 it became the first church building in the UK to meet all its primary heating needs from renewable resources.

should have a leading role in environmental responsibility. In 2003, Westray and Papay and Kirkwall East became three of the first 'eco-congregations' in Scotland, an award recognising a church's commitment to Green issues, as demonstrated by its approach to energy-use and recycling, its use of Fair Trade products, and in the content of the minister's sermons! The renovations in Westray incorporated a ground-source heat pump and wind turbine into the design, so that the church became the first in Britain to be powered entirely by renewable energy.

Although there is no longer the Victorian passion for 'Mission', in no other time has commitment of time and funds to overseas development work and to global justice issues been so high. In 2008, the Presbytery of Orkney became 'twinned' with that of the Thyolo Highlands in Malawi – one of the world's poorest countries. Instead of the Kirk dispatching missionaries to Africa, bearing Bibles and Civilisation, it is more likely to be represented by volunteers digging wells, or mixing concrete for new schoolrooms. In return, Malawi church choirs have visited Orkney, and demonstrated the astonishingly exuberant joie de vivre with which they transformed the gift of Scots Presbyterianism.

The rebuilding projects have ensured that kirk buildings will continue to be part of the physical landscape of Orkney for the foreseeable future, but it is the Kirk's prominent involvement with organisations like Amnesty International and the campaigns for trade justice, 'Make Poverty History' and Third World debt relief, that ensures it its place in the mental landscape of the islands in the third millennium.

George Mackay Brown's metaphor of the church as an Ark seems more appropriate than ever. Noah's Ark carried its cargo safely over the floods until the rain ceased and the earth dried out.[20] Presumably – after being cooped up for a year – Noah and his family and the animals disembarked as soon as possible. We never hear of the ark again: they probably scrapped it to build houses, or chopped it up for firewood. It provided transport to a safe haven, to a new life in a renewed world, but it was not an end in itself. Earl Rognvald wanted a seaworthy Ark to *carry* his people to Golden Jerusalem, not to be at anchor in the harbour, or a permanently moored museum like the royal yacht, *Britannia*, in retirement. The 'arks' that sailed through the Orkney centuries must have been truest to their purpose when they also saw themselves this way: as the vessel for the journey, not the destination.

Endnotes

Introduction

I desire an Ark...

G. M. Brown, 'Earl Rognvald Kolsson to an
Itinerant Builder of Churches' (*Travellers* 2001), Brown (2005), p. 451

1. 'Earl Rognvald Kolsson to an Itinerant Builder of Churches', Brown (2005),
p. 451.
2. Craven (1912), p. 35.
3. Goodfellow (1903), pp. 116–18.
4. Sir Herbert Maxwell.

Chapter 1

Legends of the saints endure ...

E. De Waal, *A World Made Whole* (1991), p. 48

1. See Finlay, p. 121.
2. Adomnan II, ch. 42. 'Some of our people have sailed off hoping to find a
place of retreat somewhere on the trackless sea. Commend them to the care of this
sub-king, whose hostages you hold, so that, if by chance their long wanderings
should bring them to Orkney, they should meet with no hostility within his
boundaries.'
3. Anonymous, ninth century, in D. Green and F. O'Connor, eds, *A Golden
Treasury of Irish Poetry* AD *600–1200* (London: Macmillan, 1967), p. 101.
4. Anonymous, eighth or early ninth century, trans. by R. Flower, in K. Hoagland,
ed., *1000 Years of Irish Poetry* (New York: Devin-Adair Company, 1947), p. 28.
5. See R. Fletcher, *The Conversion of Europe* (HarperCollins, 1997) p. 416.

6. Ritchie (2006), p. 7.

7. Papdale and Papil in Orkney derive from *papuli*, estate of the papar. There is literary evidence of all these papar places belonging to the earls, e.g. Earl Rognvald Brusason was murdered on Papa Stronsay, where he was collecting his yuletide malt, and buried in Papa Westray in 1046, according to *Orkneyinga Saga*, chs 29–30.

8. A mound beside the present kirk is traditionally known as Binnaskirk (Old Norse *boen-hus* or prayer-house).

9. According to the *Legend of Saint Bonifacius*, Pope Boniface travelled to Scotland from Rome, to lead a highly successful mission to Pictland. Among his followers were 'two noble virgin abbesses Crescentia and Triduana'. He performed many miracles and baptised thousands of converts, among them King Nechtan of the Picts. The *Legend* is recorded in the Aberdeen Breviary, Appendix VII in Skene (1867), pp. 421–3, and discussed in Macdonald (1992). Nechtan is reported by Bede as sending an embassy to Northumbria to ask for missionaries, in AD 710; Bede, Bk V, ch. 21.

10. Downes and Ritchie (2003), p. 8.

11. *Tigernach Annals* and *Annals of Ulster*, Anderson (1922), I, pp. 191, 212.

12. I. Simpson, 'Transitions in early arable land management in the Northern Isles – the papar as agricultural innovators?' in Crawford (2002).

13. Mackenzie p. 80, quoting Poseidonius of Apamea. Several Bronze Age hoards have also been found in Scottish bogs and lochs, for example a large hoard including a cauldron and broken swords was found in Duddingston Loch, an ale-bucket in Flanders Moss, and shields at Yetholm in Roxburghshire.

14. Ibid., p. 176.

15. Ibid., pp. 147–8; Dingwall Presbytery Minutes (1656).

16. Bede, Bk I, ch. 30.

17. *Orkneyinga Saga*, or 'The History of the Earls of Orkney' is a literary history of the Norse rulers of Orkney from the ninth to the twelfth centuries. It was written in Iceland around AD 1200.

18. For a detailed and extremely entertaining account of this process in Greece, see P. L. Fermor, *Mani* (London: Penguin, 1984), ch. 13.

19. Lamb (1973), pp. 76–80.

20. K. Brady, 'Brei Holm, Papa Stour: in the footsteps of the papar?' in Crawford (2002).

21. Lamb (1978); Brand, p. 77.

22. Lamb (1973), p. 85.

23. Psalm 139.

24. Marwick (1951), p. 112.

25. E.g. St Nicholas Chapel, Papa Stronsay; Lowe (2002). For a discussion of the problems of the Pictish–Norse transition, see Thomson (2001), pp. 40–55.

26. *Historia Norvegiae* in Anderson (1922) I, pp. 330–1; Thomson (2001), p. 14.

Chapter 2

To stand by Thor and Odin ...

G. Jones, *A History of the Vikings* (1973), p. 134

1. *Orkneyinga Saga*, ch. 12.
2. Jones, p. 134.
3. Thomson (2001), p. 64. The latest known pagan grave was excavated at Buckquoy on Mainland Orkney and dated to the third quarter of the tenth century: Ritchie (1976), p. 190.
4. *Njal's Saga*, trans. by M. Magnusson and H. Pálsson (Penguin Classics 1975), p. 19.
5. Ibid., chs 155–7.
6. *Orkneyinga Saga*, ch. 3.
7. Ibid., ch. 20.
8. Ibid., ch. 31.
9. Johnston (1907–13), p. 3.
10. Ibid., p. 1.
11. Thomson (2001), p. 67.
12. *Orkneyinga Saga*, ch. 45.
13. Ibid., ch. 39.
14. 'Tryst on Egilsay', Brown (1996), p. 147.
15. *Orkneyinga Saga*, chs 47–50.
16. Ibid., ch. 52.
17. Ibid., ch. 57.
18. Only one doorway of this building survives, in St Olaf's Wynd, but to judge from its weathered but once elaborate decoration, it must have been an impressive church.
19. Brown (1977), pp. 202–6.
20. Mooney (1928), p. 33; other bones were also missing from the skeleton but it was standard practice to give some small relic of a saint to another church. A finger-bone was found in a casket of relics built into the wall of the (now ruined) cathedral in the Faeroes.
21. Ritchie (1996), pp. 96, 103–4.
22. Clouston (1928), pp. 68–9.
23. Clouston (1932), p. 16.
24. Ibid., p. 12.
25. The round church towers in Ireland have different proportions to those of St Magnus and the North Sea examples, and are nearly all free-standing.
26. Cant (1975).

Chapter 3

I went the blue road ...

G. M. Brown, 'The Five Voyages of Arnor'
(Poems New and Selected 1971), Brown (1996), p. 36

1. *Orkneyinga Saga*, ch. 52. Pilgrims to the Holy Land wore a palm-leaf as a token of their pilgrimage, hence 'palmers'.

2. Graham-Campbell and Batey, p. 192. A complex of late Norse structures has been only partially excavated close to the church, it is not known exactly where the original Hall stood.

3. *Orkneyinga Saga*, chs 55, 66.

4. Fisher, p. 378; Ritchie (1996), pp. 96, 100–1.

5. *Eyrbyggja Saga*, trans. by H. Pálsson and P. Edwards (Penguin Classics 1989), ch. 49.

6. Mackinlay (1914), p. 428, quoting Barnabas Googe, 'Popish Kingdoms'.

7. Lowe (2002). Another piece of the same thickness (possibly from the same source) was found on the Brough of Birsay.

8. Owen, p. 324.

9. *Orkneyinga Saga*, ch. 56.

10. The church was later renamed St Ninian, after a ship wrecked on the Deerness coast.

11. Gibbon, p. 283. Orkney 'Ladykirks' included parish kirks in Westray, Sanday, Stronsay, South Ronaldsay, Rousay, Eday, Deerness and Shapinsay.

12. Gerard Manley Hopkins, 'The May Magnificat' in W. H. Gardner, ed., *Gerard Manley Hopkins* (1971), pp. 37–9.

13. Sir David Lindsay, *The Monarchy* (1554).

14. There were chapels dedicated to Bride on Graemsay, North Ronaldsay, Papa Stronsay, Rousay and Eday, and at Yesnaby on Mainland.

15. John Anderson, *OSA*, p. 318.

16. For example, Monks' House on Auskerry, Munkerhoose at Warbeth (Stromness), and Papay.

17. Gibbon, p. 273.

18. Mooney (1923), p. 12.

19. Brown (1986), p. 31.

20. Confusingly, the church is also shown on some maps as St Colme's.

21. Dryden, p. 104.

22. For example, Scott (1926), p. 51.

23. Lamb (1973), p. 94.

24. Morris and Emery (1986), p. 306.

25. Low (1879), pp. 47–8.

26. RCAHMS, no. 672.

27. Muir, p. 252.

28. Mooney (1923).

29. This is argued by Butler. The placename Grange (unusual in Orkney) occurs in Eynhallow.

30. Mooney (1923), p. 11. This is the traditional version of the story, but it is also possible that Balfour considered the island untenable with no kelp income to supplement the agriculture.

31. RCAHMS, no. 613.

Chapter 4

Rejoice. Saint Magnus Kirk ...

G. M. Brown, *Celebration for Magnus* (1987), p. 65

1. *Orkneyinga Saga*, ch. 68.

2. Ibid., ch. 57.

3. Ibid., ch. 76.

4. Ibid., ch. 85.

5. Ibid., ch. 99.

6. Fawcett, pp. 97–110; Ritchie (1996), pp. 101–3. The cathedral 'chapter', or hierarchy of canons and other clergy, was growing larger at this time – hence the need to enlarge the choir of St Magnus to accommodate them.

7. Donaldson (1987), p. 24; Hay, p. 9.

8. Peterkin 1820 (Documents), p. 21.

9. Cuthbert (1998), p. 87.

10. Thomson (2001), p. 248.

11. Ibid., p. 253.

12. Wallace, pp. 54–9.

Chapter 5

Above the ebb ...

G. M. Brown, 'Chapel between Cornfield and Shore, Stromness'
(*Loaves & Fishes* 1959), Brown (1996), p. 12

1. Donaldson (1987) p. 20. Skea is probably the same man as the chaplain from Orkney, James Ka, who in 1560 was holding 'oppynionis concerning the faith contrare the tenor of actis of parliament'.

2. Donaldson (1960), p. 72. John Knox's plan for the kirk aimed at involving all the congregation and reducing the power of the clergy: the people would choose their ministers and they would elect their elders and deacons every year, so most

of the adult male population would take their turn at representing the community. His scheme was too democratic for the time and overturned in a few years by Andrew Melville, who reinstated the divide between clergy and laity. Thereafter, elders were ordained, like ministers, and held the office for life; ministers were appointed by the patron (usually a large landowner), and the people had little say in their kirk at all.

3. Mary of Guise, mother of Mary, Queen of Scots, was Queen Regent while Mary was living in France as the wife of François, the Dauphin of France. When François inherited the French throne in 1559, he openly declared his claim, through Mary, to the thrones of Scotland and England. The result was strong anti-Catholic feeling in Scotland and an alliance between Scots and English Protestants. In 1560, an English fleet sailed into the Firth of Forth and besieged the French forces in Leith. Both the Queen Regent and François died in 1560, and Scotland became a Protestant country by Act of Parliament the same year.

4. Donaldson (1987), pp. 25–7.

5. Thomson (1987), p. 146.

6. RCAHMS, p. 115.

7. Sutherland, p. 6.

8. Ibid., p. 4.

9. The Moodies' principal residence was at nearby Snelsetter until 1628, when their debts forced them to sell off the house and most of their lands and move to Melsetter.

10. Low (1879), pp. 16–17.

11. Thomson (2001), pp. 307–8. Although the climate caused harvest failure, the famines were a man-made disaster. An enormous quantity of food was being shipped out of the islands as rent while people were dying of starvation.

12. Picken, p. 28.

13. Donaldson (1960), p. 65. To be fair, the puritanical streak had existed in the Scottish Kirk long before the Reformation. Sunday observance came from England with Queen Margaret in the eleventh century and, earlier in the sixteenth century, Archbishop Hamilton denounced dancing as a 'provocation of lechery'. The machinery of Kirk Discipline put in place after the Reformation allowed such views to be much more rigorously enforced.

14. Brown (1973), pp. 37–8.

15. Thomson (2001), p. 278.

16. Maidment and Turnbull, pp. 149, 163, 180, 185.

17. Thomson (2001), pp. 305–6. In the Orkney Archives is a Disposition by Arthur Baikie concerning a bond dated 1649 for £1,800 Scots worth of arms and ammunition received by the Earl of Morton for the support of Montrose, D29/1/13.

18. Callaghan and Wilson (2001), p. 27.

19. J. Emerson, *Poetical Descriptions of Orkney* 1652.

20. In 1643, representatives of the Scottish Covenanters and the English Parliament signed the Solemn League and Covenant. The Scots agreed to attack the royalist forces from the north, in return for money and an agreement to reform the English and Irish churches on the model of the 'best reformed churches', i.e. their own!

21. Mooney H. L. (1954), pp. 6–7; Edwin Eunson (1986), Orkney Archives D1/199, A013.

22. G. M. Brown, The Prologue to 'The Storm' (*The Storm* 1954), Brown (2005), p. 2:

> *For Scotland I sing,*
> *the Knox-ruined nation,*
> *that poet and saint*
> *must rebuild with their passion.*

Chapter 6

'Then longe folk ...'

G. Chaucer, *The Canterbury Tales* (c. 1387),
D. Laing Purves, ed. (Edinburgh 1890), l. 12

1. In the seventeenth century, Orkney had Bailie Courts in every parish presided over by a Bailie chosen from among the leading landowners. They dealt with petty crime and agricultural regulations; Thomson (1987), p. 191. Act 2 of 'The Acts of Bailiary for executing of Justice through the County of Orkney' deals with pilgrimages; Barry, Appendix IX, p. 457.

2. Mackenzie, pp. 269–70.

3. Picken, p. 17.

4. Firth and Stenness KS (1741).

5. John Armit, *NSA*, p. 118.

6. For example, the Aberdeen Breviary (see ch. 1, n. 9); Skene (1867), pp. 421–3.

7. *Orkneyinga Saga* ch. 111.

8. MacIvor, p. 251, n. 3, quoting David Chambers, *De Scotorum Fortitudine* (1631).

9. Sir David Lindsay, *The Monarchy* (1554).

10. A Peterkin, ed., *The Booke of the Universall Kirk of Scotland* (1839), p. 3.

11. MacIvor, p. 255, n. 1, quoting *Trans. Scot. Ecclesiological Soc.*, II, 2 (1907–8), p. 278.

12. Traill (1883). Among the objects Traill found in the passage were an iron spearhead, a ball of mottled green Serpentine stone and fragments of Iron Age pottery.

13. Brand, p. 82.

14. Ibid., p. 88.

15. Ibid., p. 90.

16. Traill (1883).

17. Martin, pp. 187–8.

18. Gibbon, p. 274.

19. Robertson, p. 44; Maidment and Turnbull p. 167. Katherine was burnt at the stake in 1643.

20. Wallace, pp. 40–1.

21. Ben, p. 10.

22. Marwick (1951), p. 112. Cf. Binnaskirk on Papay.

23. Brand, p. 138.

24. Morris and Emery (1986), p. 343.

25. Barry, p. 25.

26. Tudor, p. 278.

Chapter 7

The reformation in Scotland ...

King James VI, *Basilikon Doron* (1598),
Dickinson and Donaldson III, p. 50

1. King James VI, *Basilikon Doron* (1598), Dickinson and Donaldson III, p. 212.

2. NIPR (1718).

3. NIPR (1719).

4. CPR (1726).

5. Fereday, p. 30.

6. CPR (1726).

7. CPR (1730).

8. Craven (1912), p. 13, quoting George Lyon.

9. Fullerton was very popular with his pupils for encouraging games, and procuring an order from the Kirk Session that 'none in toun or paroch that marries but shall pay a foot ball to the scholars of the Grammar School'. Fullerton's Ba' Money was regularly paid until 1853. *Fasti*, p. 277.

10. Craven (1912), p. 45.

11. Ibid., p. 54.

12. Ibid., pp. 80–1.

13. Fereday, ch. 11. John Traill of Elsness, John Traill of Westness, William Balfour of Trenaby and Archibald Stewart of Brough were incriminated by their correspondence with Prince Charles Stewart. They had their houses burnt and their property looted or confiscated by government troops under Captain Benjamin Moodie; they spent months hiding in caves in Westray. Other lairds, like Thomas

Traill of Holland, were also strongly Jacobite in their sympathies, but managed to avoid being incriminated in the rebellion.

14. The bulletin is copied into the minutes of the Orkney Presbyteries, e.g. NIPR (1736).

15. The Douglas family, Earls of Morton, controlled the lands of the former Orkney earldom from 1643 (with some interruptions) until the 14th Earl sold the estate to Sir Lawrence Dundas in 1766.

16. NIPR (1746).

17. CPR (1747).

Chapter 8

The materiall Kirk lyes lyk sheip and nout faulds ...

James Melville (1584), quoted by Hay, p. 20

1. Donaldson (1960), p. 45.
2. Act of the Lords of Secret Council (1563), Hay, p. 19.
3. Pennant, p. 157.
4. Peterkin (1822), p. 58.
5. Tudor, p. 259.
6. Peterkin (1822), p. 58.
7. KPR (1700); Goodfellow (1902), p. 117.
8. Orphir KS (1744).
9. Hugh Ross, *OSA*, p. 196.
10. KPR (1797).
11. KPR (1791).
12. Ibid.
13. Hugh Ross, *OSA*, p. 197.
14. NIPR (1707).
15. NIPR (1807).
16. Brand, pp. 90–1.
17. NIPR (1719–20).
18. Pogue, p. 26.
19. Graham, p. 286.
20. Pogue, p. 115, citing Orphir KS.
21. Picken, p. 22.
22. J. Troup, *William Tomison*, Orkney View, vol. 64 (1996).
23. Hay, p. 198.
24. NIPR (1719).
25. Allen, p. 60.
26. Patrick, p. 110.

27. Victoria Street UF Church, pp. 12–13.

28. Graham, p. 291.

29. Patrick, p. 138.

30. Ibid., pp. 141–2.

31. Peterkin (1822), p. 29.

Chapter 9

'Came the minister …'

G. M. Brown, 'Funeral', Brown (1971), p. 53

1. Brand, pp. 38–9.

2. CPR (1728), p. 82.

3. Craven (1911), p. 37.

4. CPR (1730).

5. NIPR (1819, 1822).

6. CPR (1745).

7. CPR (1836).

8. *Fasti*, p. 236.

9. Cf. G. M. Brown, 'A Treading of Grapes' in *A Time to Keep* (London 1969), pp. 63–76.

10. Whyte pp. 59-60, quoting James Beattie, Letter to T. Blacklock (1768).

11. KPR (1788); Whyte, pp. 84–5.

12. NIPR (1792).

13. Whyte, p. 86.

14. Ibid., p. 93.

15. H. Walls, *A Little Sanday Church History*, Orkney View, vol. 64 (1996).

16. William Clouston, *OSA*, p. 140.

17. Ibid., p. 280.

18. Cuthbert (2001), p. 53.

19. NIPR (1791).

20. William Clouston, *OSA*, p. 128.

21. NIPR (1749). Modern equivalents of these weights are very approximate, as the Orkney measures were notoriously variable. These equivalents are based on the standardisation of weights in 1826, which defined 1 lispund as 26.625 lbs (so 1 mark = approx. ½ kg, 1 lispund 12 kg, 1 meil 72.5 kg), but the weights were probably rather less in 1749.

22. NIPR (1789).

23. Barry, p. 230.

24. Burleigh, p. 315.

25. Firth, p. 78.

26. William Clouston, *OSA*, p. 140.

27. Firth, p. 79.

28. Ibid., pp. 59–60.

29. Marwick, p. 113. Marwick was told that in Harray each 'urisland' – a medieval division of land for taxation purposes – had a separate portion of the kirkyard assigned to it for burials, and it was the duty of every man to attend any funeral that took place in his urisland.

30. Orphir KS (1722); Johnston (1940), pp. 105–6.

31. Orphir KS (1741); Johnston (1940), p. 113.

32. Victoria Street UF Church, p. 18.

33. Pogue, p. 32.

34. NIPR (1806, 1810–11).

35. Mackelvie, p. 555.

36. Goodfellow (1902), p. 128.

37. Pogue, p. 31.

38. NIPR (1797).

Chapter 10

A meeting of the North Parish ...

S. D. B. Picken, *The Soul of an Orkney Parish* (1972),
p. 35, citing St Peter's (South Ronaldsay)
Kirk Session minutes 1663

1. Johnston (1940), p. 99.

2. Extracts from the Kirkwall Session Book (1618–59), Craven (1912), pp. 102–6.

3. NIPR (1725).

4. Ibid. (1733).

5. NIPR (1746); Johnston (1940), p. 116.

6. NIPR (1719).

7. Birsay KS (1794).

8. Harray KS (1865).

9. Pogue, pp. 27–8.

10. NIPR (1707).

11. North Ronaldsay KS (1856).

12. Stromness KS (1701).

13. Hossack, p. 424, citing Kirkwall KS (1693).

14. Ibid., p. 429.

15. Deerness KS (1782).

16. Graham, p. 323.

17. Mooney (1930), citing Deerness KS (1705 and 1706).
18. Hossack, pp. 427-8.
19. Birsay KS (1799).
20. William Clouston, *OSA,* pp. 112–13.
21. Birsay KS (1798).
22. William Clouston, *OSA,* p. 129.
23. Stromness KS (1697).
24. Stromness KS (1702).
25. Hossack, p. 419.
26. Victoria Street UF Church, p. 9.
27. Orphir KS (1741); Johnston (1940), pp. 112–13; Pogue, pp. 29–30.
28. Hossack, pp. 424–6.
29. Ibid., p. 417.
30. Orphir KS (1741); Johnston (1940), pp. 114, 121–3.
31. Gibson, p. 106.

Chapter 11

Any country in the hands of an undivided church ...

B. H. Hossack, *Kirkwall in the Orkneys* (1900), p. 443

1. James Watson, *OSA,* p. 211.
2. Thomson (2001), p. 407.
3. John Malcolm, *OSA,* p. 178.
4. Haldane, p. 169.
5. Ibid., pp. 171–3.
6. Thomson (2001), pp. 408–9.
7. Bell, p. 15; Webster, p. 109.
8. Harcus, p. 65.
9. Ibid., pp. 69–73.
10. The Westray Baptist Kirk was rebuilt in 1850 and is still in use.
11. Harcus, p. 82.
12. McNaughton, p. 27, quoting John Hercus (1819).
13. Ibid., pp. 26–31.
14. Ibid., p. 51.
15. Ibid., p. 32.
16. Ibid., p. 39.
17. B. Bathurst, *The Wreckers* (2006), p. 85.
18. Goodfellow (1903), pp. 116–18.
19. Ibid., p. 128.
20. NIPR (1846).

21. The odd dedication to St Ann is explained by the fact that Ann was the laird's sister, and she had contributed and raised funds to build the kirk.

22. CPR (1849).

23. Picken, p. 65.

24. Ibid., p. 64.

25. NIPR (1843).

26. Sandwick KS (1841); William Grant, *NSA*, p. 113.

27. Sandwick KS (1843).

28. Rousay FC KS (1846).

29. Hossack, p. 443.

Chapter 12

On Sunday, the bibled elders ...

G. M. Brown, 'Hamnavoe', Brown and Moberg (1996), p. 103

1. *The Orkney Herald* (4 December 1860).

2. Ibid. (5 February 1861).

3. Ibid. (8 January 1861).

4. Ibid. (5 March 1861).

5. Gray, p. 66.

6. *The Orkney Herald* (15 January 1861).

7. Groat, p. 46.

8. Free Presbytery of Orkney Minutes (1869).

9. It was only when the Free Church changed course and campaigned for 'Disestablishment' that the way was open to negotiate union with the United Presbyterians, though the FC leader, Dr Rainy, and many of his followers, remained implacably opposed to reuniting with the Church of Scotland. Burleigh, pp. 395ff.

10. The Kirkwall UP Kirk was known as the Paterson Kirk until the congregation joined with that of the King Street Kirk in 1967.

11. E. Muir, *Paterson Church Magazine* (1952).

12. Whyte, p. 202, quoting Zachary Macaulay, *Anti-Slavery Reporter* (January 1831).

13. McFarlan, p. 12.

14. G. Brown, 'Letter from Africa', *The Orkney View*, vol. 57 (Kirkwall, 1994/1995).

15. McFarlan, p. 161. Margaret Graham is the only missionary honoured with a plaque in St Magnus Cathedral, near Baikie's tomb in the choir. It reads: 'Margaret Manson Graham, nurse and missionary: rescuer of children abandoned to die: devoted her life to Christian work in Nigeria: born Orphir 1860 + died Arochuku 1933.'

16. Hewison, p. 7.

17. The quotation is from the inscription on Baikie's tomb in St Magnus Cathedral.

18. The Zenana Mission.

19. Charles Clouston, *NSA*, p. 59.

20. Sandwick KS (1841–2).

21. Peterkin (1822), pp. 17–18.

22. Pagan, p. 199.

23. James Anderson, *NSA*, p. 25.

24. Firth, p. 73.

25. A. MacWhirter, 'Good Templars in Orkney', repr. from *The Orkney Herald* (1951).

26. Thomson (1981), p. 125.

27. Ibid., p. 52.

28. Ibid., pp. 183–4.

29. *The Orkney Herald* (24 September 1884).

30. Thomson (1981), p. 146.

31. *The Orcadian* (6 February 1886).

32. Ibid., quoting *The London Echo*. There is a sad postscript to the incident. After his judgement was overturned and severely criticised, Sheriff Mellis committed suicide.

33. For example, restitution of the lost common grazings or the breaking up of large farms to make more crofts.

34. *The Orcadian* (11 December 1886), quoting A. MacCallum.

35. *The Orkney Herald* (1 August 1888).

36. Thomson (1981), pp. 206–9.

Chapter 13

Some do not go to church …

The Rev. James Whyte, *The Missionary Record of the
UF Church in Scotland*, Orkney supplement
(July 1902), p. 2

1. Goodfellow (1925), p. 215.

2. Dabbs, p. 28, quoting Winnie Breck, Swannayside.

3. Drummond and Bulloch, p. 10.

4. Groat, p. 17.

5. J. Drever (1950) in Miller, p. 219.

6. *The Orkney Herald* (3 August 1888).

7. DeLille M. M. Diament, *Stromness Parish Church Magazine* (June 2006).

8. Peterkin (1822), p. 26.

9. Mooney (1928–9), p. 28.

10. *Representation by the Rev. Messrs Logie and Petrie to the Heritors of the Parish of St Ola and to the Magistrates of Kirkwall* (1832), p. 1.

11. Ibid., p. 2, note.

12. KPR (1823).

13. The first East Kirk was built directly behind the cathedral, where the St Magnus Centre now stands. It was used by the Free Kirk congregation for a few years after the Disruption. They were evicted by the cathedral congregation, who claimed the building, and sold it for demolition, for a fraction of the cost of building it.

14. Tudor, p. 238.

15. Muir, p. 66.

16. *The Orcadian* (9 July 1904); *The Orkney Herald* (13 July 1904).

17. Low (1879), p. 61.

Chapter 14

The Spirit moves on the deep …

G. M. Brown, 'Eynhallow: The Monastery',
Brown and Moberg (1996), p. 35

1. Alexander Ross (1834–1925) designed most, if not all, of the Episcopalian churches in northern Scotland. St Olaf's was badly damaged by fire only five years after it was completed, but rebuilt in 1881. The distinctive tower was added in 1924 to commemorate Archdeacon Craven, historian and minister of the church for nearly fifty years.

2. The medieval St Olaf's was reconstructed by Bishop Reid in the sixteenth century.

3. Craven (1912), p. 93.

4. When the foundations of the old chapel of St Colm at Osmundwall were cleared away in the late nineteenthth century, the stones were thrown on the shore. The stone incised with a cross was found there by accident but, unfortunately, lost again; see Cursiter (1897).

5. Scott-Montcrieff, pp. 104–5.

6. NIPR (1734).

7. Whyte, p. 208.

8. Gray, pp. 42–55.

9. Gray, p. 48, quoting letter from Ann Traill to Bishop Geddes (1789).

10. Scott-Montcrieff, p. 115.

11. Gray, pp 62–3, 65, quoting letters from Dr Stephan to Bishop Kyle (1860).

12. *The Orkney Herald* (18 December 1860).

13. *The Orkney Herald* (29 December 1860).

14. *The Orcadian* (16 July 1877).

15. Hossack, p. 364.

Chapter 15

We may note …

G. M. Brown, 'Introductory Poem', Brown and Moberg (1996), p. 9

1. *The Orkney Herald* (14 November 1900).

2. In 1892, the Free Kirk passed the Declaratory Act, declaring that acceptance of the Westminster Confession's doctrine on double predestination (the belief that a small number of the Elect are predestined to salvation but most of the human race to eternal damnation) was not mandatory. A few congregations in the north-west Highlands broke away in protest, forming the Free Presbyterian Kirk. It is one of history's oddities that this statement of belief, drawn up in London in 1647 but quickly abandoned in England, was (and is) most tenaciously clung to in the Gaelic-speaking Highlands.

3. *The Orcadian* (26 September 1929).

4. *The Orcadian* (12 March 1920).

5. G. M. Brown, 'Italian Chapel', Brown and Moberg (1996), p. 106.

6. Hume, p. 134.

7. Sandra Tait, P.O.W. Preservation Committee, *The Italian Chapel*, p. 19.

8. St Magnus Festival Programme (1999).

9. A. S. Johnston (1952) in Miller, p. 177.

10. Charles Clouston, *NSA*, p. 65.

11. E. Marwick, 'I meet a Minister', *Paterson Church Magazine* (1952), p. 7.

12. W. S. Hewison (1953) in Miller, pp. 87–8.

13. V. C. Pogue (1952) in Miller, p. 145.

14. The Howe of Hoxa was sold in September 2006 and the chapel closed.

15. Pope Pius X (1903–14) wanted all clergy to take an oath to reject modernism in any form. The Society of St Pius X (to which members of Golgotha belong) was founded in 1970 by the right-wing Bishop Lefebvre, opposing the reforms of Vatican II, and in dispute with the Roman Catholic Church from 1975. The reconciliation with the Roman Catholic Church was made possible by the ultra-conservative views of Pope Benedict XVI. In January 2009, the Pope rescinded the excommunication on four Catholic bishops who are members of the Society of St Pius X.

16. *The Orcadian* (13 July, 20 July, 3 August, 10 August 2000).
17. Paul Hepplestone, *Church Times* (January 2000).
18. Fatty-cutty = a traditional girdle-baked scone; see Macdonald (2003).
19. Victoria Street UF Church, p. 18; Allen, p. 9.
20. Genesis 6–8.

Note on Quantities etc. used in the Text

Measurements

Imperial measurements have been used in the text. The metric equivalents of these are:

> One inch = 2.54 centimetres
> One foot = 0.3 metres
> One (statute) mile = 1.6 kilometres

Money

Scotland's currency had been modelled on that of England by David I, but because of debasement of the coinage it dropped in value. By the time of James III (1460–88), £4 scots = £1 sterling and a century later £5 Scots = £1 sterling. At the Union in 1707, the pound Scots was officially replaced by sterling, converted at the rate of 12:1, but it continued to be used in Scotland for most of the eighteenth century.

A shilling was worth one-twentieth of a pound, and a penny was worth one-twelfth of a shilling.

Glossary

Abbreviations

Fr. = French, Lat. = Latin, ON = Old Norse

Aardvark a South African antbear.

Acolyte a junior assistant to clergy in church services, often carrying candles in a procession.

Aisle (Fr. *aile* = wing) lateral passage within a church, separated from *nave* or *choir* by an arcade. In Scots usage, a projecting wing, e.g. laird's aisle, burial aisle.

Antiburgher Church was formed in 1747 when the *Original Secession* split in two over whether or not to take the Burgess oath to uphold 'the true religion presently professed within this realm, and authorised by the laws thereof'. The *Antiburghers* refused to take the oath. The first Secession congregations in Orkney were all formed from this church.

Apostolic Church a worldwide Pentecostalist movement, in Britain originating in a mass revival in Wales in 1904. A congregation had a church in Stromness in the 1930s.

Apse semicircular or square projection at the east gable of pre-Reformation churches housing the altar and, sometimes, shrines.

Associate Presbytery alternative name for the *Original Secession*.

Aumbry cupboard or closed wall recess; in a church, used for the reserved sacrament and sometimes known as a *sacrament house*, e.g. in St Olaf's in Kirkwall.

Books of Discipline these defined the constitution of the Church of Scotland. The first was adopted by the *General Assembly* in 1560; the second, of 1578, was recognised by Parliament as establishing the *Presbyterian* basis of the Church.

Breviary book containing the daily services of the Catholic Church.

Broch (ON *borg* = fort) Iron Age defensive circular tower built of drystone walling, with galleries and stairways in the thickness of the wall, common in northern and western Scotland.

Brough a small island connected to the mainland by a tidal causeway or narrow promontory, as the Broughs of Birsay and Deerness. The pronunciation the same as for *broch*.

Burghers see *Antiburgher Church*.

Chancel east end of a church reserved for the clergy officiating at the altar, usually partitioned from the *nave* and entered through a chancel arch.

Chasuble a sleeveless outer gown worn by a priest when celebrating *Mass*.

Choir (i) the part of a church or cathedral in front of the main altar, usually separated from the *nave* by a railing or screen; (ii) singers trained to perform or lead church music.

Church of Scotland 'established' by Act of Scottish Parliament as the national Church at the Reformation in 1560; also known as the Established Church or the Old Kirk.

Cist a rectangular burial chest made of stone slabs.

Cloister a covered arcade surrounding a courtyard adjoining a monastic church.

Congregationalism (or **Independency**) a form of Church government in which each congregation manages its own affairs independently. The first Orkney congregation was formed c. 1805; thereafter churches in Kirkwall, Harray, Sandwick and Rendall.

Crannog an artificial island, or islet artificially enlarged, to form a fortified lake dwelling, e.g. in Wasbuster Loch, Rousay.

Crossing the part of the church where the *nave* intersects with the *transepts*, often (as in St Magnus Cathedral) under the main tower.

Crow-steps or **corbie-steps** stepped skews on the gable of a building, common in eastern Scotland and found on some older buildings in Orkney.

Curragh a boat made by stretching skins over a wicker frame, still used in western Ireland.

Dalmatic a wide-sleeved ecclesiastical garment.

Disruption the major schism of 1843, when many ministers, elders and laymen left the Church of Scotland and founded the Free Church of Scotland.

Elder a layman elected by a congregation to permanent office, to assist the minister and serve on the *Kirk Session, Presbytery*, etc.

Episcopalian (Lat. *episcopus* = bishop) one belonging to or supporting the Episcopal Church, in which the clergy are under the direction of a bishop.

Feudal superior the overlord of lands held from him in feudal tenure. In Orkney, the feudal superior was the owner of the earldom (the Earls of Morton from the seventeenth century until 1766, when it was purchased by Sir Lawrence Dundas). He was entitled to feudal duties, paid by the *heritors*, and also had the right of *patronage*, entitling him to appoint the minister of his choice to a vacant church.

Forestair external stair, usually of stone, rising to an upper door.

Free Church the Church formed in 1843 by the *Disruption*. Also known as the New Kirk.

Free Presbyterian Church split from the Free Church in 1892 in protest against moderation of extreme Calvinist beliefs.

General Assembly the supreme court of the Church of Scotland, consisting of equal numbers of ministers and elders elected as their representatives by the presbyteries. It meets annually in May and is presided over by an elected Moderator.

Girnel a chest for storing meal.

Glebe the portion of arable land that forms part of a minister's living.

Gogs (or **jougs***)* an iron collar fastened round an offender's neck and attached to a wall by a short chain (there was formerly one near the cathedral door and one at the Market Cross in Kirkwall).

Gothic style of medieval architecture typified by pointed arches and traceried windows. Revived and adapted in Gothic Revival buildings from the mid-eighteenth century.

Heritors the landowners in a parish, formerly obliged to maintain the church, churchyard, manse and glebe and pay the minister's stipend. In 1925, buildings held by heritors were transferred to the General Trustees of the Church of Scotland.

Hog-back stone type of tombstone of Norse origin carved to resemble a Norse long-house roofed with wooden shingles. Earlier examples are distinctively convex, hence the name. Several (of late type, with a flatter ridge) have been found in Orkney, the most complete in Skaill kirkyard, Deerness, and St Boniface kirkyard, Papay.

Jacobite (Lat. *Jacobus* = James) a supporter of the Roman Catholic Stewart king James II of England (VII of Scotland) and his son James and grandson Charles (Bonnie Prince Charlie). Finally defeated by the army of the Hanoverian King George II at the battle of Culloden in 1746.

Jougs see **Gogs**.

Kirk Session the governing body of a Presbyterian church congregation, consisting of the minister and elders.

Loft gallery forming an upper storey in a church, built across one or both gable ends, as in St Peter's, South Ronaldsay, or in a horseshoe facing the pulpit, as in St Peter's, Sandwick.

Lugs ears.

Mass the celebration of the Eucharist or Holy Communion, the central feature of worship in a Catholic church.

Nave (Lat. *navis* = ship) the main space in a church occupied by the congregation; so called because the shape and timbered roof resemble an upside-down boat.

Original Secession Church formed in 1733, the first secession from the Church of Scotland after the *Revolution Settlement*, provoked principally by resentment of *patronage*. Also known as the Associate Presbytery. Split into Burghers and *Antiburghers* in 1747.

Patronage the right of an individual (in Orkney, usually the feudal superior, or the city magistrates in Kirkwall) to 'present' the minister of their choice to a church. Lay patronage in the Church of Scotland was abolished in 1649, reimposed in 1669, abolished in 1690 and unconstitutionally reimposed by Parliament in 1712. It was finally abolished in 1874. Resentment of patronage was a major cause of secessions from the Church of Scotland.

Peregrini wanderers or pilgrims travelling through a foreign land.

Plymouth Brethren religious sect founded in Dublin in 1825 in reaction against High Church principles and unevangelical doctrine. Its first congregation was established at Plymouth in 1831 and it then spread rapidly through the fishing villages on the east coast of Scotland and reached Orkney c. 1867.

Preaching tent a portable timber booth to shelter the minister when preaching in the open air; also known as an Ark.

Prebend a property whose rent or produce formed a share of the revenues of a cathedral, and supported a resident clergyman or *prebendary*.

Presbyterian (i) system of church government by elders or presbyters developed by John Calvin in Geneva and John Knox in Scotland; (ii) a member of this Church.

Presbytery (i) the church court above the Kirk Session, consisting of the minister and one ruling elder from each church within a certain district; (ii) the eastern end of a church reserved for officiating priests.

Protestors a group that broke away from the Orkney United Secession Church in 1820 in protest at the choice of minister.

Reformation the religious revolution of the sixteenth century, in which many European countries/states/communities rejected the Roman Catholic Church and founded Protestant churches.

Relief Church formed in 1761 by James Gillespie, minister of Carnock, and followers as the Presbytery of Relief – i.e. relief from the oppression of *patronage*. United with the *United Secession* in 1847.

Revolution Settlement 1689; intended to pacify the country after the revolution of 1685, it confirmed King William's intention to accept Presbyterian government in Scotland.

Romanesque eleventh- and twelfth-century style of European architecture, characterised by round-arched doors and windows.

Sacrament house mural cupboard, usually of carved stone and dating from the fifteenth or early sixteenth centuries, for keeping the consecrated elements of the Sacrament so that it can be taken to the sick and dying at home.

Sacrist, Sacristan clerical or lay person responsible for vestments and vessels and for the maintenance of the church.

Sacristy room in or off a church where liturgical vestments and vessels are kept.

Synod a provincial court made up of all the clerical and lay members of several adjoining presbyteries. It is presided over by an elected moderator and usually meets twice yearly.

Teinds or **tithes** a tax on all landholders of a tenth part of the crops, livestock, etc. produced, intended for the maintenance of the priest and the church and the support of the poor of the parish.

Tester, or sounding board a wooden canopy above the pulpit, serving to project the minister's voice forward (rather than allow it to vanish into the ceiling).

Thirled to be bound or enslaved.

Transept wing of a church at right angles to the *nave*.

United Free Church formed by the union of the *Free Church* and the *United Presbyterian Church* in 1900. Almost all Orkney congregations reunited with the Church of Scotland in 1929.

United Presbyterian Church formed by the union of the *United Secession Church* and *Relief Church* in 1847.

United Secession Church formed by a reunion of the 'New Light' parties (the more liberal) of both the Burghers and the *Antiburghers* in 1820.

EVENTS IN ORKNEY

C7	1st Christian missionaries arrive
681	Orkney attacked by King Bridei II of Picts
Late C8	1st Viking raids
995	Earl Sigurd's baptism at Osmundwall
1046	Earl Rognvald Brusason murdered Thorfinn sole earl in Orkney
1116	Murder of Earl Magnus in Egilsay
1136	St Magnus Church built in Egilsay
1137	Foundation of St Magnus Cathedral
1192	Earl Rognvald proclaimed a saint
1349	Black Death in Orkney and Norway
1468	Orkney pawned to Scotland by Christian I
1486	James III gives Cathedral to Kirkwall
1492	1st Orkney Rental by Lord Henry Sinclair
1614	Earl Patrick Stewart executed Robert Stewart's rebellion crushed

EVENTS IN BRITAIN

c. 461	Death of St Patrick in Ireland
C5	St Ninian converting Picts in S. Scotland
c. 597	Death of St Columba in Ireland
793	1st Viking attack on Lindisfarne
849–901	Reign of Alfred the Great in England
1014	Earl Sigurd killed in battle of Clontarf in Ireland
1066	Battle of Hastings, Norman conquest of England
1216	Magna Carta
1305	Execution of William Wallace by Edward I
1314	Scots defeat English at battle of Bannockburn
1528	Patrick Hamilton burnt in St Andrews
1530s	Dissolution of Monasteries in England
1560	Scottish Reformation
1567	Mary, Queen of Scots forced to abdicate
1587	Execution of Mary, Queen of Scots in England
1588	Defeat of Spanish Armada
1603	Union of Crowns: James VI and I King of Scotland and England

EVENTS OVERSEAS

410	Rome sacked by Goths
504–604	Pope Gregory the Great
700	Irish monks in Faeroes
800	Charlemagne crowned Holy Roman Emperor
982	Eric the Red discovers Greenland
1000	Christianity voted official religion in Iceland
1000	Leif Ericsson's expedition to North America
1030	St Olaf killed at Battle of Stiklestad in Norway
1050	Earl Thorfinn in Rome
1099	First Crusade captures Jerusalem
1120	Earl Hakon in Holy Land
1152	Earl Rognvald's journey to Holy Land
1347	Black Death reaches Europe
1492	Christopher Columbus reaches America
1517	Martin Luther's '95 Theses' at Wittenberg
1522	Ferdinand Magellan circumnavigates world
1618–48	Thirty Years' War in Europe

EVENTS IN ORKNEY

1650 Montrose raises Royalist army in Orkney
1650s Orkney occupied by Cromwell's troops

1671 Cathedral steeple burns down
1679 Wreck of *The Crown* off Deerness

1774–78 Low's Tours of Orkney and Shetland

1796 1st Secession church in Kirkwall
1813 Last Great Auk in Britain shot in Papay

1830 Collapse of kelp industry
1833 1st steamship service Kirkwall–Leith
1847–9 Repairs to Cathedral
1848 Balfour Castle, Shapinsay built
1854 1st edition of *The Orcadian*
1860–1 'Revivals'
1871 St Olaf's Episcopal Church built in Kirkwall
1877 St Joseph's Catholic Church built in Kirkwall

EVENTS IN BRITAIN

1638 National Covenant signed in Edinburgh
1641 Beginning of English Civil War
1649 Execution of Charles I
1650 Oliver Cromwell's Commonwealth
1650 Montrose defeated at Battle of Carbisdale
1660 Restoration of Charles II
1666 Great Fire of London
1679 Battle of Bothwell Bridge – Covenanters
       defeated
1688 'Glorious Revolution' – abdication of James II;
       accession of William and Mary
1707 Union of Scottish and English Parliaments
1712 Act of Toleration
1715 The '15 Jacobite Rebellion
1733 1st Secession Churches in Scotland
1746 The '45 Jacobite Rebellion crushed at Culloden
1792 Freedom of worship for Scottish Episcopalians
1793 Freedom of worship for Scottish Roman Catholics
1793 Britain at war with France
1807 Britain abolishes Slave Trade
1829 Catholic Emancipation Act
1832 First Reform Act extends franchise
1837 Queen Victoria ascends throne
1843 The Disruption – founding of Free Church

1872 Education Act
1874 Abolition of Patronage
1884 Napier Commission investigates crofting

EVENTS OVERSEAS

1670 Hudson's Bay Company founded

1775–83 American War of Independence
1789 French Revolution

1805 Nelson defeats French at Battle of Trafalgar
1815 Napoleon defeated at Battle of Waterloo

1851–4 John Rae discovers North-West Passage
1853–6 Crimean War
1861–5 American Civil War

1880–1, 1899–1902 Boer Wars in South Africa
1889 Eiffel Tower built, Paris

EVENTS IN ORKNEY

1888	Crofters Commission in Orkney
1913–30	Major restoration of Cathedral
1917	*HMS Vanguard* explodes; loss of 800+ lives
1919	German fleet scuttled in Scapa Flow
1933	Fresson flies 1st airmail service to Kirkwall
1939	Battleship *Royal Oak* sunk in Scapa Flow
1943–5	Italian Chapel built
1953	January – serious damage by hurricane
1955	1st TVs in Orkney
1966	Old Man of Hoy climbed for 1st time
1974	1st ro-ro ferry to Orkney
1976	1st oil to Flotta terminal

EVENTS IN BRITAIN

1886	Crofters Holdings (Scotland) Act
1900	Union of United Presbyterian and Free Churches
1914–18	First World War
1928	Suffrage extended to all women
1929	Union of Church of Scotland and United Free Church
1934	Fresson flies 1st UK air ambulance
1939–45	Second World War
1968	1st women ministers in Church of Scotland
1968	1st British heart transplant
1971	British currency decimalised
1973	Britain joins Common Market
1999	1st Scottish Parliament since 1707

EVENTS OVERSEAS

1903	1st powered flight by Wright brothers, USA
1911	Amundsen 1st man to reach South Pole
1914–18	First World War
1917	Russian Revolution
1939–45	Second World War
1948	India becomes independent
1961	Yuri Gagarin first man in space
1963	Assassination of President Kennedy in Dallas
1969	Neil Armstrong 1st man on moon
1990	Nelson Mandela freed; end of apartheid in South Africa
1990	Iraq invades Kuwait

Select Bibliography
and Abbreviations

Adomnan of Iona, tr. R. Sharpe, 1995 *Life of St Columba* (Penguin Classics, Middlesex)

Allen, Rev. P., 2006 *Stromness Parish Church Bicentenary Memorial 1806–2006* (Stromness)

Anderson, A. O., 1922 *Early Sources of Scottish History* vols I & II (Oliver & Boyd, Edinburgh)

Bardgett, Rev. F. D., 2000 *Two Millennia of Church and Community in Orkney* (The Pentland Press, Durham)

Barry, Rev. G., 1805 *History of the Orkney Islands* (facs. repr. The Mercat Press, Edinburgh 1975)

Batey, C. E., J. Jesch and C. D. Morris, eds, 1993 *The Viking Age in Caithness, Orkney and the North Atlantic: Select Papers from the Proceedings of the 11th Viking Congress* (Edinburgh University Press)

Bede, ed. B. Radice, 1955 *A History of the English Church and People* (Penguin Classics, Middlesex)

Bell, D. R., 1946 *Paterson Church Kirkwall* (Kirkwall)

Ben, Jo, c. 1529 *Descriptio Insularum Orchadiarum* (repr. *The Orkney Herald*, Kirkwall 1922)

Brand, J., 1701 *A Brief Description of Orkney, Zetland, Pightland Firth and Caithness* (repr. Edinburgh 1883)

Brown, G. M., 1971 *Fishermen with Ploughs* (Hogarth Press, London)

——, 1973 *An Orkney Tapestry* (Quartet Books, London)

——, 1977 *Magnus* (Quartet Books, London)

——, 1986 *The Loom of Light* (Balnain Books, Nairn)

——, 1987 *Celebration for Magnus* (Balnain Books, Nairn)

——, 1996 *Selected Poems 1954–1992* (John Murray, London)

Brown, G. M., 2005 Bevan, A., and B. Murray, eds, *The Collected Poems of George Mackay Brown* (John Murray, London)

——, 1996 and Moberg, G., *Orkney, Pictures and Poems* (Colin Baxter Photography Ltd, Grantown-on-Spey)

Burleigh, J. H. S., 1983 *A Church History of Scotland* (OUP)

Butler, M., 2004 *The Landscapes of Eynhallow* (unpublished MA thesis for the University of Bristol)

Callaghan, S. and B. Wilson, eds, 1981 *The Unknown Cathedral* (Orkney Islands Council, Kirkwall)

Cant, H. W. M. and H. N. Firth, 1989 *Light in the North* (The Orkney Press, Kirkwall)

Cant, R. G., 1975 *The Medieval Churches and Chapels of Shetland* (Shetland Archaeological and Historical Society, Lerwick)

Clouston, J. S., 1928–9 'Three Norse Strongholds in Orkney', POAS VII, pp. 57–74

——, 1932 'Tammaskirk in Rendall', POAS X, pp. 9–16

——, 1932 *A History of Orkney* (Kirkwall)

CPR = Cairston Presbytery Records (Orkney Church Records)

Craven, Rev. J. B., 1911 *Church Life in South Ronaldsay and Burray in the 17th Century* (Kirkwall)

——, 1912 *History of the Episcopal Church in Orkney 1688–1912* (Kirkwall)

Crawford, B. E., ed., 1988 *St Magnus Cathedral and Orkney's 12th Century Renaissance* (Aberdeen University Press)

——, ed., 2002 *The Papar in the North Atlantic* (University of St Andrews)

Cursiter, Rev. J. W., 1897 'Note on a stone bearing an incised cross from the site of St Colm's Chapel, Walls, Orkney', PSAS XXXII, pp. 50–2

Cuthbert, Olaf D., 1998 *A Flame in the Shadows* (The Orkney Press, Kirkwall)

——, ed., 2001 *Low's History of Orkney* (Orkney Heritage Society, Kirkwall)

Dabbs, C. M. M., 2004 *The Kirk Abune The Hill* (Birsay Publications, Orkney)

De Waal, E., 1991 *A World Made Whole* (HarperCollins, London)

Dickinson, W. C., G. Donaldson and I. A. Milne, eds, 1954 *A Source Book of Scottish History* vol. III (Thomas Nelson & Sons Ltd, Edinburgh)

Donaldson, G., 1960 *Scotland: Church and Nation through 16 Centuries* (SCM, London)

——, 1987 *Reformed by Bishops* (Edina Press, Edinburgh)

Downes, J. and A. Ritchie, eds, 2003 *Sea Change: Orkney and Northern Europe in the later Iron Age AD 300–800* (The Pinkfoot Press, Balgavies)

Drummond, A. and J. Bulloch, 1978 *The Church in Late Victorian Scotland 1874–1900* (Saint Andrew Press, Edinburgh)

Dryden, Sir H. E. L., 1870 *Ruined Churches in Orkney and Shetland 1867–1870* (notebook in Orkney Archives)

Fasti = Fasti Ecclesiae Scoticanae see Scott, H.

Fawcett, R., 1988 'Kirkwall Cathedral: An Architectural Analysis' in Crawford 1988, pp. 88–110

FCKS = Free Church Kirk Session Minutes (Orkney Church Records)

Fereday, R. P., 1980, *Orkney Feuds and the '45* (Kirkwall Grammar School, Kirkwall)

Fernie, E., 1988 'The Church of St Magnus, Egilsay' in Crawford 1988, pp. 140–62

Finlay, I., 1979 *Columba* (Richard Drew Publishing, Glasgow)

Firth, J., 1974 *Reminiscences of an Orkney Parish* (Orkney Natural History Society, Stromness)

Fisher, I., 1993 'Orphir Church in its South Scandinavian Context', in Batey et al 1993, pp. 375–80

Gibbon, S. J., 2006 *The Origins and Early Development of the Parochial System in the Orkney Earldom* (unpublished PhD thesis for the UHI Millennium Institute)

Gibson, W. M. 1991 *Auld Peedie Kirks* (Kirkwall)

Goodfellow, Rev. A., 1902 *Sanday Church History* (Kirkwall)

——, 1903 *Birsay and Harray Church History* (Kirkwall)

——, 1920 *Dr Robert Paterson* (Edinburgh)

——, 1925 *Two Old Pulpit Worthies of Orkney* (Stromness)

Graham, H. G., 1928 *The Social Life of Scotland in the 18th Century* (London)

Graham-Campbell, J. and C. E. Batey, 1998 *Vikings in Scotland* (Edinburgh University Press)

Gray, A., 2000 *Circle of Light: The History of the Catholic Church in Orkney since 1560* (Birlinn, Edinburgh)

Groat, T., 1939 *Thirty Years A Colporteur* (Kirkwall)

Haldane, A., 1852 *The lives of Robert Haldane of Airthrey and of his brother James Alexander Haldane* (London & Edinburgh)

Harcus, Rev. H., 1898 *The History of the Orkney Baptist Churches* (Ayr)

Hay, G., 1967 *The Architecture of Scottish Post-Reformation Churches 1560–1843* (OUP)

Hearn, E. H., ed., 1911 *The Sagas of Olaf Tryggvason and of Harald the Tyrant* (London)

Hewison, W. S., 1998 *Who Was Who in Orkney* (Bellavista Publications, Kirkwall)

Hossack, B. H., 1900 *Kirkwall in the Orkneys* (facs. repr. The Kirkwall Press 1986)

Hume, J., 2005 *Scotland's Best Churches* (Edinburgh University Press)

Johnston, A. W., ed., 1940 *The Church in Orkney, Miscellaneous records of the 16th, 17th and 18th centuries* (repr. from *The Orcadian*, Kirkwall 1889–92)

Johnston, A. W. and A. Johnston, 1907–13 *Orkney and Shetland Records* vol. 1 (Viking Society for Northern Research, London)

Jones, G., 1973 *A History of the Vikings* (OUP)

KPR = Kirkwall Presbytery Records (Orkney Church Records)

KS = Kirk Session Minutes (Orkney Church Records)

Lamb, R., 1973 'Coastal settlements of the North', *Scottish Archaeological Forum* 5, pp. 76–98

——, 1978 'A Stack Site off Stronsay, Orkney', PSAS 110, pp. 517–19

Low, G., 1879 *A Tour through the Islands of Orkney and Schetland in 1774* (Kirkwall)

Lowe, C., 1998 *Coastal Erosion and the Archaeological Assessment of an Eroding Shoreline at St Boniface Church, Papa Westray, Orkney* (Historic Scotland)

——, 2002 'The Papar and Papa Stronsay: 8th Century Reality or 12th Century Myth?' in Crawford 2002

Macdonald, A., 1992 *Curadan, Boniface and the Early Church of Rosemarkie* (Groam House Museum Trust, Rosemarkie)

Macdonald, I., 2003 *Labour of Love: A Tale of Faith, Fabric and Fatty Cutties* (Westray Parish Kirk)

McFarlan, D. M., 1957 *Calabar: The Church of Scotland Mission Founded 1846* (Edinburgh)

MacIvor, I., 1962 'The King's Chapel at Restalrig and St Triduana's Aisle: A Hexagonal Two-Storied Chapel of the Fifteenth Century', PSAS 96, pp. 247–63

Mackelvie, Rev. W., 1873 *Annals and Statistics of the United Presbyterian Church* (Edinburgh and Glasgow)

Mackenzie, D., 1922 *Ancient Man in Britain* (Blackie & Son, Glasgow)

Mackinlay, J. M., 1914 *Ancient Church Dedications in Scotland: Non-Scriptural Dedications* (Edinburgh)

McNaughton, W. D., 2006 *Early Congregational Independency in Orkney* (Kirkcaldy)

Magnusson M. and H. Pálsson, eds, 1975 *Njal's Saga* (Penguin Classics, Middlesex)

Maidment, J., and W. Turnbull, 1837 'Trials for Witchcraft, Sorcery and Superstition in Orkney', in Abbotsford Miscellany vol. 1, pp. 135–85 (Edinburgh)

Martin, M., 1716 *A Description of the Western Isles of Scotland* (facs. repr. Mercat Press, Edinburgh 1981)

Marwick, H., 1951 *Orkney* (Robert Hale Ltd, London)

Miller, R., ed., 1985 *The Third Statistical Account of Scotland. The County of Orkney* (Scottish Academic Press, Edinburgh)

Mooney, H. L., 1954 'The Wreck of the "Crown" and the Covenanters in Orkney', *Orkney Miscellany* 2, pp. 1–8

Mooney, J., 1923 *Eynhallow, the Holy Island of the Orkneys* (Kirkwall)

——, 1928 'Further notes on Saints' relics and burials in St Magnus Cathedral', POAS VI, pp. 33–7

——, 1930/31 'Deerness: The Kirk Session', POAS IX, pp. 49–55

——, 1934 'Some Further Kirk Session Records', POAS XII, pp. 41–5

Morris, C. D., and N. Emery, 1986 'The chapel and enclosure on the Brough of Deerness, Orkney: Survey and excavations 1975–77', PSAS 116, 301–74

Muir, T. S., 1885 *Ecclesiological Notes on some of the Islands of Scotland* (Edinburgh)

NIPR = North Isles Presbytery Records (Orkney Church Records)

NSA = *New Statistical Account* 1842; *The Statistical Account of the Orkney Islands by the Ministers of the Respective Parishes* (Edinburgh)

OCR = Orkney Church Records (Orkney Library and Archive)

OHS = Orkney Heritage Society

Orkneyinga Saga, see Pálsson H., and P. Edwards 1978

OSA = *Old Statistical Account*, see Storer Clouston, J., 1928

Owen, O. A., 1993 'Tuquoy, Westray, Orkney. A Challenge for the Future?' in Batey et al 1993, pp. 318–39

Pagan, A., 1988 *God's Scotland? The Story of Scottish Christian Religion* (Mainstream Publishing, Edinburgh)

Pálsson, H., and P. Edwards, trans., 1978 *Orkneyinga Saga* (Penguin Classics, Middlesex)

——, trans. 1987 *Magnus' Saga* (The Perpetua Press, Oxford)

——, trans. 1989 *Eyrbyggja Saga* (Penguin Classics, Middlesex)

Paterson, Rev. J., 1874 *Memoir of Robert Paterson DD* (Edinburgh)

Patrick, M., 1949 *Four Centuries of Scottish Psalmody* (OUP)

Pennant, T., 2000, *A Tour of Scotland 1769* (Birlinn, Edinburgh)

Peterkin, A., 1820, *Rentals of the Ancient Earldom and Bishoprick of Orkney* (Edinburgh)

——, 1822 *Notes on Orkney and Zetland*, vol. 1 (Edinburgh)

——, ed., 1839 *The Booke of the Universall Kirk of Scotland* (Edinburgh)

Picken, Rev. S. D. B., 1972 *The Soul of an Orkney Parish* (Kirkwall Press)

Pilgrimage Sites of the Orkney Isles 2004 (Solo Publications, Harray, Orkney)

POAS = *Proceedings of the Orkney Antiquarian Society* (Kirkwall)

Pogue, Rev. V. C., 1954 'Church Life in Orphir 200 Years Ago', *Orkney Miscellany* 2, pp. 24–33

POW Chapel Preservation Committee, *Orkney's Italian Chapel* (Kirkwall)

PSAS = *Proceedings of the Society of Antiquarians of Scotland* (Edinburgh)

RCAHMS = Royal Commission on the Ancient and Historical Monuments of Scotland

Ritchie, A., 1976–7 'Excavation of Pictish and Viking Farmsteads at Buckquoy, Orkney', PSAS 108, pp. 174–227

——, 1996 *Orkney* (HMSO)

——, 2006 *People of Early Scotland* (The Pinkfoot Press, Brechin)

Robertson, D., 1924 'Orkney Folk Lore', POAS II, p. 44

Royal Commission on the Ancient and Historical Monuments of Scotland, 1946 *Inventory of Orkney* (Edinburgh)

Scott, Rev. A. B., 1926 'The Celtic Church in Orkney', POAS IV, pp. 45–56

Scott, H., 1928 *Fasti Ecclesiae Scoticanae* vol. VII (Oliver & Boyd, Edinburgh)

Scott-Montcrieff, G., 1960 *The Mirror and the Cross: Scotland and the Catholic Faith* (London)

Skene, A., 1989 *Stromness Church of Scotland* (Stromness)

Skene, W. F., 1867 *Chronicles of the Picts, Chronicles of the Scots* (Edinburgh)

Storer Clouston, J., 1928 *The Orkney Parishes, containing the Statistical Account of Orkney 1795–1798, drawn up from the Communications of the Ministers of the Different Parishes by Sir John Sinclair, Bart.* (Kirkwall)

Sutherland, R. T., 1928 *St Magnus Cathedral* (repr. from *The Orkney Herald*, Kirkwall)

Thomson, W. P. L., 1981 *The Little General and the Rousay Crofters* (John Donald, Edinburgh)

——, 1987 *History of Orkney* (Mercat Press, Edinburgh)

——, 2001 *The New History of Orkney* (Mercat Press, Edinburgh)

Traill, W., 1883 'Donations to the Museum', PSAS 17, pp. 136–8

Tudor, J., 1883 *The Orkneys and Shetland* (facs. repr. Edinburgh 1987)

Victoria Street United Free Church Stromness 1906 *Centenary Memorial 1806–1906* (Stromness)

Wallace, Rev. J., 1693 *A Description of the Isles of Orkney* (repr. Edinburgh 1883)

Webster, Rev. D., 1910 *The History of the Kirkwall United Presbyterian Congregation* (Kirkwall)

Whyte, I., 2006 *Scotland and the Abolition of Black Slavery 1756–1838* (Edinburgh University Press)

Index